Lost Innocence

Lost Innocence

Folk Craft Potters of Onta, Japan

Brian Moeran

UNIVERSITY OF CALIFORNIA PRESS

Berkeley / Los Angeles / London

University of California Press
Berkeley and Los Angeles, California

University of California Press, Ltd.
London, England

© 1984 by The Regents of the University of California

Printed in the United States of America

1   2   3   4   5   6   7   8   9

Library of Congress Cataloging in Publication Data
Moeran, Brian.
  Lost innocence.
  1. Hita-shi (Japan)—Rural conditions—Case studies.
  2. Villages—Japan—Case studies. 3. Potters—Japan—
  Case studies. 4. Onta Pottery. I. Title.
HN730.H57M63   1984   306'.47'095213   82-23840
ISBN 0-520-04692-7

For Anchan

Fuji no shirayuki
Asahi ni tokete
Tokete nagarete
Mishima ni ochiru.
Mishima jorōshu no
Keshō no mizu.

The white snow on Mt. Fuji
Melts in the morning sun,
Melts and flows down,
Flows down to Mishima.
And in Mishima
The prostitutes use it
In their makeup.

Popular Ballad

Contents

Maps, Tables, and Figures

FIGURES

Preface

This book would never have been written but for the intervention of an old friend, Chance. In April 1974 I was engaged in a part-time job as interpreter—lucrative employment which supplemented my student grant as I struggled toward the completion of my undergraduate degree. This particular job promised to be exciting. I was being paid by a Japanese television company to do exactly what I always liked doing—leave England for the sunny shores of the Mediterranean. There I was to interpret for a camera crew filming an interview with a member of one of Europe's royal families. Glamour had come into the life of a third-year student of Japanese, and I had even bought a tie for the occasion.

But I was destined never to act as interpreter for royalty. Upon arrival in the south of France I discovered that our announcer had offended palace officials and that the interview had been summarily canceled. Required to find an immediate replacement for the princess concerned, we decided to approach the English potter Bernard Leach. Permission for the interview was granted, and a few days later, on a beautifully clear morning in St. Ives, Cornwall, I first laid eyes on some of Bernard's work. It was then that I decided to take up pottery.

Although my research was thus initially inspired by Bernard's pots, this book would probably never have come into print but for another twist of chance. My original intention when I went out "to the field" was to apprentice myself to a potter in Sarayama (Onta). I hoped to proceed with my research more as a participant than as an observer and, if all went well, to become a professional potter rather than an anthropologist. I did not realize at the time that the method of preparing clay in Sarayama prevented apprentices from being taken into the community. Fortunately, Bernard Leach had put me in touch with friends of his in Tokyo, who advised me to forget my potting ambitions—in Sarayama (Onta) at least. I took their advice, finished my research, and wrote a thesis which duly received academic approval.

This book is addressed to people of widely differing interests—to potters and to anthropologists—and consequently is in danger of failing to appeal to either professional group. Whereas potters will be looking for detailed technical information on clay and glaze compositions, for example, anthropologists may be wondering why I have chosen not to discuss aspects of symbolic classification. One problem that I have wrestled with—for the most part unsuccessfully—is "structural." This book started out as a doctoral thesis in social anthropology. But when I began to rewrite the dissertation, I discovered that its argument was too closely woven for me to chop and change with ease. I was dealing with a piece of anthropological knitting—undo one stitch and a whole section unraveled itself into nothing. It was unfair of me to expect potters to wade through long sections on Japanese rural society, and yet it was precisely these that were important to an appreciation of Onta pottery in the context of the Japanese folk craft movement. If I were to rewrite the work entirely for potters, I would produce yet another in a long line of "arty" books on Japanese ceramics. By concentrating on technical and "purely" aesthetic, rather than social, detail, the new book would have ended up supporting that point of view which its thesis contents had indirectly criticized. All of which means that potters are here asked to wade through an "anthropological" tome, and anthropologists to read a "potty" monograph.

And since it is the potters who deserve most encouragement, I shall address their problems here. My own view is that for too long potters in the West have been given nothing but an ideological vision of Japanese folk crafts. They—and I myself—have been taught to perceive the work of the potters of Onta, Tamba, Okinawa, Mashiko, and so on as they "ought" to be perceived, not as they actually are. We have rarely, if ever, been given the opportunity to hear what potters in Japan themselves think of a "movement" in which they have become, often involuntarily, involved. *Mingei* aficionados will doubtless say that I am blind to beauty and that I have failed to understand what Yanagi was trying to say. With the conviction of converts to a new faith, they will proclaim that Onta pottery really *has* deteriorated over the years. This may be so, but I would remind such people that it is not for the social anthropologist to make value judgments of this kind.

What is more, if Onta pottery really has "gone to the dogs," then the potters of Sarayama deserve to be given a hearing as to why this may be so before judgment is passed. This has been my sole aim. I hope that some positive results may come of it all.

Acknowledgments

My greatest debt is, of course, to the people of Sarayama it-self. They permitted me to live in their community, endured my presence with remarkable equanimity, and answered my persistent questions with patience and good humor. Realizing my difficulties in grasping some of the technical aspects of production, the potters gave me special permission to throw my own rather bad pots, to join in the glazing and loading, firing and unloading of kilns. They also invited me to play in their softball games, run in their "marathon" races, and get drunk at their not infrequent sake parties. Although it would perhaps be injudicious to praise certain individuals within Sarayama it-self for the help that they gave me in my research, I should like to thank in particular all members of the Yamamaru household for the kindness with which they treated me as a guest in their house during the first year of my fieldwork in the community. I am sure that my presence made life difficult for everyone there in one way or another. To Tsuruyo and Moriyuki I owe a special word of thanks.

On the academic side, neither this book nor the doctoral thesis upon which it is based could have been written without the help of a number of scholars and institutions. In Tokyo, Professor Chie Na-kane, of the Institute of Oriental Culture at the University of Tokyo, undertook to act as my supervisor during fieldwork. Despite an extremely busy schedule, she invariably managed to find the time to see me during my infrequent visits to the capital. The clarity with which she was able to discuss certain problems that I had encountered and the interest that she took in the progress of my fieldwork were both sociologically and psychologically invaluable to me.

Others who have read this manuscript in one or another of its various forms and who have given me criticism and instruction include

Ronald Dore, Nelson Graburn, Robert Smith, and Lionel Caplan. I thank them all for their time and trouble.

My gratitude, too, to Masao Imai for allowing me to use almost all the black-and-white photographs produced here. So many monographs disappoint by the quality of their photographs that I feel myself exceptionally fortunate to be able to include such excellent plates.

I should like also to pay tribute to the Social Science Research Council of Great Britain for funding my research for three years; to the Japan Foundation for granting me a fellowship that enabled me to do an invaluable second year's fieldwork in Sarayama; and to the Suntory Foundation for providing a generous grant toward the publication of this book.

Others who have been most helpful over the past few years, and for whom I hope this book will be of some help in return, include Janet Leach, Kim Schuefftan, Mihoko Bekku (Okamura), Yōko Tanaka, and Toshio Sekiji. They do not agree with some of the opinions that I have expressed here, but they have never failed to give me their support and assistance when I needed it. My debt to them will be repaid, at least in part, if this work succeeds in clarifying a few of the many problems that now beset the Japanese folk craft movement.

I have left to the end the name of the man who has had to suffer the most, Dr. Rodney Clark. It is impossible to express adequately the thanks that I owe him for his untiring patience, his perseverance through adversity, his encouragement, and a sense of humor which was at times the only thing that kept me—and, I suspect, him—from insanity. Although this book may not meet his exacting demands, I hope that its quality in some way reflects the time and energy which, as my Ph.D. supervisor, he devoted to it.

Introduction

This book is about a group of potters who live in a small community called Sarayama in the south of Japan and who make what is known as Onta ware. It concerns certain problems arising from the production, marketing, and aesthetic appraisal of a kind of stoneware pottery that is generally referred to as a "folk art" or "folk craft" (*mingei* in Japanese).

People have been making pottery in Sarayama for well over two hundred and fifty years. Until recently, however, hardly anybody had ever heard either of the community or of the wares that it produced. The pottery was sometimes called "Hita thing" (*hitamono*), Hita being the name of the nearest town to Sarayama. It was bought mostly by local farmers, who used it as domestic ware because it was considerably cheaper than, what was for them "superior," light porcelain china.

In 1927 a black teapot made in Sarayama was picked up by Yanagi Muneyoshi (1889–1961) off a dusty shelf in a wholesaler's shop in Kurume, some fifty kilometers away from the pottery community. Yanagi was philosopher, critic, and founder of what has come to be known as the Japanese folk craft movement. He admired the teapot from Sarayama because it accorded with his aesthetic ideals of what constituted beauty. He resolved to visit the community and see for himself where and how such beautiful pottery was being made. This was the first time that anyone from the "outside world" had taken the trouble to find out about Sarayama's wares, and the older men in the community remember Yanagi's first visit very well. It was the beginning of a complicated relationship between potters and folk craft aficionados, which has continued to this day and which is the focus of much of this book.

Over the years, Yanagi and others involved in the Japanese folk craft movement have written about Sarayama's pottery, praising it for its "natural," "traditional," and "cooperative" beauty. Consequently, hundreds of thousands of people have visited Sarayama's fourteen households, situated in the mountains to the north of Hita. Many of these visitors have passed through the neighboring hamlet of Onta (of which Sarayama was once an administrative part), and it is this name—written somewhat poetically with Chinese characters meaning Small Deer Field—which is now used for the community's pottery. Most people go there as tourists; but for a significant few the trip to Sarayama is a kind of pilgrimage because the community and its pottery represent in their minds Yanagi's ideal of what true folk crafts should be.

In many ways, this book would seem to be just one more in a long line of Japanese community studies. The reader will have noticed that it contains many of the words and phrases that haunt other anthropological works on Japanese rural society. *The household system, the hamlet, community solidarity, environmental change, tradition,* even the dreaded *dōzoku*—all these have had enough scholarly print devoted to them, it might be thought, to deserve no further attention. There are two points that I should like to make here in justification of their further discussion.

First of all, Japanese rural society is what may be called an "irrigation culture" (Wittfogel 1955:46), in that a large majority of people in the countryside have grown rice in irrigated paddy. Almost all studies hitherto undertaken of Japanese rural society, and most of the data upon which analysis of its social institutions have been made, have been of such agricultural communities. However, it should be realized that a considerable number of people in rural Japan are either only "half" farmers, or not farmers at all, but craftsmen, shop owners, teachers, commuters, and so on (cf. Plath 1967:519–20). The fact that a large number of households in any one community may not practice farming as a full-time occupation may influence the social organization of that community in a manner hitherto undocumented by scholars of Japanese society. This study, concerned as it is with a pottery community, aims to show precisely that. I intend to argue that the social structure of Sarayama (Onta) and the organization of its households depend mainly on the way in which water is used to prepare clay for use at the potter's wheel.

My second point is that those studying Japanese rural society have rarely managed to make comparisons or deductions of theoretical interest to anthropologists in general. Rather, they have at times appeared to form as close-knit and introverted a clique as do the very communities they have studied. It may be that the closed-in nature of Japanese society as a whole has determined the form that the studies of its social institutions have taken. Or perhaps there is not much of general theoretical interest to be said about country farmers. At any rate, I have been fortunate enough to discover a community that is linked to the outside world through the pottery that it produces. This pottery has been subjected to a form of appreciation whose content, as I shall show, has itself been influenced by a European aesthetic theory. I describe not only the relation between ecology and social organization in a Japanese pottery community, but the interpretation of that relationship in the context of the Japanese folk craft movement. Ultimately, it is the general relation between folk crafts and social organization that is of interest to me.

My use of the phrase "folk craft" is deliberate. When it comes to studying art, anthropologists are often deceived by their own ideological prejudices. Unable to take a consistently objective view of the art forms of other societies, they have generally failed to clarify whether the criteria they use to determine the worth of an object as art are in fact their own or those of the people in whose culture the art object is found. About the only thing that has become clear from the so-called anthropological approach to art is that nobody is quite sure what art is.

I feel that, as anthropologists, we might have made more progress in our studies of art forms if we had concentrated on finding out what it is that makes them art—that is, if we had analyzed more fully the role of aesthetics in the organization of society. My argument here is that, for an object to be termed "art," the aesthetic appraisal of that object cannot be made by a single individual. The aesthetic criteria by which it is judged should not be those of the artist (cf. Haselberger's "artistic-aesthetic intention," 1961:342) or the critic (cf. Bohannan 1961:86) alone, but should include the opinions of artist and critic alike, and very often a host of others involved—patrons, traders, gallery owners, literary editors, and other kinds of art promoters (Mendieta y Nunez 1957). This point is straightforward, but tends to be overlooked in anthropological studies of art.

It is, then, the experience of art, rather than the art object per se, in which I am interested here. Whether Japanese *mingei* is art or not is a moot point. Ideally, Yanagi Muneyoshi stressed that his concept of *mingei* (which literally means "popular art") was not an art form. However, as I shall show, many people nowadays do regard *mingei* as a kind of art. *Mingei* objects are seen to cover a broad spectrum that includes Art (with a capital A), on the one hand, and that delightful term "ethnokitsch" (Graburn 1976:6), on the other. Onta pottery lies approximately midway between these two extremes. It is subject to the same social processes as those that surround the appreciation of a Rubens oil painting, a Chippendale chair, or that pile of bricks in the Tate Gallery in London. In other words, it is the existence of a set of conscious and publicized aesthetic premises which is important to the sociological study of art.

One theme pervading this book about the Japanese folk craft movement and Sarayama's community of potters is that of nostalgia. In certain respects it might be said that the Japanese feeling for nostalgia, or *natsukashisa*, is a peculiar cultural trait. From very early times, Japanese literature has reflected the people's concern for the passing of time—epitomized perhaps by the sense of *mono no aware*, or "sadness of things," that pervades *The Tale of Genji*. People can frequently be heard exclaiming how wistful they feel upon encountering an old acquaintance, revisiting a haunt of the past, or simply doing something that they have not done for some time. To some extent, I would suggest, this concept of *natsukashisa* helps the Japanese strengthen tenuous personal relationships. But there is more to nostalgia than this. One thing that struck me during fieldwork was that both critics and craftsmen seemed to be looking wistfully to the past in an attempt to come to terms with the present. Yanagi Muneyoshi himself saw the medieval European guild as the perfect example of the way in which "beauty" was created by craftsmen who cooperated in a particular social and moral order. Potters in Sarayama did not have to refer so far back in time in their search for community. For them, there had always been a social and moral order until the community was broken up by the effects of the boom in Japanese folk crafts during the 1950s and 1960s.

Nisbet (1970) has shown that this nostalgia for community is to be found in a large body of European thought, especially of European sociology, during the nineteenth century. It would appear that in any society undergoing the sort of radical changes that were induced by the Industrial Revolution in northern Europe, people are likely to fall back on the concept of community as a means of restoring social order. This leads me to a general premise about the relation between folk art and social organization. I would argue not only that the Industrial Revolution has affected the way in which we see art, but that the rise of industrialism, and its concomitants, urbanization and mechanization, has led many of us to look back with a certain nostalgia to those forms of art or craft which evoke a preindustrial, golden age of simplicity. When established art forms fail to meet the criteria of simplicity, new forms are likely to be invented by those with a special interest in the arts. At this stage what has hitherto been seen as "rubbish" may be elevated to the more durable category of "art" (Thompson 1979). This is precisely what has happened to Japanese folk crafts.

The term "folk art" was originally applied to arts and crafts made in the peasant villages of Europe (Graburn 1976:21; Harmon 1974:470), and was for some time used to refer specifically to European folk art (Gerbrands 1957:19). The term "folk" has been used interchangeably with "popular," although the distinction is not absolute. In Japan, Yanagi Muneyoshi himself at one stage used the phrase "people's art" (Yanagi 1949:7) to describe the kind of artisan work that he later preferred to call *mingei*, or "folk craft."

The following characteristics of folk arts have been noted: (1) their utilitarian aspect; (2) the role of continuous tradition; (3) the use of readily available natural materials, and often the use of simple techniques in production; (4) their collective aspect: "without considerations of the group involved and of the circumstances of folk culture in general, the art can scarcely be interpreted;" and (5) a style evolving naturally out of the craftsman's repetitive use of established patterns, leading in many cases to simplicity (Harmon 1974:471–474). Tomars (1940:167) has also argued that folk arts have (1) no professional specialist who lives by practicing the folk art concerned; (2) in general, a concern for "communal growth" rather than for individual work; (3) a comparatively slow rate of change; (4) no aristocratic patrons; and (5) no abstract theory regarding technique.

Tomars' list of folk art characteristics expresses an ideal, perhaps, that no longer exists, for over the past few decades artists, museum curators, anthropologists, and traders have patronized folk arts all over the world. As a result, craftsmen have often become professional specialists and may well be known by their individual names. "Communal growth" is overlooked as craftsmen continually experiment with new shapes and designs. Although a stylistic simplicity may be retained, this is frequently only because it is an essential part of an abstract theory of folk art. Craftsmen find themselves involved in a definition of folk art which may well include an emphasis on beauty (Becker 1978:865–866), put forward by outsiders not directly involved in the craft concerned.

These are problems faced by the potters who live in the community of Sarayama, where I conducted fieldwork for two years from April 1977.

From the late 1920s, Yanagi Muneyoshi published a series of essays in which he argued that, ideally, "beauty" derived from the fact that folk crafts were functional, made by craftsmen who relied on traditional methods of production and on the use of natural materials. These were not individual "artists" but "unknown craftsmen" who worked "unconsciously" in a spirit of cooperation with one another, without regard for financial gain.

Onta potters found themselves involved in the Japanese folk craft movement because their work and the social organiztion of their community closely conformed to Yanagi's aesthetic ideals. However, since the mid-1950s, a rapid expansion in domestic consumption has brought on an equally rapid growth in the Japanese economy as a whole. What Dore (1967:24) refers to as "the landslide into Westernization" has affected all sections of Japanese society. The community of Sarayama has been brought into more immediate contact with the outside world by an improvement in communications; potters have been able to adopt one or two technological innovations in production as a result of developments in the ceramic industry. Such advances, together with a sustained increase in the market demand for folk crafts (itself a product, as I will argue, of the process of Westernization), have led to a number of changes in Sarayama's social organization. These social changes have been interpreted as aesthetic changes by the present leaders of the Japanese folk craft movement, who have suggested that the standard of Sarayama's pottery has thereby deteriorated. The potters, for their part, argue that they cannot now fulfill *mingei* aesthetic ideals, because they have to take technical aspects of production and consumer demand into account when making pottery. They find themselves caught between the expectations of their critics, on the one hand, and those of their buyers, on the other. This book is an account of the extent to which they satisfy and fail to satisfy the two groups, of how they try to adapt to changes in-

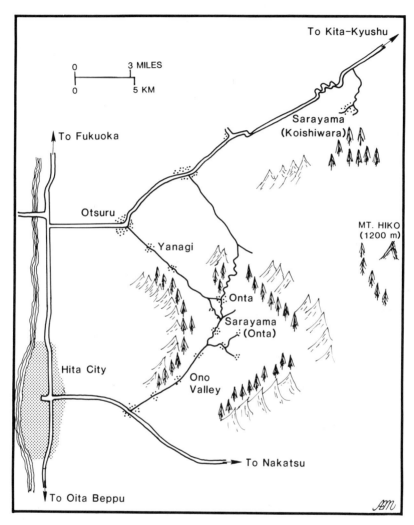

MAP 1.   *Japan*

duced by national economic growth, and of what happens to their community as a result.

This study, therefore, concerns the total social processes surrounding the production, marketing, and appreciation of a type of stoneware pottery which is known in Japanese as *ontayaki*, or Onta pottery, and is made in the community of Sarayama, Kyushu, Japan (see map 1). In chapter 1 I shall give an outline of the historical background of the Japanese folk craft movement, including details of some aspects of its founder's ideology. I shall then discuss the organization of a Japanese rural society in general and provide a more detailed study of the social structure and organization of Sarayama itself (chapters 2–5). From chapter 6 I shall turn to the general theme of social change and the aesthetic appraisal of Onta pottery. I hope to show how environmental changes and improved economic conditions lead to a breakdown of community solidarity and to the emergence of individualism, and how these changes are seen by leaders of the folk craft movement to give rise to a deterioration in the quality of Onta pottery (chapters 6–8). In chapter 9 I intend to examine Yanagi's folk craft ideology in more detail and to show how many theoretical premises cannot be fulfilled because of problems arising in the production and marketing of Onta pottery. In the Conclusion, I shall sum up the main points made in the book and speculate about possible links between the concept of folk art and the nature of the society in which such a concept is found.

1

The Japanese Folk Craft Movement

Two events seen to be of vital significance to the development of nineteenth-century European thought were the French Revolution and the Industrial Revolution. The development of Japanese thought in the late nineteenth and early twentieth centuries was influenced by no less dramatic an event. In 1868, the Meiji Restoration brought an end to the feudal system that had characterized the country's government for the previous three centuries, and laid Japan open for the first time to the influences of modern Western civilization. During the next few decades the country underwent a number of political, administrative, and economic changes that were the prelude to Japan's emergence as an advanced industrialized nation in the mid twentieth century.

THE BRITISH ARTS AND CRAFTS MOVEMENT

So far as I can judge, the earliest example of a folk art movement is that which occurred in England during the second half of the nineteenth century, approximately one hundred years after that country had industralized. What is known as the arts and crafts movement flourished in Britain during the 1880s and 1890s and aimed to counter some of the social, moral, and aesthetic disintegration that was seen to have been brought about by the Industrial Revolution. One of the first to speak out against the way in which, in his opinion, crafts were being destroyed by industry appears to have been Thomas Carlyle. In 1829 he published a diatribe in *The Edinburgh Review*, in which he deplored what he was as the mechanization of man's hand, head, and heart:

Our old modes of exertion are all discredited, and thrown aside. On every hand the living artisan is driven from his workshop, to make room for a speedier, inanimate one. The shuttle drops from the finger of the weaver, and falls into iron fingers that ply it faster. For all earthly, and for some unearthly purpose, we have machines and mechanical furtherances. . . . We remove mountains and make seas our smooth highway; nothing can resist us. We war with rude Nature; and by our restless engines, come off victorious and loaded with spoils. . . . Not the external and physical alone is now managed by the machinery, but the internal and spiritual also. Here, too, nothing follows its spontaneous course, nothing is left to be accomplished by old natural methods. . . . The same habit regulates not our modes of action alone, but our modes of thought and feeling. Men are grown mechanical in head and in heart, as well as in hand. They have lost faith in individual endeavor, and in natural force, of any kind. Not for internal perfection, but for external combinations and arrangements, for institutions, constitutions—for Mechanism of one sort of other, do they hope and struggle. Their whole efforts, attachments, opinions, turn on mechanism, and are of a mechanical character. (From *Sign of the Times*, in the *Works of Thomas Carlyle*, vol. 2, pp. 233–236)

The real precursor of attitudes that were later adopted by the arts and crafts movement may be said to be the architect A. W. N. Pugin (1812–1852) who, in the late 1830s, published books in which he aimed to combat "the present decay of taste." Pugin was also responsible for two ideas that were taken up by such later critics as Ruskin and Morris, and by Yanagi in Japan: first, that of the functional approach to beauty; second, the idea that the art of a period could be used to judge the quality of the society that was producing that art.

John Ruskin (1819–1900) was essentially an art critic before he became a social critic, but the two aspects of his writings should be taken together and seen as a whole. His central concern was with beauty, a word that he usually spelled with a capital B and that was virtually interchangeable with Truth. Beauty was the absolute standard of perfection, not only in works of art but in man as well.

Ruskin followed Pugin in thinking that there was a close relation between the quality of a society and the quality of its art. His conception of art and society may be said to be organic in that he stressed their interrelation and interdependence. The beauty of form in art was connected with the fulfillment of its function; the fulfillment of function depended on the coherence and cooperation of all parts of the social organism. Ruskin argued that if a society was not regulated in such a way as to permit each man to fulfill his function, then the system was to blame. It was here that he took issue with the idea that production should be geared to the laws of supply and demand.

> We have much studied and much perfected, of late, the great civilized invention of the division of labour; only we give it a false name. It is not truly speaking, the labour that is divided, but the men:—Divided into mere segments of men—broken into small fragments and crumbs of life; so that all the little piece of intelligence that is left in a man is not enough to make a pin or a nail, but exhausts itself in making the point of a pin or the head of a nail. (Ruskin 1963:180, from *The Nature of Gothic*)

William Morris (1834–1896), poet, designer, critic, and socialist, also argued that man was being destroyed by industrialization. He saw people deprived of all joy in their work, saw them desecrating arts inherited from the time when that joy had been present in all its vitality. He called for a popular art, simple and functional, that was "to be made by the people and for the people, as a happiness to the maker and the user" (Morris 1902:33). Art was for everyone, not simply for a "narrow class who only care for it in a very languid way" (1947:115), and the best things were "common wares, bought and sold in any market."

Morris bitterly objected to what he called "the wretched anarchy of commercial war," for he felt that commerce had by its supremacy entirely suppressed art. He also realized that nature was being polluted and destroyed by the competitive society in which he lived:

> Is money to be gathered? Cut down the pleasant trees among the houses, pull down ancient and venerable buildings for the money that a few square yards of London dirt will fetch; blacken rivers, hide the sun and poison the air with smoke and worse, and it's nobody's business to see to it or mend it: that is all that modern commerce, the counting-house forgetful of the workshop, will do for us herein. (Morris 1902:16)

To Morris the laws of nature were the laws of art, and wherever nature worked there would be beauty. This connection between nature and beauty is just one of a number of parallels in the aesthetic theories of Morris and Yanagi Muneyoshi, founder of the Japanese folk craft movement. It also plays a large part in my study of the pottery community of Sarayama (Onta).

One of the effects of industralization in Britain was the emergence of a stream of social criticism which advocated a utopian sense of community to counteract what was seen as the moral disintegration of capitalist society. In Japan a number of people began to propound similar moral theories, partly in response to, but increasingly more as outright reaction against, the rapid industrialization and urbanization of Japanese society following the Sino-Japanese War in 1894–1895. These theories were for the most part highly romanticized, calling for a return to the sort of rural communalism whereby high and low, young and old, rich and poor would all live together as one large organic family. The countryside came to be seen as a repository of such "true" values as frugality, altruism, harmony, and cooperation. Such social criticism led, on the one hand, to the establishment of the Tolstoy-inspired "new village" movement and, on the other, to the development of agrarianism (*nōhonshugi*) as an ideology for Japan's militarists in the early Shōwa period. It may also be said to have had some influence on Yanagi Muneyoshi's concept of *mingei*.

The whole idea of "folk craft" began in Japan in the late 1920s, when Yanagi published his first book, *The Way of Crafts* [Kōgei no Michi]. Yanagi was born in 1889. His father was of high rank in the Japanese navy, but died when Muneyoshi[1] was only two years old, and the boy was brought up by his mother. He was sent to the Peers' School (Gakushūin Kōtōka) before entering the Department of Philosophy and Letters at the Tokyo Imperial University in 1911.[2]

It was during his final year at the Peers' School that Yanagi joined a number of friends and acquaintances, who were all interested in lit-

---

1. Later in life, Yanagi sometimes made use of the Chinese pronunciation of the characters with which his name, Muneyoshi, was formed to call himself Yanagi Sōetsu. This is the name by which he is generally known in the West.

2. For biographies of Yanagi, see Tsurumi 1976 and Mizuo 1978. Bernard Leach has given a somewhat more subjective account of his friendship with Yanagi in the Introduction to *The Unknown Craftsman* (Leach 1972). Further facts may be gathered from a reading of Leach's conversations with the Japanese potter Hamada Shōji (Leach 1976). I am grateful to Yanagi's son Munemichi for giving me further information about his father's activities during the early part of his life. I have decided not to include here references to Yanagi's works where words or short phrases only are quoted. Those readers interested in tracing the exact sources are referred to my Ph.D. dissertation, *Social Aspects of Folk Craft Production, Marketing and Aesthetics in a Japanese Pottery Community*, University of London, 1980.

erature and art, to start publication of the now famous magazine *Shirakaba* [Silver Birch]. Several members of this group, including Shiga Naoya, Mushakōji Saneatsu, Arishima Takeo, and Satomi Ton, later became well-known writers as a result of their contributions to this magazine. Although Yanagi himself was not at the center of the group, he wrote more than seventy articles for the magazine, including poems, translations, and critical essays. Publication of the *Shirakaba* continued monthly for fourteen years, until the great Kantō earthquake of 1923. During this time the *Shirakaba* group saw itself as "children of the world" and sought to introduce to its Japanese readers a wide range of Western artists and writers. These included Rodin, Cézanne, Van Gogh, Blake, Whitman, Ibsen, and Tolstoy. It was undoubtedly Tolstoy's work which inspired Mushakōji to set up the first of the "new villages" (*atarishiki mura*) in Hyūga, Kyushu, in 1916.

In 1919 Yanagi was appointed Professor of Religious Studies at Tōyō University, and in the same year he published the first of a series of articles on Korean culture. Despite being harassed by the police, Yanagi persisted in his praise of Korean things. His fondness for that country led to his planning, and eventually opening, the Korean Folk Art Gallery (Chōsen Minzoku Bijutsukan) in one of the old palace buildings in Seoul.

Yanagi's early interest in Korea stemmed primarily from his liking for ceramics of the Yi dynasty. Indeed, the Japanese folk craft movement might be said to be a result of Yanagi's enthusiasm for Korean pottery,[3] for when he learned that Yi dynasty wares had for the most part been made by nameless craftsmen, he felt that there had to be a similar sort of art in Japan. He thus became interested in what he initially called "people's art"—for the way in which it accorded with his ideals of beauty. Once he discovered that there was a popular art in his own country, Yanagi started planning a folk craft museum for Japan.

Although, finally, Yanagi's folk craft ideal was a combination of philosophical, religious, and aesthetic elements, in the early days he appears to have been primarily concerned with beauty. While he went around collecting all sorts of objects that fitted his idea of what was beautiful, he began to realize that his taste was hardly that of the average, educated person, and that his collection was not of the kind

---

3. Yanagi's praise for Korean pottery, and in particular his linking *mingei* beauty to the "sadness of white glazed wares," has been effectively criticized by Kim Yang-gi (see Kumakura 1979).

that could be seen displayed in the museums and art galleries of his time. Reflecting upon the matter, he gradually realized that all the objects that he liked had been made to be used in ordinary people's everyday lives. In other words, they had a "common" nature which was a far cry from the "aristocratic" *objets d'art* favored by art critics, historians, and dealers in antiques. Moreover, these practical, everyday utensils had not been made by famous artists, but were the work of unknown craftsmen who produced things cheaply and in quantity. This was what gave them, in his opinion, a "free" and "healthy" beauty.

Yanagi was particularly fond of looking for this kind of craft work in the street and temple markets of Kyoto, to which city he had moved with his family in 1923 after the Kantō earthquake. The word that the women stall-operators in these markets used for such common or garden items was *getemono* (vulgar thing). Yanagi himself adopted this word for some time, before finding that it was picked up by critics and journalists and sometimes given unfortunate nuances evoked by the concept of vulgarity (*gete*). In order to overcome such misunderstanding, he had no alternative but to think of some other word to describe his "people's art." In 1925, after considerable discussion between Yanagi and two potter friends, Hamada Shōji (1894–1978) and Kawai Kanjirō (1890–1966), the term *mingei* was coined to describe the craftsman's work. This was an abbreviated term, derived from *minshū*, meaning "common people," and *kōgei*, "craft." Yanagi translated it into English as "folk craft" (not "folk art"), since he did not wish people to conceive of *mingei* as an individually inspired "high" art.

The term *mingei* was applied to things that were functional, used in people's everyday lives, "unpretentious," "pure," and "simple." Yanagi argued that *mingei* was characterized by tradition and not by individuality. Art should not be associated with the individual creator; it should be unassuming, the work of "non-individuality." Beauty could exist "without heroes."

Enquiries soon revealed, however, that the "unknown craftsmen" had all but disappeared. Mass production and competitive pricing had effectively put a stop to public demand for craftwork. Yanagi deplored the was in which communities of craftsmen, such as potters or lacquerers, had been forced to give up their work and take up some other occupation for a livelihood. He felt that it was precisely because such people had worked together over the centuries, patiently, with humility, using methods of trial and error in an "abandonment of egoism and pride," that their work had great aesthetic value.

The general public needed to be educated in the beauty of Japanese crafts. Yanagi set about propagating his views in a series of articles, books, and lectures, and his first complete work, *Kōgei no Michi* [The Way of Crafts], was published in 1928. In 1931 he started a magazine, *Kōgei* [Crafts], in which he and a close circle of friends who thought like him were able to air their views. The folk craft movement, as such, really began with publication of this magazine, and the number of Yanagi's followers increased considerably as a result of their reading its contents. The first edition of *Kōgei* ran to 500 copies; the last (volume 120), to 2,000 copies. In 1952 *Kōgei* was absorbed by a second magazine, *Mingei* (first published in 1939). *Mingei* remains the official organ of the Japan Folk Craft Association (Nihon Mingei Kyōkai), which was founded in 1931 by Yanagi and friends—mainly potters like Kawai Kanjirō and Tomimoto Kenkichi.

Yanagi did not confine himself to literary activities, but spent some considerable time traveling round Japan, seeking out and actively encouraging craftsmen to continue or go back to their work. Indeed, it was on one of these trips, in 1931, that he visited the potters' community of Sarayama (Onta). Yanagi was himself encouraged in his evangelical work by a director of Takashimaya Department Store, Kawakatsu Kenichi, and received some financial support from private sources, wealthy businessmen such as Yamamoto Tamesaburō, owner of the Royal Hotel in Osaka, and Ōhara Magosaburō, president of the Kurashiki Rayon Company. It was the latter who provided the ¥100,000 needed for the purchase of land and the building and furnishing of the Japan Folk Craft Museum (Nihon Mingeikan), opened in Tokyo in 1935.

There are three manifestations of the folk craft movement: The Folk Craft Museum exhibits objects that are seen to be "truly *mingei*"; Yanagi intended the Museum to establish a standard of beauty. The Folk Craft Association promotes Yanagi's ideals throughout the country and publishes two monthly magazines. The folk craft shop, Takumi, acts as a major retail sales outlet in Tokyo. Although Takumi was founded as long ago as 1933, it was only in the 1950s that sales began to show a noticeable increase, and the movement as a whole began to receive national, and even international, attention. By about 1960, Yanagi's ideas had become known, not just to a small group of people living in Tokyo, Kyoto, and Osaka, but—as a result of publicity in the media—to almost everyone in Japan. There was an enormous demand for handmade folk crafts, which many people thought included such things as toothpicks and log cabins. This demand came to be labeled the *"mingei* boom" and continued until about 1974– 1975, after which it gradually declined. Craftsmen who had been struggling to make ends meet before and just after the Pacific War, suddenly found themselves comparatively well-off; potters in particular benefited financially from the boom. With all the publicity surrounding folk crafts, new kilns were set up everywhere. So far as the purists were concerned, the day of the "instant potter" had come to accompany the other "instants" of everyday life in Japan—coffee, noodles, and geisha. The average craftsman was interested in *mingei*, not for its beauty, but for the money that was to be made from it.

One of the problems currently facing leaders of the folk craft movement is the way in which the meaning of *mingei* has come to be interpreted by people who are not directly acquainted with Yanagi's works. It is the interpretation by the average man in the street of what constitutes *mingei* that saddens and frustrates the movement's leaders. What is perhaps worse, so far as the latter are concerned, is that it has also affected the way in which craftsmen themselves have come to view their work.

A second problem lies in the varied interpretations of Yanagi's ideals within the movement itself. In the beginning, potters such as Tomimoto Kenkichi and Kawai Kanjirō were closely involved with the concept of *mingei*, but in time their own work developed in such a manner that they felt it necessary to dissociate themselves from the folk craft movement. Tomimoto actually went so far as to set up his own organization, the Shinshōkai (New Craftsmen's Association), in 1947. Yanagi had in part expected this sort of thing to happen; Tomimoto and Kawai were, after all, artist craftsmen in search of a new means of expression in their own idiom. What really upset Yanagi and others close to him was the decision by one of his non-craftsmen followers, Miyake Chūichi, to break away and form his own group with its separate ideology. In 1949 Miyake built his own Japan Craft Museum (Nihon Kōgeikan) and then, ten years later, founded the Japan Folk Craft Society (Nihon Mingei Kyōdan). He also started publishing a monthly magazine, *Nihon no Mingei* [Japanese Folk Crafts], and in this he time and again took issue with Yanagi, arguing that the latter had made folk crafts into an art form by stressing beauty over function, by promoting such artist-craftsmen as Leach, Kawai, and Hamada, and by refusing to take economic issues into account when referring to the functional aspects of *mingei*. To a certain extent, perhaps, Miyake's criticisms were not ill-founded, but the manner in which he made them was regrettable. Yanagi, to his credit, did not want to involve the whole folk craft movement in what was mainly a personal vendetta against himself. He therefore remained silent in the face of criticism that during his lifetime was, and still is, often vitriolic.

Miyake died in April 1980, after running a "one man band," which many people think will fade away with its leader's death. The Folk Craft Association, for its part, has survived since the death of Yanagi in 1961, but its new leaders—consisting of people like Yanagi's son Munemichi and the art historian Mizuo Hiroshi—are now faced with a variety of problems. Some of these are financial: the Folk Craft Museum in Tokyo is in need of repair; its magnificent collection of items (most of which have never been shown to the public) urgently requires proper storage facilities. But the Folk Craft Association has not the financial wherewithal to carry out such major tasks. Its private backers have long since died, and a request to the national government for funds appears to be the only way to meet such financial problems.

Other problems are ideological. The Folk Craft Association's magazine, *Mingei*, is published monthly and distributed to about five thousand of its members all over the country. Yet, Yanagi Munemichi and Mizuo Hiroshi know that people are not really reading the magazine. Subscription is a form of passive membership; craftsmen, in particular, take the magazine to keep the "people in Tokyo" happy.

By far the most active members of both the Folk Craft Association and the Folk Craft Society are women. Young housewives regularly attend summer seminars; they travel round the country visiting craftsmen's workshops and buying much of their work. Yet many will argue that the housewives do not understand the meaning of true *mingei* and cannot appreciate proper beauty. It is perhaps not surprising, therefore, to find that rural craftsmen now dismiss the folk craft movement as another urban elitist fashion whose followers have failed to come to grips with their problems. The new leadership somehow has to counteract disinterest, remain faithful to Yanagi's original ideas, yet update them to present-day realities. The intensity with which many craftsmen now criticize the folk craft movement reveals, paradoxically, how much they had pinned their hopes on Yanagi's ideology.

THE JAPANESE FOLK CRAFT IDEAL

We turn now to the nature of the ideals that Yanagi expounded. Inasmuch as he was concerned with the "beauty" of objects that
he labeled "folk crafts," and outlined the various criteria which in his
opinion created such "beauty," Yanagi may be said to have written
about aesthetics. However, the Japanese folk craft movement was envisaged not simply as an art movement, but rather as something more
fundamental to man's existence:

> This movement of ours is most active in the field of crafts, but it is not
> simply a craft movement. Rather what we are really aiming at is a clear-
> ly spiritual movement. Thus the folk craft movement cannot be said to
> exist without its ethical and religious aspects. . . . I am not suggesting
> that a craftsman has to be a moralist or religious preacher; each man
> can keep to his own profession. What I do say is that a craftsman is first
> and foremost a human being, and as a human being his life has to be
> founded on spirituality. . . . When one reviews the history of crafts, one
> cannot avoid the fact that every great period of craftsmanship was
> founded on an ethical and religious doctrine. . . . The problem of beau-
> ty is not simply a problem of beauty; beauty cannot exist unless it con-
> tains elements of truth, goodness and holiness. If we reflect on this, we
> will realize that it is impossible to come to terms with a folk craft move-
> ment that is not spiritual. In this sense, the folk craft movement should
> try to be a cultural movement. (Yanagi 1946:21–22)

I should like to stress here that Yanagi's primary concern was with
what I shall call modern man's "spiritual" attitude, and that he chose
to express his vision of spirituality through the medium of folk crafts.
He was, therefore, concerned with *how* folk crafts were made, rather
than with these crafts as objects in themselves. Provided they were
made according to a certain set of rules laid down by himself, they
would naturally accord with his concept of beauty. This is a point not
fully understood by many devotees of *mingei*, who concentrate on the
aesthetic effect of craftwork and ignore the spiritual attitude of the
craftsmen.

How, then, did Yanagi think that *mingei* ought to be made, and on
what basis was he able to determine the difference between good and
bad crafts? Yanagi himself emphasized that he did not intend to start
a movement; he did not begin with a preconceived theory of art
which he then tried to apply to Japanese folk crafts. Things were

much simpler. He had no aesthetic ideas at all, but just looked at craft objects and experienced a certain "mental shock." It was from his own personal experience in "just looking" at crafts that Yanagi developed his *mingei* theory. This experience he called "direct perception" (*chokkan*), which he variously referred to as "the absolute foot rule," "the selfless foot rule," and "the foot rule that is no foot rule" and which he used to determine beauty. Let me quote a free adaptation of what Yanagi wrote about *chokkan*:

> When you look at things, your eyes can be clouded by knowledge, by habit, or by the wish to assert yourself. But this is not the way to look at things. There should be nothing coming between the person who is seeing and the thing that is seen. A thing should be seen for what it is. This is "direct perception"—just seeing things. You enter into the thing; the thing communicates with your heart. When the two become one, you have direct perception. To know about something, without seeing it directly, gives rise to pointless judgment.
>
> In order to see things properly, you should look at them directly. But to do this, you must not prejudge them. Direct perception must come before criticism. If you allow your learning to come before direct perception, then your eye will be dulled. To know and then to look is the same as not looking at all. In order to come into contact with beauty itself, you have no need of intellectual analysis, for this only impedes your perception. Without direct perception, you will never understand beauty. (Yanagi 1932:56, 58)

Direct perception, then, defies logical explanation. Yanagi argued that it was "beyond the self" and that it offered a means of seeing crafts without the intrusion of subjectivity and all its possible prejudices. In his appreciation of Japanese folk crafts, therefore, Yanagi aimed at putting aside all concepts of what did and did not constitute beauty, and at allowing a thing to be seen for what it was and to speak for itself. Direct perception was a method of aesthetic appreciation that could be applied by *anyone*, and "good" and "beautiful" folk crafts could be recognized as such by *anyone*, provided that he or she made use of direct perception. Yanagi argued that if *chokkan* was subjective or arbitrary, then it was not "direct" perception at all.

As we have seen, so far as crafts were concerned, Yanagi's main emphasis was on beauty. Beauty was, in his opinion, unchanging, created by an immutable spirit. Sung-period ceramics and medieval Gothic churches were products of the same spirit; "true" man was unchanging, unaffected by cultural or historical background. The present and the past were linked by beauty.

Mingei has been roughly defined by Hamada Shōji, the world-famous artist potter and friend of Yanagi's, as "health, naturalness and beauty." Two broad categorizations of the content of Yanagi's folk craft theory may be useful. I shall call them the "moral" and "utilitarian" aspects of *mingei*. The first is, strictly speaking, extra-aesthetic, since it concerns the way in which folk crafts are made; the second centers on their social use. The moral aspect concerns the craftsman; the utilitarian aspect, the craft itself as object.

Let us look first at the moral aspect of folk craft theory. One word that occurs frequently in Yanagi's writings is "nature" (*shizen*), for all craftwork should, in his opinion, be focused on nature. Craftsmen should ideally make use of natural materials, and these materials ought to be obtainable locally. The beauty of folk crafts, therefore, depended largely on the natural environment in which the craftsman worked.

But Yanagi's concept of nature had two meanings: one referred to the environment, the other to the inner self, or God. Yanagi did not accept the notion that nature was but a shadow or reflection of a higher reality. For him, nature *was* the higher reality; it sustained the masses, made them great, and gave them strength. He directly linked nature, beauty, and selflessness, and it is here that his thought differs most radically, perhaps, from Western art theories and shows close affinity to Buddhist ideas. Beauty was, in his opinion, born of the natural, of the unconscious in man. For crafts to be beautiful, the craftsman should let nature do the creating; salvation came from outside himself, from what Yanagi called "self-surrender" (*tarikidō*). *Tariki* was not denial of the self so much as freedom from the self. Just as an Amidha Buddhist could be saved by reciting the *nenbutsu* prayer and denying his or her self, so the craftsman could attain a "pure land of beauty" by surrendering his self to nature. No craftsman had within himself the power to create beauty; the beauty that came from "self-surrender" was incomparably greater than that of any work of art produced by "individual genius."

This argument led Yanagi to suggest that only in a communal society in which people cooperated with one another would beauty be born. Cooperation bound not only one man to another, but man to nature. There was always a communal beauty in good craftwork, and behind this beauty flowed the blood of love—the love of God, of nature, of justice, of other men, of work, and of things. Cooperation was built on mutual love, which was itself brought about by crafts. Folk crafts could only be called the "communal arts" (*sic*).[4]

In the light of this emphasis that beauty derived from nature and from cooperation, it is not surprising to find Yanagi criticizing modern industrialized society. Three things in particular incurred his displeasure: mechanization, greed, and individualism. He felt, therefore, that the more a society shifted from a cooperative to a capitalist system of relations, the more its crafts deteriorated. With industrial capitalism, mechanized means of production replaced handwork, and people became isolated from one another. Naturalness yielded to artificiality, and man was unable to be creative; while the joy of work could be found in handicrafts, it was absent in machine-made things.

Yanagi further argued that there was a close connection between the incentive for profit and the quality of work produced under a capitalist system of wage labor relations. A craftsman had to feel love for his work, and this was impossible when he made things merely for sale. "Love of profit robs a work of its beauty." Beauty could not, in his opinion, be born under conditions of wage labor. In the twentieth century people were working because they had to, not because they wanted to, whereas in the past the opposite had been true. In the world of crafts, a master had loved his apprentices, and they in turn had responded by doing their utmost to please their master; consequently, their work had been good. In modern times, however, profit had become the sole motivation behind work; it was this greed for money that was destroying crafts, beauty, the world, and man's spirit.

Yanagi claimed that it was impossible for "bad" craftwork to be created in a "good" society, and he concluded from this that "a system which does not guarantee the existence of beauty cannot be called a right and proper system." In short, he equated the beauty of crafts with the beauty of society. The concept of folk craft beauty was, therefore, clearly dissociated in Yanagi's mind from the idea of indi-

---

4. The word used here by Yanagi was *bijutsu*, "art." It is interesting to note that in the early days of the folk craft movement, neither Yanagi nor any of his friends had fixed on the idea that *mingei* was a "craft" rather than an "art" form. In a letter to Bernard Leach in 1927, Hamada calls the planned museum in Tokyo the Nihon Mingei Bitjutsu-kan, or Japan Folk Art Museum (Leach 1976:91). Leach himself always referred to *mingei* as "folk art," and Yanagi has often been criticized for setting *mingei* on a pedestal and making it into an art form, despite his theoretical emphasis on the notion of craft.

vidual talent. Anyone could create beautiful things, provided he was prepared to surrender his self and live in a "proper" spiritual manner within the bounds of morality. "The greatest crafts are born of the nameless masses," wrote Yanagi, who was convinced that real beauty could only be appreciated once one forgot all about names—names of *who* had produced an object, of *what* particular period or civilization or style that object belonged to. The commonly held theory that beauty could be produced by only a few highly talented people was, in his opinion, entirely wrong.

It is at this point that we come back to the nonintellectual approach to beauty which, it will be remembered, Yanagi argued was essential to his concept of direct perception. As far as he was concerned, intellectualism gave rise to art, while crafts were a result of "unlearnedness" (*mugaku*). Craftsmen did not create beauty; beauty was "born." An intellectual understanding of beauty, and a conscious attempt to produce beauty, merely produced what Yanagi thought was ugliness.

He was particularly concerned that folk crafts would in fact end up as one of the arts, and he prophesied—correctly, as we shall see—that the intrusion of the craftsman's "self" in his work would lead to high prices, self-consciousness, elevation to the status of art, and an emphasis on decoration rather than on function. It is here that we come to my second broad categorization of Yanagi's folk craft theory: its utilitarian aspect. Yanagi argued that it was because folk crafts were used that they were beautiful. A pot, for example, was made not to be looked at but to be used; only when it was used could it be said to be beautiful. If a craft was not used, it would lose its *raison d'être*. It was use which gave a thing life; it was misuse that destroyed it. The more a thing was used, the more beautiful it became. That was why, in Yanagi's opinion, the act of creation alone was not sufficient to give a thing beauty. All crafts had an afterlife, and beauty to a large extent derived from the way in which things were used in this afterlife.

Yanagi's concept of beauty deriving from function extended to the pricing of folk crafts; he felt that if things were to be used by the average man on the street, they would have to be cheap, and this was only possible if they were made in large quantities. He therefore rejected the generally held idea that there is an inverse relation between quality and quantity in the appreciation of beauty and art. In his opinion, works by individual artists were highly evaluated precisely because they were produced in limited numbers. Because there were so few of such artistic works, people became afraid to use them; they lost their function and became entirely decorative and expensive works that could be bought by only a few rich people. Consequently, these "art" objects became divorced from the common people. Folk crafts, on the other hand, had to be made by and for ordinary people; they were born of the unlearned, of the unknown masses. *Mingei* was not an art but a craft.

CONCLUSION

There are four main points that I should like to make in conclusion to this introductory chapter on the Japanese folk craft movement. The first two of them concern the social circumstances surrounding Yanagi's concept of folk art; the other two concern his aesthetic doctrine of direct perception.

First of all, let me repeat my suggestion that the concept of a "folk" art or craft generally occurs in highly urbanized societies at a certain stage following their industrialization. This point is important because Yanagi himself at one stage tended to emphasize the uniqueness of *mingei* and to suggest that the Japanese folk craft movement had no parallel elsewhere in the world (Yanagi 1946:3–4). I would argue that, on the contrary, there have been similar aesthetic ideals put forward in other societies, notably by the leaders of the British arts and crafts movement in the late nineteenth century.

Although there has been some argument to the contrary, it seems to me that much of Yanagi's theory of *mingei* has developed from the work of William Morris.[5] There are several parallels in the thought of the two men, both of whom advocated that (1) simplicity and fitness for purpose gave rise to beauty; (2) crafts belonged to the common people rather than to an aristocratic elite; (3) crafts were not created by individual genius, but resulted from a cooperative tradition; (4) the craftsman relied on natural materials, remained close to nature, and (5) took pleasure in his work; and (6) commerce destroyed good craftwork. I will return to Yanagi's attitude toward the uniqueness of *mingei* and to my suggestion regarding the connection between a folk art and urbanized industrialized societies in my Conclusion to this book.

---

5. See, for example, Jugaku 1935; Tonomura 1973; and Mizuo 1978:20-23. My own critique of this position has been printed in *Ceramic Review*, no. 66, December 1980.

Second, I think that the content of Yanagi's thought should also be viewed at a more specfically national cultural level. Japanese aesthetics are in general frequently imbued with subconscious Shinto beliefs. Practicality and beauty, for example, are commonly associated in Japanese aesthetics, since they conform to the Shinto concept of creative action. In this respect, the combination of spirituality, aestheticism, and utilitarianism found in Yanagi's thought is close to the three creative characteristics of Shinto religion (cf. Mason 1938:195). But Yanagi himself was not a Shinto but a Confucian scholar. It is not surprising to find, therefore, that his concept of *mingei* reflects a number of Confucian principles which were expounded, in a different context by Japan's nationalist leaders during the 1920s and 1930s. I am not convinced that Yanagi was himself aware of the parallels between his *mingei* aesthetics and the ideology upon which Japanese imperialism was founded; on the contrary, it is evident that he deplored Japanese military expansion abroad. But I think that these parallels might profitably be pointed out here as an example of my contention later on that aesthetic philosophies are never absolute, but are invariably socially relative.

The contrast running through Yanagi's thought between Western "material" culture and Asian "spiritual" culture had been made periodically from the end of the Edo period, but its appeal appears to have been particularly strong when Japan suffered from both internal and external crises. This was true of the late 1880s when certain Western countries were unwilling to revise their treaties with Japan. It was true once more in the early 1930s, when Japan was going through a period of economic depression and isolation. Confucianism came to play an increasingly important role in Japanese nationalism because it opposed Western materialism and provided a useful ethical ideology with which to explain Japan's expansion abroad. At the same time, it gave those in power more opportunity to strengthen their authority by upholding the Confucian concepts of loyalty, filial piety, and service to sovereign and state.

These ideals emphasized the unity of society, in which everyone fulfilled his duties and responsibilities, thus bringing about peace and prosperity for all. They became the national goal after 1931 when cooperative effort was seen to be the means by which the nation would become strong, and the notion of a corporate society included the holding up of the family as the foundation of the state. Relations between ruler and subject were seen to be the same as those between

father and son; those between superior and inferior, like those between elder and younger brothers. Economic relations were interpreted in a similar manner. Confucianists objected to the Western labor/
capital, management/worker type of relation and advocated instead,
as did Yanagi, a return to the medieval guilds where master craftsmen
looked after their apprentices and there was unity of interest in the
work of both parties.

Because of its anti-Western content, it was almost inevitable that
Confucianism would become associated with Japanese nationalism
and be used to stimulate the national consciousness. From the mid to
late 1920s, Confucianism gradually came to be seen as an integral
part of the "national policy" (*kokutai*), in which harmony and selflessness were stressed (W. W. Smith 1973:103–145). This is not to say that
it was ever accepted by the mass of Japanese people. Rather, Confucianism remained a philosophy which appealed to the ruling classes,
to a cross section of the Japanese elite consisting of businessmen, poli-
ticians, high-ranking military officers, university professors, and
scholars. All these men advocated a return to traditional ways, for
they believed, like Yanagi, that emphasis should be placed on an inner spiritual transformation. It was only a short step from this spiritual change to a revival of the "Japanese spirit" demanded by the na-
tionalists. The association between Confucianism and imperialism,
therefore, was coincidental, unfortunate, but—from this intellectual
vantage point of half a century's history behind us—not entirely un-
expected.

My third point concerns Yanagi's emphasis on direct perception as
the main guide to understanding beauty and here again I am concerned with the problem of absolute and relative values in the appreciation of art. The idea of "perception" is not new to aesthetic criticism, for, as Bourdieu points out (1968:601), "the work of art only
exists as such to the extent that it is perceived." Theoretically, therefore, "artistic criticism is always determined by the quality of first-
hand perception; obtuseness in perception can never be made good
by any amount of learning, however extensive, nor any command of
abstract theory, however correct" (Dewey 1934:298).

The concept of "perception" is very often religious. The identification between knower and known advocated by Yanagi is a belief that
was also prevalent in Europe during the Middle Ages. Thomas Aquinas, for example, argued that the apprehension of beauty was non-
conceptual knowledge, but that if it were conceptualized, it would

cease to be direct intuition; the aesthetic joy would vanish and with it the awareness of beauty.

The problem is, therefore, that logically "perception" as such cannot define either art or beauty. In theory,

> so long as we are considering the purely perceptual act involved in becoming aware of complicated constructs of perceptual stimuli to the exclusion of emotional response, imaginal associations and reverie . . . it is to be assumed that any two ideally competent observers would actualize in awareness exactly the same work of art when looking at the same picture or listening to the same performance of a musical composition. (Osborne 1955:33)

In practice, however, as Osborne admits, one cannot make a critical judgment on the basis of direct perception because that judgment will not be a "direct" comment but a later reflection upon the original experience. It would appear inevitable, therefore, that Yanagi's concept of direct perception (*chokkan*) cannot in fact logically provide a standard of beauty; extra-aesthetic values are bound to occur in the appreciation of Japanese folk crafts.

I have already outlined these extra-aesthetic values in my discussion of Yanagi's emphasis on the way in which he felt that folk crafts ought to be made. In his opinion, beauty could be adversely affected if (1) the craftsman preferred to make use of modern technology in production, rather than use only local natural materials; (2) he put his own individual interests before those of the community in which he worked; (3) he became too interested in financial reward and increased production beyond a given point of "equilibrium"; (4) he allowed his work to be priced beyond a reasonably low level; and (5) he produced work that was decorative rather than purely functional. Throughout the rest of this book, I will come back to each of these points as I attempt to show how the methods by which pottery is made in Sarayama, and the social organization of the community, have affected folk craft leaders' critical appraisal of Onta pottery.

My fourth and final point stems from Yanagi's concern for social and moral attitudes in his discussion of *mingei*. By emphasizing such theoretical concepts as "direct perception" and "self-surrender," Yanagi made it clear that beauty could be understood and created by *anyone* in Japanese society, regardless of his or her rank or education. Moreover, in his description of the content of beauty, Yanagi set out an ideal image of society in which people lived in cooperation and self-denial. I have already commented on how Confucianist ideals were taken up by Japan's militarists during the period leading up to the Pacific War. However, Yanagi's image is even more interesting to us now in that it closely parallels the ideal of present-day Japanese society as portrayed by sociologists and by most Japanese people themselves. What I intend to show throughout this book is the extent to which the practice of folk crafts, and the way in which a potters' community actually lives its day-to-day life, conform—or fail to conform—to these aesthetic and social ideals.

2

The Fieldwork Community

A number of places are called Sarayama in Kyushu, the southernmost of Japan's four main islands. Almost all of these are connected with pottery. There is one Sarayama in Koishiwara, another in Shiraishi, yet another in Nishijinmachi in Fukuoka City, and a fourth in the ceramic complex of Arita in Saga Prefecture. Literally meaning "plate mountain," the name of Sarayama has been given to places where deposits of clay have been found and pottery made. Because of the number of such sites, the wares made in each need to be identified by some other name, usually that of a nearby community or of a larger administrative unit that includes the Sarayama concerned within its boundaries. Hence pottery is called after the town of Arita, the ward of Nishinjin, the village of Koishiwara, and, in this case, the neighboring community of Onta.[1]

The exact date of the founding of Sarayama, and the date from which pottery has been made there, is not known, but is put at approximately 1705 (Hoēi 2). In that year a potter called Yanase Sanuemon is said to have left the hamlet of Sarayama in Koishiwara, about nineteen kilometers away, and to have set up a kiln in Onta where he

---

1. To avoid confusion, I will, from now on, refer to the fieldwork community as Sarayama when the community is being discussed independently, and as Onta when it is being compared with another pottery community, such as that of Koishiwara, or when the pottery—rather than the community as such—is being discussed. This is because pots made in the fieldwork community are known as Onta pottery (*ontayaki*).

had discovered deposits of suitable clay.[2] Koishiwara itself was founded by a Korean potter in the mid-seventeeth century not long after
Hideyoshi's invasions of that country between 1592 and 1598.

Three things were necessary to set up a pottery kiln: technical skill,
capital, and land. It is said that the first of these was provided by Yanase Sanuemon, and the second by one Kurogi Jūbē, who came from
Yanase hamlet near Ōtsuru (see map 2) and was not originally a potter
by trade.[3] Permission to settle was granted by the headman of the
hamlet of Onta, for it was on this hamlet's land that the clay deposits
had been discovered. The headman, called Sakamoto, apparently
agreed to the establishment of a new community provided he be permitted to join the two men whenever he pleased. Sarayama thus began with two households, those of Yanase and Kurogi, which were
later joined by a Sakamoto household that had branched from Onta
buraku. All fourteen of the households now in the community origi-
nate from these three families.

Little is known of the history of Sarayama between the founding in
1705 and its discovery by Yanagi in 1931. It has been suggested that
in the eighteenth century the potters made their wares for Kuroda, the
feudal lord who controlled Koishiwara (Koyama 1967:100), but there
is no evidence to support this assertion. Indeed, since Sarayama was
not located in Kuroda's fief, it is unlikely that the potters were called

----

2. Miyake Chūichi, leader of the Japan Folk Craft Society, has argued in his magazine, *Nihon no Mingei* (114:3-11), that Sarayama was founded in 1665 (Kanbun 5). At
the same time, however, he accepts that Yanase Sanuemon and Kurogi Jūbē (see main
text below) were founders of the community. But the Kurogi household mortuary tablets (*ihai*) show that Jūbē died in 1756. It is unlikely that Jūbē was old enough to walk,
let alone found a community, in 1665, ninety-one years prior to his death. That
Miyake's argument is more than suspect may be seen from the fact that the same edition of the magazine advertised in 1965 Onta's 300th anniversary festival—a festival
devised and arranged entirely by the Folk Craft Society (despite assertion to the contrary by Miyake, cf. *Nihon no Mingei* 114:34-35). Yanagi himself says that the old people in Sarayama told him in 1931 that their ancestors had come from Koishiwara some
186 years earlier (Yanagi 1931:6). This would mean that Sarayama was founded in
1745.

3. Umeki (1973:27) supposes that the two men were in some way related. While
proof is lacking to substantiate this view, it is known that Jūbē's mother (d. 1707) was
the daughter of one Yanase Mataemon. Whether Mataemon was related to Sanuemon,
however, remains unclear. Unfortunately, all genealogical records of the Koishiwara
and Onta Yanase households were lost when the temple in which they were kept was
destroyed by fire.

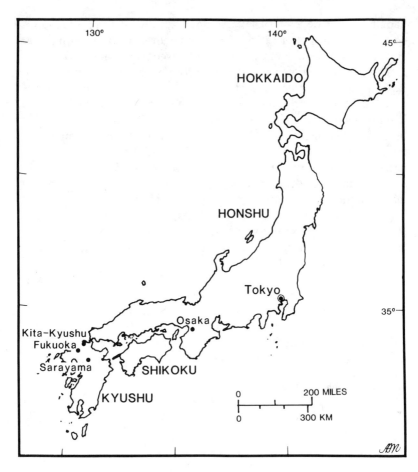

MAP 2.   *Hita City, Showing Onta and Koishiwara Pottery Communities*

upon to fill orders for the feudal lord. They may, however, have occasionally fired pots on behalf of the sheriff (*daikan*) in charge of the imperial domain of Hita. All that is known for certain is that Onta potters did not make tea ceremony wares, but concentrated on functional pots for everyday use by local farmers, such as water crocks, lidded jars for pickled fruit and vegetables, ash burners, and *unsuke* pouring vessels.

During the Edo period (1603–1868), potters used to hawk their wares around the countryside, and it was only toward the end of the nineteenth century that they began selling them through wholesalers—one in Hita and another in Kurume, some fifty kilometers away in Fukuoka Prefecture. It was at the latter's shop that Yanagi Muneyoshi, on one of his trips around Japan searching for "unkown craftsmen" and their folk crafts, first learned about Onta pottery. At the pottery dealer's he saw a black teapot that immediately appealed to his sense of beauty. Asking where the pot had been made, he was told that it was a "Hita thing" (*hitamono*) from some inaccessible pottery hamlet up in the mountains.

Yanagi's interest was aroused. He consulted various books about Japanese pottery, but failed to find any mention of *hitamono*. He realized that if he wanted to discover more about what kind of pottery was made in Sarayama, and how it was made, his only alternative was to go and see the community for himself. This he finally managed to do four years later in the spring of 1931. He had to walk most of the way up the valley from Ōtsuru, a distance of twelve kilometers. When he finally reached Sarayama, nobody there had any idea who their distinguished-looking visitor was, but he had to be pretty well up in the world to be able to buy all sorts of pots (even ones that the potters were using in their kitchens) and pay for them and their postage to Tokyo in *cash*. They asked him to spend the night in Sarayama, but Yanagi excused himself, saying that he had an engagement elsewhere the next day, so the potters accompanied him en masse down the valley to the nearest bus stop. There Yanagi boarded a bus bound for Hita, promising to return as soon as he could.

Yanagi published an account of his visit to Sarayama in the Saga edition of the Mainichi newspaper on July 13, 1931, under the title, "Kita Kyūshū no kama o miru" [A survey of pottery kilns of north Kyushu], and later that year the article was republished in the craft magazine *Kōgei* (no. 9) as "Hita no Sarayama." Onta pottery was praised because it had always been functional rather than decorative.

Potters were ordinary craftsmen, who had no pretensions to fame, simple people whose work was clearly lacking in self-consciousness. The community of potters and their work were "all tradition," unchanging since the first kiln had been fired back in 1705. They were also "close to nature"; clay was prepared and pounded by water-powered crushers; pots were thrown on a kick-wheel, dried in the sunshine, then glazed with local raw materials and fired in a wood-fueled climbing kiln. All this was "natural." Modern machinery was not used at all (Yanagi 1931:6–11).

In spite of Yanagi's praise for Sarayama and its pottery, potters still struggled to sell their work. Local people in Hita for the most part disdained these dull-colored wares with their black clay and glazes, which very often did not prevent moisture from seeping through to the outside of the pot. Mass-produced china from Arita was, in their opinion, much better. It was light and thin; it was white and had pleasant floral designs painted on it; it didn't leak; and it was cheap. As a result, Sarayama potters found their market limited to country people living far away from towns where the Arita china was not readily available. Then came the war with its blackout restrictions; kilns were not allowed to be fired at night. As there were very few people wanting to buy their pots anyway, potters stopped production entirely until about 1947.

After three or four years, they started firing their kilns again. One advantage from the war was that a road was constructed between the Ono valley and Sarayama, and it was now possible to drive a jeep or heavy vehicle, somewhat bumpily, up from Hita to the community. It was along this road that Yanagi, true to his promise, came on a second visit to the community in 1951. This time he was not alone; the potter Hamada Shōji accompanied him and was as impressed by Sarayama's pots as Yanagi himself had been. The potters' reputation began to be firmly established in Tokyo and Osaka.

Sarayama's next visitor marked a turning point in the community's history. Bernard Leach (1887–1979), the English potter who had been closely connected with the folk craft movement throughout its early stages, expressed a desire to pay an extended visit to Sarayama. With the cooperation of both potters and prefectural authorities, Leach came in 1954 and stayed for twenty days, learning from the potters their techniques of chattering and brush decoration and teaching them in return his technique of pulling handles for their pitchers.

There was wide press coverage of Leach's visit to Sarayama, and this helped make "Onta ware" well known to those interested in folk crafts. During the next few years, visitors to the community became more frequent, and the publication of Leach's own description of Sarayama (Leach 1960) led to the arrival of foreign visitors as well. Potters expressly attribute their improved economic conditions and newly acquired fame to Leach's decision to stay for so long in Sarayama.[4]

There were, of course, other reasons for the potters' better financial position, not least of these being the improvement in the Japanese economy as a whole. It was from 1954 that the Japanese economy began to grow with great rapidity; over the next ten years, the net national product increased at an annual rate of 9.8 percent, while the annual growth rate of the G.N.P. averaged 14.5 percent between 1957 and 1967. As Okada notes (1976:170–171), "innovations in textiles, improvements in household appliances, and rationalization of 'home living' which all took place in the late 1950s were elements that helped bring about a revolution . . . in the appreciation of handcrafts on the part of the consumer."

So, an increase in market demand brought about greater sales of Onta pottery. But to Sarayama potters, improved transportation facilities were also very important. A bus started plying between Sarayama and the town of Hita three times a day in 1956; and in this year also the railway line between Kokura, in northern Kyushu, and Hita was opened, thereby facilitating travel to Sarayama by visitors from the main island of Honshu. Communications were further improved when a communal telephone was installed in the hamlet's sake shop in 1957.

By the late 1950s, the media had started promoting widespread interest in Japanese folk crafts, an interest that developed into what came to be called the "*mingei* boom." Busloads of visitors began pouring into Sarayama, and potters soon found that their production was hardly sufficient to meet demand. The more they made, the more they sold. They spent less and less time in the fields, and finally from the mid–1960s began full-time specialization in pottery. The boom has brought economic stability to potter households; but it has also led to a number of problems in social relations between the community and the outside world and within the community itself. These problems will be the focus of most of the rest of this book.

---

4. Nelson Graburn has pointed out that it is intriguing that the Japanese should think it so important that Leach has visited and described Sarayama, and that in effect they are using him as an ultimate reference to judge the quality of Onta pottery.

GEOGRAPHICAL BACKGROUND

The community of Sarayama lies near the northeastern border of Oita Prefecture in central Kyushu. It is part of the hamlet (*buraku*) of the same name and is situated within the administrative confines of Hita City (population: 65,253 people; 17,573 households).

Hita is a world apart from such cities as Tokyo, Osaka, and Fukuoka. Indeed, it is not really a city at all, but a town. For the moment, at least, a rice field is still being farmed along the main shopping street. Here, in this basin of land surrounded by mountains, with its sprawling fogs in autumn and winter, with its deep haze during those sultry, humid days of summer, people live in what the city officials like to promote as Kyushu's "Little Kyoto." Although it cannot rival that great capital architecturally, Hita does attract the tourists, and the town is posted in the travel brochures as a place of "water, greenery, and hot springs." It has all the trappings of tourism: hotels and traditional Japanese-style inns, bars and nightclubs, and plenty of souvenir shops for those who wish to purchase gifts to take home to their families, fiancées, friends, and neighbors. It is in these shops that Onta pottery is sold, along with buckwheat sweet-cakes, bamboo baskets, cedarwood paper knives, and a host of other local products.

Sarayama is located about 17 kilometers from the town center and about 460 meters above sea level in the foothills of the Hiko-Gakumeki mountain range. These mountains effectively cut off Oita Prefecture from the north of Kyushu with its industrial urban complexes of Hakata (Fukuoka), Tobata, Yahata, and Kokura.

Sarayama is as clean, as quiet, as physically attractive as most of Japan's cities are polluted, noisy, and ugly. Situated in a narrow valley which is hardly 200 meters across at its widest point, the community consists of just fourteen households, ten of which make pottery.

Sarayama looks much bigger than it actually is. Many buildings line the narrow road that winds up from Hita, and it is only at the top of the valley that the thickly wooded mountain slopes leave enough room for a dozen terraced fields. These fields are no longer used to grow rice; some have been planted with cedar, others are used for stacking wood for the potters' kilns; still others have been leveled into a car park and a softball ground. Most of the buildings in the village are for purposes other than living in: garages and workshops, sheds for storing materials and pots, lean-tos for wood, and the kilns. There are six of the last in all, climbing kilns between twelve and twenty-five meters long, built on thirty-degree inclines. The black, gaping mouths of their arched chambers are covered by asbestos corrugated roofs, and from the top of these, red-bricked chimneys rear against the backdrop of the mountains' wooded greens.

The houses have for the most part been rebuilt. There is still one old thatched farmhouse at the bottom of Sarayama, to remind potters of how they lived before the days of the folk craft boom and their newfound prosperity. Most people now live in spacious dwellings with prestigious tiled roofs, and each household has a selection of gadgetry that has come to be thought of as essential in Japan: a color TV, a stereo set, an automatic washing machine, a rice cooker, a self-defrosting refrigerator, and very often other luxuries such as a piano, an oven, a gas-heated bath, and a large stove in the workshop.

The workshops, too, have been rebuilt. Each forms an L-shape with its main house and faces downhill toward the south and sunlight. In front of each house is the drying yard, now concreted over, where pots are placed on their trays to lie all day in the sun. The garages are occupied by new and expensive cars, and several potters also have light vans for transporting wood or fired pots.

Yet, for all this obvious prosperity, one thing remains unchanged and is, therefore, somehow incongruous—the use of the clay crushers. Ever since Sarayama was founded, wooden crushers have been used to pound the clay with which generation after generation of potters have worked. The two streams running through the village have been stepped in a series of five-to-six-foot dams the whole length of the valley, and water is drawn from these along channels to the crushers. Each crusher is made from a large pine-tree trunk between four and five meters in length, with one end hollowed out into a scoop. Into this the river water is directed. The crusher is critically balanced on a cross-axle of wood, so that when the scoop is filled the weight of the water makes the crusher seesaw down toward the river bed. As the other end of the pine beam rises high into the air, the water flows out of the scoop and the crusher falls back with a thud onto a mound of clay piled under the far end.

The sound that the crushers make cannot be expressed adequately in words. It is this sound that dominates everything that goes on in the valley, all day, all night, every day and every night, except for one respite of twenty-four hours from New Year's Eve. The potters can tell from the changes in the thudding rhythm of the day how much water is in the streams, whether their crushers are working, and if so, how efficiently. These pounding pine trunks are an endless source of delight to Sarayama's countless visitors, who will stop for minutes on end to gaze at these "primitive" machines. They belong to a world of which people living in an industrialized urban Japan can only dream. The continued use of this method preparing the potters' clay has become incorporated into the folk craft ideal with regard to Onta pottery; it has also had considerable effect on the social structure of the community of Sarayama.

PEOPLE

What sort of people live in Sarayama? Who are the buyers who purchase Onta pottery? Who are the leaders of the folk craft movement who give potters the supposed benefits of their advice?

One of the most important people in Sarayama, and a man who will often make an appearance during the course of this book, is Haruzō. Haruzō, or Harusan, as he is often called, was born in 1914. At the age of twenty, he was sent to study pottery in Kurume, where his father, who was not much of a potter, had eventually succeeded in getting him apprenticed. Apprenticeship in those days theoretically went on for five years, but, before two of them had passed, Haruzō found himself called up and sent to join the army in Manchuria. Although he returned to Sarayama after his stint of "imperial service," he soon found himself back in uniform with the outbreak of war. He managed to stay in Japan, in charge of supplies, and once he had been demobilized he returned home to help run the Yamani household. He married Matsue from Kanemaru down the road and had five children. His eldest son, Masami, has married now and has four children of his own, and they all live together in the one house, which includes Haruzō's own father and mother, both healthy and still able to work at the ages of ninety-three and eighty-eight respectively.

Haruzō has always taken pride in acting on behalf of others, and it was his ability to take on the role of intermediary sucessfully that led to his being looked up to as a leader. It was he who approached the Folk Craft Association and arranged for Bernard Leach to come and stay in Sarayama during his visit to Japan in 1954. As leader of the potters' cooperative, Haruzō also managed to get Sarayama's annual pottery festival under way. As rural district councillor, he has more recently inaugurated an Ono valley softball competition. In the practical matters of everyday life, it is Haruzō who is asked to act as go-between in marriages, land disputes, and community problems.

Haruzō's leadership, however, is often resented by his fellow villagers, who accuse him of being bossy, of being a dictator. Haruzō points out in defense that it is because nobody will speak his mind (except when drunk) or take the necessary decisions that he has to do the deciding for the others. His ability to act arouses a certain amount of resentment among others, who can only recite, with some relish, any of Haruzō's misdemeanors that come to light. Potters also object to the unashamedly mercenary manner in which Haruzō carries on his profession, with overlong hours, high prices, and shoddy goods. Now that he is getting old and his power is on the wane, others in Sarayama are beginning to speak out against what has often been little short of dictatorship. Haruzō is becoming an isolated figure in the community.

One of those who has never been afraid to speak his mind is Shigeki. At forty-two years of age, Shigeki is not, in theory, old enough to be of much consequence in community affairs, but in fact he is already seen as Sarayama's next real leader. He is naturally gifted: third grade at *kendō* fencing, fifth grade at archery, second in the Hita *shigin* singing contest, the all-important position of fourth when it comes to batting at baseball. Whatever he decides to do, Shigeki does well. But, as we have already seen with Haruzō, talent can lead to envy, and life in a small community like Sarayama can be very frustrating.

Shigeki's life has never been easy. The eighth of nine children, Shigechan was brought up by stern parents to believe that he was less than good for nothing. This was because he was second and not eldest son of the household. Shigeki's elder brother, Kunio, began to study pottery before Shigeki was born. During the war he was killed in action somewhere in the Philippines, and Shigeki suddenly found himself in favor with his father, for as eldest surviving son he was now due to take over the running of the household. He was sent, at the age of fifteen, to study pottery at Haruzō's and stayed there for two years. Every month he handed over one *shō* of rice in payment for his education and living expenses. He was not, however, by most accounts, properly taught. Haruzō sat the lad down at the wheel head only one day a month; the rest of the time Shigeki was made to prepare the clay, or cut wood for the kiln in the mountains, or even weed the rice paddies.

Although he was hardly able to make any pottery at all when he returned home from Haruzō's, Shigeki devoted himself to his work. This devotion paid off when, a few years ago, he was awarded the major prize for folk craft potters at a national ceramics exhibition. Even before this he had opposed some of Haruzō's schemes—such as his trying to put in machinery with which to pound the clay, or arranging for potters to report the same incomes to tax authorities each year—but Shigeki now found that he was being called upon by those concerned with the folk craft movement to act as spokesman for the Onta potters. He realizes the problems that this causes within the community, however, and is for the moment prepared to bide his time. He hopes that if he does emerge as Sarayama's leader, he will be able to do things more democratically than they have been done so far. He knows it takes time for things to change, though, and does not hold out much hope for the future. Another generation will grow up with its own ideas, which may oppose Shigeki's plans. But so long as things are done by decision of the majority, instead of on the spur of the moment by one or two individuals to further their own private interests, Shigeki will remain content.

Isae is Shigeki's sister-in-law, his brother Kunio's widow. Although, after Kunio's death, she could have returned to her natal home in Kusu, halfway between Hita and Oita, she decided to stay on in Sarayama. Her father-in-law once entertained the idea of marrying Isae to Shigeki, who was fiteen years her junior, but things did not turn out that way, and Isae has remained a widow. Her two children by Kunio were brought up in the Yamaichi household, and have now married and live in Fukuoka. They still come back three or four times a year, bringing with them their own children to visit Granny. Granny is barely five feet tall, with wrinkled, sunburnt skin and a merry laugh. She has helped look after the house, the fields, the pottery, even Shigeki's own children, and has thereby been a constant help and companion to Fumichan, his wife. She has in recent years taken charge of growing the vegetables, weeding and fumigating the rice fields, stacking the wood for drying, then tying it in bundles and taking it to the kiln before every firing. Isae also works at the back of the house doing the endless task of sifting glaze materials—wood and straw ash, feldspar and iron oxide—until they are fine enough to be mixed for use in the workshop. She still sleeps with Shigeki's teenage children in their second-floor room behind the kitchen, and very often it is Isae, and not their mother—who is just as busy helping Shigeki in the workshop—who nurses them when they are ill.

Machiko lives in the house opposite Shigeki's. The youngest of four grown-up children, she is one of two girls in Sarayama who are considered ready for marriage. Her father has already approached Osamu, who is a relative and runs the noodle shop across the river from them, asking him to keep an eye out for a suitable young man. Machiko is "open-hearted," a quality that in the opinion of the older women of the community would make her an excellent wife, but things haven't turned out well so far. Hisae, Machiko's mother, has insisted that her daughter does not marry into a farming household. The girl would be worked like a horse from morning to night, and she is too good for that. After all, she has spent several years learning how to knit in Hita and she is now qualified to teach. Her skills with the large and expensive knitting machine bought by her parents are often put to use as she mends heavy sweaters or designs and makes cardigans or woolen coats for her relatives and neighbors.

It is not as if Machiko is a burden on the household and her parents want her to leave. Indeed, she does many jobs that would normally be left to her elder brother's wife, Hideko. Most mornings of the week Machiko sets off for her knitting classes in a battered and rusty Honda mini. In the town, she acts as errand girl for members of the household, buying meat and eggs from the supermarket, paper diapers from the chemist's, a pencil case or an eraser from the stationery store for one of her nieces. When one of the children falls sick it is Machiko who drives the girl to the doctor's. If she is around during a storm and the elementary school calls to say that Miyuki is afraid of the thunder, Machiko will pick up the girl and bring her home. She does the household cooking and bathes and sleeps with the children every night. Neighbors comment wryly that her sister-in-law Hideko is going to have to work a lot harder once Machiko gets married and leaves home.

Those with whom the potters have to deal when selling their work live well away from Sarayama. Mr. K. is in his early thirties and runs a pottery shop downtown near Hita station. He himself has been adopted into his wife's family and does not claim to know much about Onta pottery. It was his wife's father who started buying and selling pots as a sideline before the war, when he was running a coffee shop. The old man used to play around with clay himself as a hobby and is known to have made suggestions to the potters about shapes and designs. He was, however, more interested in stock than in saleable items. The K. family has a large collection of old pots stacked away in its storehouse.

Now that his father-in-law is dead, Mr. K. has taken over. He does not buy much, but he does not need to, since the family's main business is in real estate. Like many other Hita buyers, Mr. K. sells Onta pottery because he wants to, rather than because he has to. He admits that, as a result, he can afford to sell at fairly high prices. He realizes that this is not in accordance with folk craft ideals, which emphasize that pots should be cheap, but he reckons that the media are much to blame for the increase in prices. As for the potters, they are not as honest as they should be in their dealings with buyers. Mr. K. would like to see them sell their pots through the cooperative; that would help fix retail prices in Hita and make the potters maintain a reasonable standard in their work.

Mr. T. is probably the nearest to having what might be called a patron-client relationship with the potters of Sarayama. Now in his mid-sixties, he lives with his wife in a small house in the western part of Hita. His connection with Sarayama also started through his father, when the latter was director of the town's Industrial Crafts Institute and took a personal interest in promoting the potters' work. Mr. T.'s father became involved with the folk craft movement when he made arrangements for Bernard Leach's stay in Sarayama in 1954. Although his father has died, Mr. T. made use of his connections to start buying pots from all the potters in the community except Haruzō, whom he has always made it clear he dislikes. At the opening of every kiln, Mr. T. goes up to Sarayama by taxi, and with his back very straight from his early military training, he walks from one workshop to the next and selects the pots he likes. In each pottery he is served tea and cakes, but these he tends not to touch, for he is more interested in conversation. Sometimes he will talk about the war; at other times he will enter into a monologue concerning Japan's early industrialization and contact with the West; more often he will concentrate on what he refers to as "the great problem" besetting the folk craft movement. Potters will try to look attentive and adopt a fairly humble attitude in front of Mr. T., but as he has a habit of saying nasty things about people behind their backs, they tend to ignore most of what he tells them. There is general agreement among the potters that they would like to stop selling their work to Mr. T. But they still feel a sense of obligation toward his dead father, who really did his best to help them in the old days when pots did not sell. Mr. T. is "stuck up"; he spends his whole time corresponding with the folk craft leaders in Tokyo and telling them, and the media, that Onta is in "dire crisis" and "headed for destruction." As far as potters are concerned, community affairs are none of Mr. T's business. Nevertheless, because he is important, Mr. T. usually manages to get his way with potters, who appear unable to join in concerted action against him.

One of the people Mr. T. likes writing to is Tonomura Kichinosuke, director of the Folk Crafts Museum in Kurashiki, halfway between Hiroshima and Osaka. Tonomura is in his mid-seventies and one of the last surviving members of the "old school" of people like Yanagi, Hamada, and Leach who helped found the Folk Craft Movement. He now spends a lot of his time commuting between Kurashiki and Kumamoto, where he has set up a new *mingei* museum, run by his daughter. He is frequently called upon to act as judge at exhibitions containing folk crafts, or to give speeches, very often at the summer seminars held by the Folk Craft Association all over Japan. He may be seen at such events wearing what is to some a very folksy outfit, which almost invariably includes the incongrouous combination of farmer's *mompe* (baggy trousers) and highly polished black leather shoes. Tomomura is a lay priest; he speaks good English and has a nice sense of humor. The potters in Sarayama respect him highly; he has "character" in their opinion. On one of his rare visits to the community, the potters make sure that they are all there to meet him at the entrance to Sarayama, even though they may have to wait for more than half an hour in the rain. They obviously enjoy listening to him talk, even though Tomomura has a habit of repeating the same anecdotes. He is, after all, the last of a generation of men who have made the community what it is.

Mizuo Hiroshi is very much one of the second generation of folk craft leaders. Born in 1931, five years after the publication of Yanagi's first major work, *The Way of Crafts*, Mizuo is now professor of art history at Musashino University in Tokyo. He is also, strictly speaking, the folk craft movement's only professional critic. He has written several works on Japanese art in general, but is recognized as a leading exponent of the meaning of *mingei*. In the 1950s he acted as secretary-cum-translator to Bernard Leach, and has now written a full biography of Yanagi Muneyoshi. Following the death of the potter Hamada Shōji in January 1978, there was a shuffle of personnel in the Folk Craft Museum in Tokyo. Yanagi's eldest son, Munemichi, was appointed director; Mizuo found himself taking over the editorship of the Association's monthly magazine, *Mingei*. Followers of the folk craft movement are conscious that things are about to change, but none of the potters in Sarayama is optimistic about the future. In their opinion, Mizuo is too much of an ivory-tower scholar, too much the parrot of Yanagi's philosophy, to be able to understand the real problems that craftsmen such as themselves now face. While potters are, perhaps justifiably, apprehensive, it is too early to tell how the Folk Craft Association's new leadership will affect the movement as a whole.

3

Social Organization of a Pottery Community

One of the themes running through this book concerns the inconsistencies to be found in the theory and practice of folk crafts, on the one hand, and of Japanese rural society, on the other. The way in which a potter ought to make his wares may not be the same as he actually does make them; the way that he ought to participate in community life may well differ from the way in which he actually does so. What is more, these discrepancies tend to interact one upon the other. Sometimes a potter is unable to make his pottery according to folk craft theory precisely because of community ideals; on other occasions he fails to fulfill community ideals because of the way in which he is obliged to make and market his pottery.

My premise is quite straightforward: the production, marketing, and aesthetic appraisal of pottery are all social activities. Each affects, and is affected by, the other two. To understand how and why this is so, we must look at the kind of social organization that supports the production and marketing, and at the kind of people who are interested in the appreciation, of folk craft pottery. It is here that we will encounter a dichotomy between the ideals held by people living in rural and in urban Japan.

Since I am concerned with the way in which the Japanese folk craft movement has affected social relations—and hence the pottery—in the community of Sarayama, I will begin by giving a brief account of some of the institutions that are to be found in Japanese rural society. I will then show how Sarayama itself is organized. I must emphasize here that the description of Sarayama's social organization outlined here and in the following two chapters is in part idealized. Later, I will show how this "model" of rural society compares with the reality of people's everyday lives in the community.

THE HOUSEHOLD (*IE*)

Enough has been written about Japanese society that I need not go into a detailed description of its organization. I will deal first with two general concepts—the household (*ie*) and the hamlet group (*buraku*)—which have been the focus of considerable attention by both Japanese and Western scholars. I will then discuss these same concepts in the context of the pottery community of Sarayama.

In agricultural villages, the *ie* has been seen as the fundamental unit of Japanese rural society. *Ie* literally means "house," but should perhaps be translated as "household," for the word refers to the people living in a house as well as to its physical frame. The *ie* is a corporate group in that (1) it continues through time, regardless of any change in its membership; (2) it is a political and economic unit, whose members work together on land, making use of common property and of the household's right to irrigation water; (3) it is widely conceptualized as such by those who do and by those who do not belong to the household concerned; (4) it is a religious group, as may be seen in common ancestor worship, temple affiliation, and burial site; and (5) it was, until quite recently, a legal entity.

Membership of an *ie* generally consists of an "elementary family"—husband, wife, and children, and possibly one or both of the husband's or the wife's parents. An *ie* may also be formed by just one man. It is also possible for non-kin, such as servants or laborers, who live in the household and form part of its work force, to be members of the *ie*. At the same time, kin who have moved out of the physical household to work permanently in a different area are not included in membership of the *ie*.

Household Head

The most important person in an *ie* is the household head, who acts as trustee of the property of the *ie* and makes use of it in a way that he thinks is most advantageous for all its members. The household head used also to hold absolute authority over the affairs of members of the *ie*, but this is no longer legally permitted. Nevertheless, he still has enormous influence in the running of the *ie* and over the activities of its members.

Ideally, succession to the headship of the *ie* is based on patrilineal descent.[1] The successor should be the son[2] and not any other kind of kinsman, this son often—but not necessarily—being the eldest son of the household head. Where the household head has no male successor, adoption is frequently resorted to. There are three possible alternatives: (1) a man is adopted as son; (2) a husband for a remaining daughter is imported as son-in-law and is then adopted as son; and (3) a woman is first adopted, then married to a man who is adopted as son. In all three cases, the man will succeed to the name of the *ie* as well as to its headship. Thus, although the Japanese say that the *ie* is continued by rules of patrilineal descent, we must realize that in fact the *ie* is first and foremost a corporate group.

Household Branching (*honke-bunke*)

A second rule of succession to the headship of the *ie* is that the post should not be held by more than one person at the same time. The rule of residence, which is closely related to that of succession, is that there can be no more than one married couple in each generation in the house. As a result, although it is possible for two married couples of the same generation to live in a single *ie* on a temporary basis, those who do not succeed to the post of household head generally leave their home. Very often these individuals will go to live and work in urban areas, in which case they will have no more than a tenuous relationship with their natal *ie*. When these individuals live nearby in a new residential unit established by the *ie* and financed out

---

1. Kitano (1963) calls the *ie* the "traditional Japanese family" and emphasizes its genealogical aspect. Befu, who takes the same approach, argues that "patrilineal descent in Japan performs what may be called the corporate function, that is, the function of perpetuating the kinship unit called the family" (Befu 1963:1330). There is thus some controversy concerning the exact interpretation of what an *ie* is—probably because of the variety of its forms. The interpretation presented here is based on the views of Yoneyama (1965), and of Nakane (1967), who herself follows the Japanese scholar Ariga Kizaemon.

2. Suenari (1972:123) suggests that "a patrilineal rule of inheritance, succession and descent are not so dominant in Japanese society as was once thought." He argues that an eldest daughter can have rights of succession transmitted to her either temporarily or permanently, and cites figures from the Tōhoku area which suggest that first-child, and not first-son, inheritance did exist before the Meiji period (1868-1912).

of property belonging to the *ie*, a relationship is often set up between the two households. This is known as the *honke-bunke*, or main-house/branch-house, relationship.

The decision by the head of an agricultural *ie* to set up a branch household for his second son (for example) will depend largely on the amount of land owned by the main household. The personal relationship between father and son is secondary, but it may affect consideration of how much land, if any, the son will be given. If an economic tie is not established, however, the relationship between main household and branch household will soon become tenuous. Branch households may be formed not only for younger sons but for elderly parents (as in the *inkyo* system of retirement), daughters, and servants.

THE HAMLET (*BURAKU*)

The Japanese word *buraku* is generally translated as hamlet. In the past, it was considered to rank in importance next to the *ie* as a social unit for group activity among farmers. The *buraku* has no legal existence now, even though in Tokugawa times (1603–1867) it conducted economic and political activities. Nowadays the village (*mura*)—or, group of hamlets—is the smallest unit of government.

Whereas the *ie* is a property-owning group, the *buraku* is primarily a water-controlling unit. It is because agricultural households grow rice in their fields and because water has to be used to irrigate these fields that owners of land within a certain area have to form a group. The hamlet cannot, therefore, be viewed in isolation from the use of water (Nakamura 1977:190; R. J. Smith 1978:224–228; Sumiya 1953:47). It is not simply a residential but an economic group (Nakane 1970:60).

The nature of the hamlet's organization has been discussed at length by Japanese scholars, who have argued that it is essentially hierarchical. Wet-rice agriculture requires the use of a lot of water over a limited period, and hamlet life is formed around the irrigation associations which control this water. As ownership of land is usually not equally distributed among households in a hamlet, the use of communal water is likewise unequal, and it is not possible to run the *buraku* along democratic principles. In other words, power is based on the right to water (Nakamura 1956:78; 1977:187–188; Sakamoto 1953:161; Shimpo 1976:1–7).

Not all hamlets throughout Japan, however, are organized in this hierarchical manner. Not every *buraku* consists predominantly of full-time farming households; there are some hamlets whose constituent households engage in forestry, fishing, or some kind of craft. Japanese scholars have noted that there is a tendency for hierarchically structured hamlets to exist in the northeast of Japan, and democratically structured ones to be found in southwestern parts of the country. They have accordingly made a distinction between what Isoda (1951) has called "household ranking" and "non-household ranking" types of hamlet.[3]

A number of general features distinguish these two types. The "household ranking" type of hamlet is usually geographically isolated. Its organization depends on the common ownership of mountain land, on the administration of irrigation water, and on the landlord-tenant system of rice cultivation. Branch households maintain close social and economic relations with their main houses. This relation is one of dependency between the two types of household and may develop into a *dōzoku* group,[4] in which the kinship system is based on household (rather than individual) ties. It is also the household to which prestige status and power attach. Members of branch households and upper-ranking households usually marry out from the hamlet.

The "non-household ranking" type of community is generally found in the southwest of Japan. It is more directly affected by industrialization and improvements in communications and is consequently not nearly so isolated. Diffusion of the cash economy into rural areas has ensured that agriculture is carried out under better economic

---

3. Various terms have been used for this distinction between two types of hamlet. Fukutake (1956) has referred to the two types as the *tōhoku-gata* (northeast) and *seinan-gata* (southwest); Ariga (1956) uses the term *dōzoku-gata* (extended household) and *kōgumi-gata* (association), and Gamō (1962) *jūzokuteki* (dependent) and *dokuritsuteki* (independent), respectively. Johnson (1967) talks of "hierarchical" and "egalitarian" types. Dore (1959) has translated Isoda's terms as "family status" and "non-family status."

4. "The *dōzoku* . . . is a set of households which recognize their relationship in terms of *honke* and *bunke* and which, on the basis of this relation, have developed a corporate function as a group" (Nakane 1967:190–191). The *dōzoku* is rarely expected to exceed half a dozen households; nor does it usually last for more than about three generations (p. 119).

conditions; chemical fertilizers are now readily available, a fact which has enabled farmers to cultivate a greater area of land, so that they have been able to divide up hamlet common land among individual households. Branch households do not remain socially or economically dependent on their main houses, and the *inkyo*, or retirement system, of branch-house formation is commonly practiced. The hamlet is often organized according to principles of age grading and governs itself by a non-kin system of seniority rather than through a *dōzoku* type of kin group. The status of individuals participating in hamlet self-government is not determined by hereditary factors so much as by present economic standing and personal qualities. There are few restrictions on marriage partners, and relations with in-laws are close. It is the individual's, rather than the household's, kindred that are often important to alliances between households in the hamlet. The "non-household ranking" type of hamlet is particularly common in fishing communities (Dore 1959:364–366; Fukutake 1949:34–48; 1956:14–18; Gamō 1962:255–257; Isoda 1951:62–64; Johnson 1967:156–159; Seki 1962:173; Takahashi 1958:137–138).[5]

There is some argument about the extent to which the hamlet is disintegrating in the face of administrative changes, on the one hand, and of the development of technology and the market, on the other. This argument tends to concentrate on the concept of community solidarity, the density of which is measured by what is seen to be nascent individualism in rural society. This is an argument of some relevance to this book since Sarayama's potters, folk craft critics, and students of Japanese society all appear to value highly the notion of "community" and take the wistful view that any change in its organization must of necessity be for the worse. The latter have always emphasized that ideally the individual is expected to subordinate his or her interests to those of the primary group to which he or she belongs; in rural society, this means to the household and the hamlet. It is the household that provides "the frame of organization in which individ-

5. It should be made clear that "household rankings" and "non-household ranking" hamlets are ideal, rather than actual, types. The distinction is certainly useful, but not absolute. For example, it is possible for an age-grade system to operate alongside a *dōzoku*-type of authoritarian organization of households in the same hamlet (Takahashi 1958:138). It is also probable that a hamlet consisting entirely of a single *dōzoku* will have some kind of horizontally structured alliance between its constituent households (Ariga 1956:25–26). Ariga has therefore suggested that we distinguish "ranking" from "non-ranking" relations between households in a hamlet, rather than between hamlets as such.

uals are classified" (Nakane 1967:28); it is a "continuing entity transcending individuals" (Fukutake 1967:40), who are all but obscured by it. An individual participates in community activities only as a representative of his household. It is further argued that relations between individuals—such as those of an extended kin group or of a patron-client (*oya-ko*) nature—are effectively regarded as relations between households (Fukutake 1967:68; Nakane 1967:125).

The importance of the hamlet, and the loyalty and support that it ideally commands of its members, is also stressed. "The individual is ready to set aside personal interests in favor of the community. Households within a *buraku* may feud and a man always has his enemies, but it is customary to subordinate such considerations to requirements of community interest in what are defined as important matters" (R. J. Smith 1961:522). Fukutake (1967:84) has argued that restraints on the individual are reinforced by the isolation and exclusive nature of the hamlet.

Because of the administrative and technological changes alluded to above, however, the ideals of both the household and the hamlet are sometimes seen to be yielding to that of individualism (Steiner 1956:197; Norbeck 1961:320; R. J. Smith 1978:202–228). Perhaps the institutions of the household and the hamlet no longer suppress individuality in the way that they used to, but it should not be inferred that "rational" or "liberated" individualism (Fukutake 1967:216) reigns in rural Japanese society. The individual is still expected to subordinate his or her private interests to those of the household or the hamlet.

In the chapter on the ideals of the folk craft movement, I pointed out that Yanagi Muneyoshi emphasized the fact that, in his opinion, beauty derived from cooperation and self-denial, rather than from individual genius. In this respect, Yanagi's aesthetic ideal closely parallels the principles according to which Japanese rural society is organized.

THE HOUSEHOLD IN SARAYAMA

The *buraku* of Sarayama consists of two *koaza* (subhamlet group), Sarayama and Ikenzuru. These settlements consist of fourteen and five households respectively and lie about a kilometer and a half apart. Ikenzuru, which cannot be seen from Sarayama, lies further up the mountainside, and all five of its households are inhabited by families called Kinoshita. None of them has ever intermarried with any of the four name groups living in the community of Sarayama below. Nobody in Ikenzuru has ever made pottery, although there do appear to be some deposits of suitable clay. One or two women from Ikenzuru are occasionally employed by Sarayama potters to help prepare clay and glaze materials, as well as do other odd jobs around the potteries. Both communities participate in recreational activities together on monthly rest days, but otherwise there is very little contact between people living in Sarayama and Ikenzuru. Their households do very different jobs, and they are situated too far apart.

Of the fourteen households in Sarayama, ten make pottery. The other four are involved in selling pottery, keeping a sake store, building houses, plastering, forestry work, part-time agriculture, and running a noodle shop for tourists. None of the younger men from these nonpotting households is around very much during the day, and building work may take the two carpenters away from Sarayama for two or three weeks on end. By contrast, men from the potter households, father and son, work in Sarayama, making pots from morning to night. Their wives prepare the clay and glazes; they turn the pots that are drying outside in the sunshine and bring them in before they are too hard if they are to be decorated. The women put handles on the coffee cups and spouts on the teapots. When the smaller pots are completely dried, they will pack them in the bisque kiln and take charge of the preliminary, low-temperature firing. They will also glaze the smaller pots, while the men, who have worked continuously at the wheel for five or six weeks, glaze the larger wares. Together they load them into the multichambered climbing kilns, which the men then fire. After the firing, the whole household rests for two days.Then everyone turns out to unload the kiln, sort the fired pots, and pack those that have been ordered by people in places like Tokyo and Osaka. Any pots that are left over, after dealers have made their purchases, are put on the display shelves outside the potters' workshops. Then the men start throwing at the wheel again; the women return to the heavy tasks of clay and glaze preparation. Each household completes six or eight cycles of work every year.

In Sarayama, the household is the basic unit of cooperation, and each individual is first and foremost a member of his household. The corporate nature of the household may be seen in the way *all* members of one household will greet, thank, or apologize to *all* members of another household for any *one* of its members' behavior in relation to any one member of that latter household.

Household composition in Sarayama varies from a nuclear family of parents and children (Irisai), to an extended family of parents, grandparents, children, and grandchildren (Yamani). For reasons that will be explained in due course, no household includes servants or laborers (such as pottery apprentices) among its members. Kin who have moved out of the household are not considered to be household members. This does not, however, apply to schoolchildren who are being educated elsewhere.

Each household is also a religious group which performs common ancestor worship[6] and possesses an ancestral altar (*budsudan*), to which rice and water are offered before every morning meal. When gifts are presented to members of the household, they are customarily placed first of all before the *butsudan* as an offering to the ancestors. The importance in country life of household ancestors—and by implication the emphasis placed on the institution of the *ie*—may be seen in the way in which visitors to a household frequently pay their respects to the ancestors before greeting their host and hostess.

The value placed on the ancestors in Sarayama may further be seen in all households' strict observation of *o-bon* (August 13–15). Ancestors are "met" at the households' communal graves and "brought back" to their homes, where they are believed to reside for the three days of the festival. Household property, and in particular land, is closely associated with the ancestors (by whose endeavors such property was originally obtained), who are said to be enraged should a living household head for any unnecessary reason decrease household land holdings.

All households in Sarayama are affiliated to one of two temples (*o-tera*). The Yanase, Kurogi, and Kobukuro name groups belong to the Nishi-Hongan-affiliated Kyōeiji in Ashikari *buraku*, four kilometers down the Ono valley from Sarayama. The Sakamoto name group belongs to the Higashi-Hongan-affiliated Saizenji in Kirio *buraku*, five kilometers southwest of the hamlet.

The head of the household (*sewayaki*) is the most important person in the *ie*, and he usually represents the household in community matters. Although he cannot legally hold absolute authority over the affairs of members of the household, he does exercise considerable con-

---

6. Those who are celebrated as ancestors include only those who die as members of the household, back to the founder of the *ie* (Nakane 1967:106).

trol over them. Household finances are entirely in his hands,[7] and members of the household often have to obtain the household head's permission for any purchases other than those made on necessary food and daily household supplies. The household head also controls the activities of members, and his permission generally has to be obtained before any extra-household activity is indulged in. Finally, the household head is primarily responsible for the selection of spouses for his children, who are expected to accede to his wishes.

Succession to the headship of a household in Sarayama is based on the ideal of patrilineal descent. Theoretically, the successor should be the eldest son of the household head. These rules are, however, flexible, and a wife or a younger son may take over the running of the household. In Yamasai, the widowed Fusae has controlled household affairs since the death of her husband, despite the presence of a son now in his early thirties. In Yamako, the second son agreed to take up pottery and eventually to succeed to the headship of his household after his elder brother had made it clear that he wished to live and work in Tokyo.

It is generally agreed among all those living in Sarayama that only men are physically strong enough to become potters and work at the wheel full-time. A male successor is thus an absolute essential. Over the years many household heads have failed to father a son and so adoption has been frequently resorted to.

Two methods of adoption are commonly practiced in Sarayama: either a man is adopted as son; or a husband is brought in as son-in-law for a remaining daughter, and is then adopted as son. In both cases, the male will take the name of the household as well as succeed to its headship in due course. There is also a third method of succession to the headship of the *ie*. This involves what is known as "secondary adoption" (*junyōshi*), whereby a younger brother will become head of the household upon the (usually premature) death of an elder sibling. In this case, the latter has often, but not always, left no surviving children. Shigeki, the present head of Yamaichi, succeeded to the headship by this means of adoption.

When someone is adopted from outside the household as son, he is usually closely related to the present head of the adopting household.

---

7. Compare this with the urban salary-man's household in which the wife has control over everyday financial affairs (Fukutake 1967:57). It is said that Kyushu men are particularly authoritarian in their dealings with household money matters.

Very often, he will be the son of the household head's brother or sister (cf. Cornell 1956:160; R. J. Smith 1956:65).

When only girls are born to a household head, a son-in-law is married to one of the daughters (generally the eldest) and adopted into the household. In the past such adopted sons-in-law have tended to come from other households within the community (Yamani to Yamako, for example), but in exceptional circumstances an "outsider" has been adopted, even though the arrangement is not usually considered to be satisfactory. The control exerted by the adopting household head over the "son" with whom he has no blood ties tends to lead to confrontation and on occasion to the adopted son's returning to his natal home (as in the case of Irisai's father).

Household Branching in Sarayama

It will be remembered that, because of the rule that the post of household head should not be held by more than one person at a time, those who do not succeed are forced to leave the household as they grow older. If economic circumstances permit, these individuals may be given a small amount of household land and property and establish a subsidiary, or branch, household nearby. Branch households are formed not only for younger sons of a household head, but also for daughters or servants. There is also what is known as the *inkyo* system whereby the head of a household may form a branch house for himself, his wife, and possibly a younger child upon retirement from active life.

In Sarayama it has been customary for those children not succeeding to the position of household head to go to live and work in other areas, such as Hita, Fukuoka, and Kita-Kyushu. Very often they have been adopted into agricultural and trading households in these regions.

Since Sarayama was founded in 1705, a considerable number of branch households (*shintaku*) have been formed. Although in 1978 there were fourteen households in the community, altogether seventeen branch households have been set up by the original three main households, Yamasan, Yamasai, and the Sakamoto *sō-honke* (overall main household). See figs. 1 and 2.

It can be seen that two basic types of branching have occurred. In one, second or third sons have been allowed to form branch house-

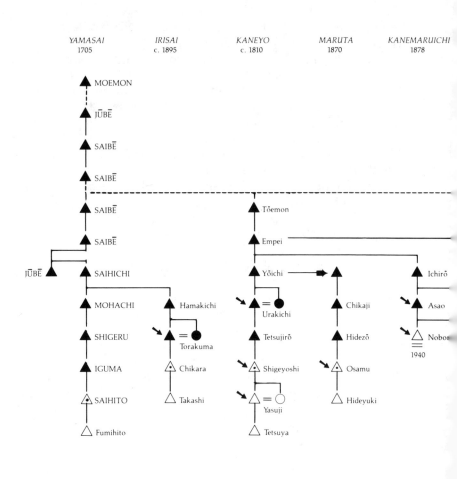

FIGURE 1. *Genealogical relations of household heads of the Kurogi and Kobukuro name groups*

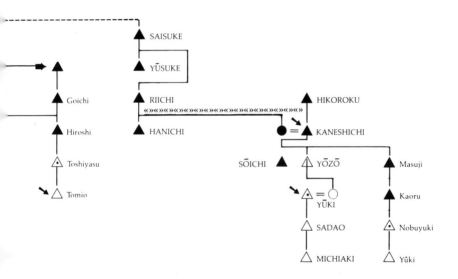

KANEMARU   YAMAKO   YAMAMASU
   1866   c. 1810   1906

SAISUKE

YŪSUKE

Goichi   RIICHI   HIKOROKU

Hiroshi   HANICHI   KANESHICHI

Toshiyasu   SŌICHI   YŌZŌ   Masuji

Tomio   YŪKI   Kaoru

                                SADAO   Nobuyuki

                                MICHIAKI   Yūki

➡ Retirement house (*inkyo*)   《》《》《》《》 Kurogi becomes Kobukuro
                                                (*nakatsugi*) c. 1885

= Household moves elsewhere   ----- Line of succession unclear

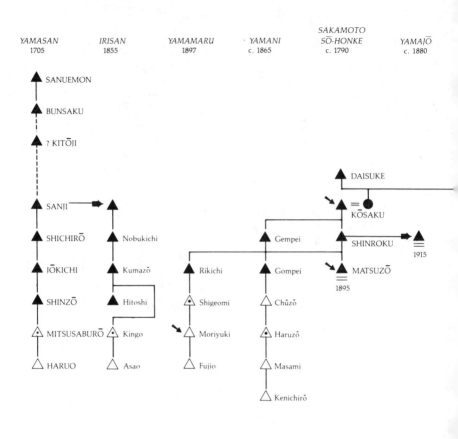

| YAMASAN | IRISAN | YAMAMARU | YAMANI | SAKAMOTO SŌ-HONKE | YAMAJŌ |
| 1705 | 1855 | 1897 | c. 1865 | c. 1790 | c. 1880 |

FIGURE 2. *Genealogical relations of household heads of the Yanase and Sakamoto name groups*

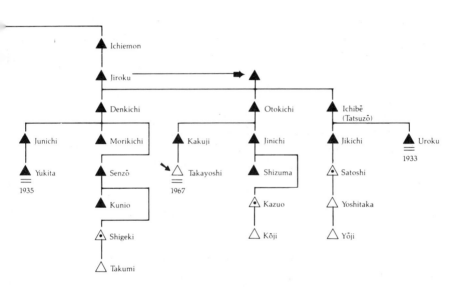

MARUMOTO   YAMAICHI   IRIKA   IRIICHI   KANEICHI   YAMAU
  1905   c. 1820   1924   c. 1872   1875   1907

Ichiemon

Jiroku

Denkichi   Otokichi   Ichibē
                                (Tatsuzō)

Junichi   Morikichi   Kakuji   Jinichi   Jikichi   Uroku
                                                         1933

Yukita   Senzō   Takayoshi   Shizuma   Satoshi
1935   1967

Kunio   Kazuo   Yoshitaka

Shigeki   Kōji   Yōji

Takumi

➡ Retirement house (*inkyo*)   ---- Line of succession unclear

= Household moves elsewhere   △ Household head

holds of their own. In this case, as described above, the main household has provided some form of accommodation and some agricultural and mountain land. I have managed to obtain information about land distribution for only one household, Yamamasu, which was formed in 1906 for a second son (Masuji) of the household head of Yamako (Kaneshichi). According to Masuji's brother, father of the present head of Yamako, the main house provided the second son with a place to live, together with some rice fields and mountain land. There was not enough paddy to feed Masuji and his family, but Masuji was a carpenter by trade and thus had a cash income, which compensated for shortage of homegrown food supplies. He was able to buy more rice fields a few years later. At no time was Yamamasu economically dependent on Yamako, and there was no obligation for the former to give labor services to the main house. The *shintaku* started out and remained a self-supporting unit.

Second, what is known as the *inkyo*, or "retirement," system of forming branch households was frequently practiced between 1855 and 1872. In this case, the head of the main household handed over authority to one of his sons and, taking his (second) wife and youngest remaining son (*suekko*), left the main house to set up a branch household (*inkyoya*).[8] The retiring head of the main household often made sure that his own branch household received a major portion of land, so that the main house was left just enough capital with which to make a living.

Of the branch households originally formed in Sarayama, five no longer exist, either because no satisfactory successor to the household head could be found or because household members moved out of the community to make a living elsewhere. The Sakamoto *sō-honke* collapsed when the adopted household head went bankrupt; it is said that he emigrated to Brazil in 1895. There are now, therefore, altogether fourteen households in the community (fig. 3).

Extended Kinship Relations

Because branch houses are not economically dependent on their main households, there is no *dōzoku*, or extended household

---

8. Generally, the eldest son succeeded to the headship of the main household, though there are exceptions. For example, in Yamaichi, the eldest son formed a branch household (Kaneichi), the second son succeeded to the headship of the main household (Yamaichi), and the third son was taken into the *inkyo* household (Iriichi) by his father.

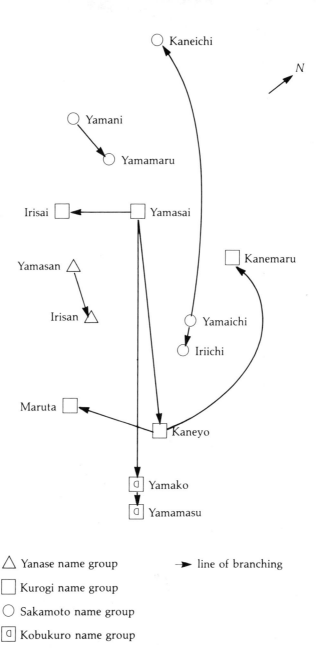

FIGURE 3. *Spatial relations between* honke *and* bunke *in Sarayama*

group, in Sarayama. Kinship relations do play an important part in people's everyday lives, however, for it is through them that individuals participate in the wider activities of rural life. Such kinship ties are often framed as household relations; this is particularly so of people related to one another through the practice of household branching. We now look at the way in which personal kinship ties, in particular those formed as a result of adoption and marriage, may further serve to link one household to another.

As was mentioned above, adoption has frequently been resorted to in Sarayama, and on a number of occasions the adopted son (son-in-law) (*yashinai-go*) has been taken from another household within the community. In figure 4(a), two households—Yamani and Yamako— which would not normally unite because of household kinship ties or residential proximity (see next section), are brought together through adoption. In figure 4(b), Kaneyo and Maruta are main and branch households respectively, but this household relationship is reinforced by close-personal-kin adoption. At the same time, Irisan becomes linked to both households owing to the previous adoption of a younger son into Kaneyo.

Marriage ties (*engumi*) have also served to link or reinforce links between households within the community (fig. 5). Close personal kinship ties can be seen to exist between the household heads of Yamasai (*honke*) and Irisai (*bunke*) (nephew and uncle); Kanemaru and Kaneichi (brothers-in-law); Kanemaru and Yamani (brothers-in-law); Irisai and Kaneichi (brothers-in-law); and Kaneichi and Yamani (first cousins). More distant kinship relations brought about by marriage exist between and are recognized by Yamasai and Kanemaru, Kaneichi and Kaneyo, Kaneyo and Yamasan, and Yamasan and Yamasai.[9]

As we shall see in the following chapter, personal kinship ties form an extremely convenient secondary means by which labor may be recruited by a household. For example, Yamani and Yamamaru are main and branch households respectively, Chūzō and Shigeomi being first cousins. At the same time, Yamani is closely tied to Kaneichi, since Satoshi's mother was Chūzō's younger sister. Finally, Kaneichi and Yamamaru are related by personal kinship ties (even though as *households* they are formally separate), since Satoshi's brother married the sister of Moriyuki. Moriyuki was himself adopted into Yamamaru

---

9. Further recognized marriage ties exist between households, one of which has since left the community—e.g., Yamaichi and the Sakamoto *sō-honke*, and Yamasai and Yamau.

(a) Yamani　　　　Yamako

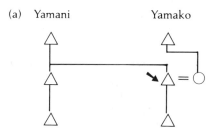

(b) Irisan　　　　Kaneyo　　　　Maruta

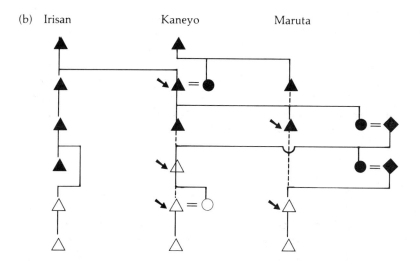

 △ Adopted

◆ Man living outside Sarayama

FIGURE 4. *Households linked through personal kinship adoption ties*

by Shigeomi, who is Satoshi's sister-in-law's uncle (fig. 6).

While Yamani and Yamamaru are primarily related as main and branch households and hence cooperate for such *household* ceremonies as ancestor memorial rites (*hōji*), when it comes to other kinds of cooperation (such as the weeding of rice fields), personal kin ties between Yamamaru and Kaneichi, on the one hand, and between Yamani and Kaneichi, on the other, facilitate the grouping of all three households. Similarly, Yamamaru may on occasion cooperate with Iriichi or Yamamasu because of past marriage ties (fig. 7), even though in both cases kinship relations are becoming tenuous. Almost all households in Sarayama are thus able to form links on the basis of the past exchange of women (and men, through adoption).

Finally, it should be noted that personal kinship ties can be used to increase the number of households linked through household kinship ties. For example, Yamasan is linked to Kaneyo, and Kaneyo to Maruta, by marriage; household kinship ties exist between Yamasan and Irisan, Irisan and Kaneyo, and Kaneyo and Maruta; but there is no household or personal kinship tie between Yamasan and Maruta. However, these households, together with Kaneyo and Irisan, almost invariably form a quartet for cooperative work or labor exchanges.

Residence Associations

Another means by which households in the community may be linked is that of residence associations (*kumi; tonari dōshi*). Such associations are based on principles of residential proximity and act primarily as methods of recruiting labor for community (as opposed to household) activities, such as road repairs, river weeding, recreation, and the appointment of community officials.

Although residence associations tend to strengthen *honke-bunke* household ties, in that main and branch households are almost always located on adjacent plots of land, they do provide an opportunity for nonrelated households to cooperate in community tasks or sports. Yamaichi and Irisan, for example, will join together in one team to play a softball match or have an archery contest with a second team that includes Yamamaru and Yamasai. Associations are designated with reference to the top and bottom houses of the community, and households within each assocation are enumerated from top to bottom according to their location down the mountainside.

To some extent, perhaps, residence associations tend to isolate those

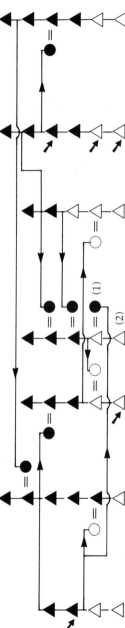

Irisai   Yamasai   Kanemaru   Kaneichi   Yamani   Kaneyo   Yamasan

▶△ Adopted son   (1) First wife

——▶ Direction of virilocal marriage   (2) Son by second wife

FIGURE 5. *Households linked through personal kinship marriage ties*

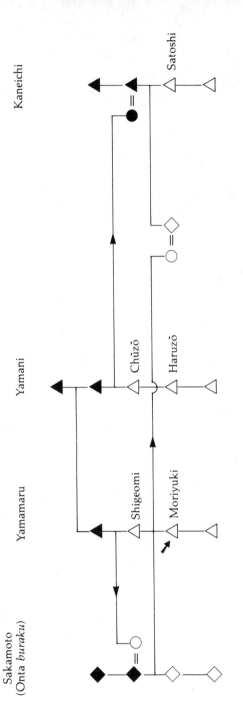

FIGURE 6. *Personal kinship ties between Sarayama households (1)*

◇ Man living outside Sarayama

△ Adopted

➤ Direction of virilocal marriage

Yamamaru   Sakamoto   Iriichi   Yamamasu
                   (Onta *buraku*)

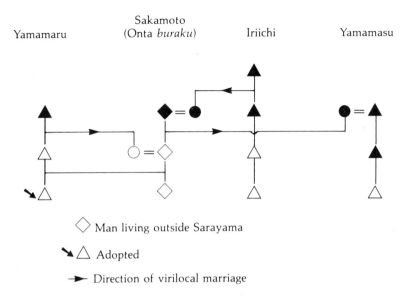

◇ Man living outside Sarayama

◥△ Adopted

➤ Direction of virilocal marriage

FIGURE 7. *Personal kinship ties between Sarayama households (2)*

households at the top and bottom of the community into fixed combinations (Kaneichi-Yamani-Yamamaru, and Yamamasu-Yamako-Maruta-Kaneyo). Those households located in the center of Sarayama, however, have more fluid relations with other households around them. Certain households, not otherwise connected by household or personal kinship ties, are able to form links with other households through the residence associations. As a result, there are very few households that have no connection at all with other households within the hamlet (fig. 8). Residence associations prevent kin-related households from forming exclusive groups.

AGE ASSOCIATIONS

Another method of social organization—age associations—provides crosscutting ties within the hamlet and also serves to link those living in Sarayama with people from other communities nearby. These associations have been given some attention by Japanese scholars, who have shown that various types of age associations exist all over Japan, although they are most commonly found in the south-

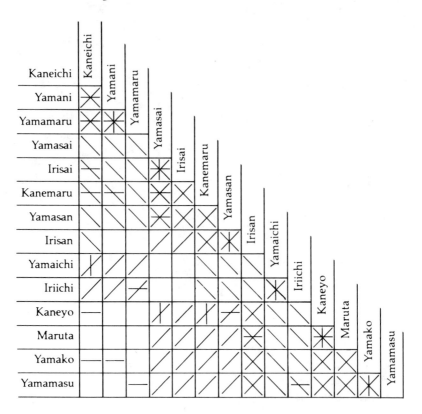

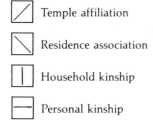 Temple affiliation

Residence association

Household kinship

Personal kinship

FIGURE 8. *Household connections through temple affiliation, kinship, and residential ties*

western part of the country. In general, there are three factors which may affect the membership of an age group: (1) topography, which may lead to the existence of two groups, not just one, in a hamlet; (2) household status, which may give rise to a distinction between original residents and more recently settled households; and (3) individual status, which may permit only firstborn sons to join an age group. Any community, hamlet, or village may be divided into four age associations—child, youth, adult, and aged—of which the eldest or the youngest may be missing. The actual age limits and the internal structuring of each age association also vary from place to place (Seki 1962:131–139).

Sarayama is divided into three age associations: youth (*seinen*), adult (*sōnen*), and aged (*toshiyori*). In the past, young people, both boys and girls, regardless of whether they were eldest or youngest in their households, were required to join the youth association after leaving school. They would remain members until the time they were married at about twenty-five years of age. They then automatically became members of the adult association. The age at which men and women joined the old people's association was ill-defined, and members were recruited from their early sixties to late seventies, depending on the individual's own concept of what constituted old age.

The youth association has always been the best organized of the three associations in Sarayama. Because members used to meet regularly, friendships were formed between young people who would remain close to one another through the busier and less well organized years of adult life. In the past, members of the youth association would participate in such activities as communal reading, abacus practice, discussions, and *utai* chanting. They were also required to clean the hamlet graveyard at the *o-bon* ancestor ceremony and were generally assigned the least pleasant community tasks, such as gravedigging.

During the past fifteen to twenty years, however, the youth association has come to occupy a less and less important position in young people's lives. This is partly because the youth association of Sarayama has been absorbed into a national organization of youth groups, whose membership is not compulsory. But there has also been an improvement in communications, giving access to entertainment (such as television, films, bowling, pachinko, baseball, and so on) not previously readily available, and many young people prefer not to join the youth association. As a result, there is only one fully active member of the Ono youth association from Sarayama, and young people in the community only get together for such rare events as the *bon* dance (which is not held unless there has been a death in Sarayama that year). The custom of cremating rather than burying the dead has also relieved young men of the unpleasant job of grave-digging, so that their community activities tend now to be limited to the occasional, haphazard fire practice.

The adult association has never been well organized. It is the only age association formed entirely of men, for many of the boys and girls who were members of the youth association leave Sarayama to get married or find work elsewhere. Women who are married into Sara-yama join the women's association (*fujinkai*), which has acted as the female equivalent to the adult association (*sōnenkai*). The women's association meets twice a month, and also goes on an overnight trip to one or another of the nearby spas once a year, but, by all accounts, it is not as active as it used to be. Members of the adult association have, for their part, usually been too busy with household affairs to partici-pate regularly in leisure or study activities, but friendships forged dur-ing their time in the youth association have continued and have served to bring about fresh ties between households.

Traditionally, it has been the old men who have maintained au-thority in hamlet affairs. When household members gather for cere-monies or discussion, men are seated in order of age. The eldest men place themselves with their backs to the *tokonoma*—according to Shinto beliefs, a sacred alcove and the "highest" point in the room. In the past, the elders customarily commanded silence when they spoke and did not expect to be questioned or argued with by members of the youth or adult associations. They controlled their household purse strings, and particularly wealthy members were known to contribute money for projects that benefited the whole hamlet. Such action natu-rally enhanced their status (cf. Dore 1978:205–207) and made it more difficult for younger household heads to argue with their often auto-cratic decisions.

In the past, the old people's association was essentially administra-tive, although there were occasions, of course, when the old men par-ticipated in leisure activities with their womenfolk. However, postwar education, based on ideals of democracy, has led to a weakening of the position of the old men, and some of the younger men in the ham-let have begun to speak out against the more blatantly dictatorial acts of their seniors. (The way in which the power of the elders has been gradually erased over the past two decades is the subject of a later chapter.) Membership is more or less fixed by the national pension scheme, which decrees that a man is old at sixty-five. Nowadays, the old people's association meets periodically for a game of "gateball" (a kind of croquet) or a "tea" party during which plenty of alcohol is also consumed. Once a year, all the old people in Sarayama are entertained and banqueted by the rest of the hamlet's residents.

THE POTTERS' COOPERATIVE

The Onta Potters' Cooperative (Ontayaki dōgyō kumiai) is a loose association which serves basically to help individual potter households deal with extra-hamlet bodies. Only those households which fire kilns are members of the cooperative; other households in Sarayama may not participate. The cooperative is strictly limited to residents of Sarayama and is not legally recognized, nor is it affiliated with any larger, nationally organized, potters' cooperative, in the way that farming households are with the Agricultural Cooperative.

The cooperative appears to have been formed sometime between 1935 and 1937, at about the time of the China Incident, when the central government tried to stimulate the Japanese economy. All those of the same occupation (*dōgyō*) were required to form a cooperative association. Tetsujirō, the father of the present head of Kaneyo, was the first leader of the cooperative, since he was employed in the local village office and was also hamlet chief at the time. But his household stopped potting, and from 1945 Chūzō of Yamani took over the job. Eight years later, however, Mr. T., director of the Hita Industrial Crafts Institute, suggested on one of his visits to Sarayama to buy pots that Chūzō was too old to do the job and that a younger man was needed. As a result, his son, Haruzō, was appointed and remained leader of the cooperative for more than twenty years. In 1975, after some argument, two of the younger potters, Shigeki of Yamaichi and Chikara of Irisai, persuaded Haruzō to resign, and his place was taken by Yūki of Yamako, who was next in line of seniority, but was also Haruzō's brother.

Potters say that the post of leader of the cooperative is necessary, but they realize it is an unpleasant duty, which they do not see as prestigious (cf. Cornell 1956:175; Norbeck 1977:98). Its occupant is required to act as spokesman for the potters, to relay information, and in general to mediate between them and the outside world. Increasing contact with the media, local government officials, and various folk craft organizations has made the job of cooperative leader rather more time-consuming than it used to be, and outside bodies tend to look upon the position as one of importance. The potters' attitude toward the selection of their cooperative leader may, therefore, begin to alter in the near future, especially since the potters have now come to be differentiated as an occupational group from the remaining nonpotting households in the community.

CONCLUSION

In my description of the social organization of the potters' community of Sarayama, I have concentrated on the household as an economic, political, and religious institution, and have traced the ways in which households in Sarayama are linked through household and personal kinship ties. I have also outlined further means of social organization, such as residence associations, age groups, and the potters' cooperative.

In this discussion of household alliances in Sarayama I have shown that the community is essentially of the "non-household ranking" type. This may be seen in the facts that (1) there is no evidence that there was ever economic dependence between a branch household and its main house; (2) the *inkyo* system of branch-house formation was frequently resorted to (cf. Takahashi 1958:136); (3) an individual-oriented type of kinship system may be found alongside a house-oriented system (Gamō 1962:255); (4) endogamy has been practiced among households in the community (Gamō 1962:256); (5) age associations exist, and their membership is not affected by territorial or status considerations (Seki 1962:131–133; Isoda 1951:63); and (6) religious and social events in the community are the responsibility of each household in turn (Fukutake 1949:37).

I will go into further details of the egalitarian nature of household relationships in Sarayama in the following chapter; but here I should like to note that the "non-household ranking" system has been to some extent upheld by the age-grade system of gerontocracy. Although government by older men may be seen as somewhat undemocratic, it should be realized that the system is cyclical and that those who are young now will in due course grow old and take over the reins of community power. Thus *every* household should in theory take its turn at the top of the gerontocratic hierarchy, as its head gradually grows older, retires, and is replaced by his son, who in turn grows older. Ideally, this rotating system of authority prevents a household ranking system based on such criteria as wealth—a point to which I shall return when I discuss the decline of community solidarity.

Another point concerns the way in which the social organization of Sarayama might differ from that of a purely agricultural hamlet. I have already mentioned that the data for most of the sociological explanation of Japanese rural life has come from studies of farming villages. The household has been seen as a landholding, and the hamlet as a water-controlling, unit. This study, however, focuses on a community that has been only partly agricultural; people living in Sarayama have also been making pottery there since the community's founding in 1705. What interests me, therefore, is the possibility that the organization of households in the community of Sarayama may differ from that found in purely agricultural hamlets.

There are two features in particular which contribute to egalitarian relations in the community and which may also add to our knowledge of the hamlet and the household as social institutions: (1) the way in which water is used by potter households to prepare clay for use at the wheel; and (2) the way in which pots have to be fired in kilns. I intend to argue that the method by which the clay is prepared for use at the wheel has in fact affected the composition of the potter's household and limited the number of potter households in Sarayama. I will also show that the ownership of kiln rights—rather than of land or water rights—has affected the economic development of potter households and their relations with other households in the community. I also hope to show how these means by which potters make their wares in fact affects the critical appraisal of Onta pottery by leaders of the folk craft movement.

4

Ecological Aspects of Social Structure

The Japanese hamlet, as I have pointed out, is not simply a residential group, but a water-controlling unit, which is often hierarchically organized. The vertically structured hamlet is most frequently found where landlord-tenant relations have existed. It is access to water rights associated with ownership of rich paddy that has in effect "ecologically" structured the organization of the rural hamlet.[1]

It has been suggested that the size of the hamlet has been largely determined by the limited amount of land available for farming and building on. During the Tokugawa period (1615–1868) the proliferation of households in a hamlet depended on the distribution of land and water rights; the latter may be said to have been the decisive fac-

---

1. In this book, I use the term "ecology" to refer to the "environment," even though I realize that strictly speaking they are not equivalent (cf. J. Anderson 1973:182). Anderson has defined ecology as "the study of entire assemblages of living organisms and their physical milieus, which together constitute integrated systems." Such a broad view involves too many variables to be accounted for in any comprehensive study of man's social and biological relations with the environment in which he lives.

Two problems arise from this. In the first place, there is little agreement as to what exactly constitutes an ecological approach in anthropology (Ellen 1979:1). A number of terms have been used to describe limited aspects of particular environmental-cultural relations: for example, "cultural ecology" (Steward 1955), "ethnoecology" (Frake 1962), "cultural (or, 'vulgar' [Friedman 1974]) materialism" (Harris 1968), "anthropological ecology" (J. Anderson 1973), "ecological anthropology" (Rappaport 1971), and so on. Second, anthropological research into the relationship between "ecology" and "society" has so far left us with "a wealth of facts but a paucity of principles" (Freilich 1963:21). I remain unconvinced by the evidence provided hitherto that cross-cultural "ecological" regularities do in fact exist (cf. Ellen 1978:298-299), but I hope that such regularities may one day be found. In this spirit of optimism I present my "ecological" argument about clay, water, and social structure.

tor in the formation of branch households (T. C. Smith 1959:24–25; 56–57; Johnson 1967:163).

Those living in the community of Sarayama have, until very recently, been both farmers and potters. One of the questions of theoretical interest for students of Japanese rural society, therefore, concerns the extent to which the structure of this community and the organization of the households making up the community differ from those of purely agricultural settlements studied so far (Beardsley et al. 1959; Cornell 1956; Dore 1978; Embree 1939; Shimpo 1976; R. J. Smith 1956, 1978; and Yoneyama 1967a, 1967b). Although the answer is "not much," the reasons underlying that answer are significant.

Since the community has until very recently relied on wet-rice agriculture for its livelihood, it is like other agricultural communities in two important ways: not only is Sarayama's household system similar to that found elsewhere in Japanese rural society, but the community as a whole may be seen as a water-controlling unit. However, most households in Sarayma also make pottery. The clay used for this is extremely hard and has to be powdered before being thrown on the wheel. Clay crushers, powered by the water flowing in two streams that run through the community, are used to prepare the clay, but they can prepare only enough for two men in each household (i.e., father and one son) to work with at the wheel. The nature of the clay therefore affects the composition of each potter household. But it also affects the expansion of potter households, since each must have access to water in order to prepare its clay. The limited amount of land available for building on, together with the angle of slope of the streams flowing down through Sarayama, have thus determined the number of households in the community able to practice agriculture *and* pottery.

I have already argued that Sarayama may be classed as an egalitarian type of community such as is found in the southwest of Japan. There are three reasons for the lack of hierarchical organization in Sarayama. In the first place, there have never been any landlords in the community, nor have households there been tenants to large landlords in neighboring hamlets. Ownership of rice paddy and dry fields has been fairly evenly distributed among all households; their holdings are comparatively small, averaging about 2,900 square meters of paddy and 238 square meters of dry field, scattered within a three kilometer radius of Sarayama. Second, since all the paddy that has been cultivated is situated in narrow valleys in the mountains, it has not been necessary for farmers to build complicated or lengthy irrigation systems. Many streams provide a constant source of water supply, and farmers have generally taken water directly from these streams to their fields by way of split-bamboo pipes. There was only one irrigation channel supplying as many as a dozen small fields and this was found in the valley immediately above the community. In general, however, not more than four or five narrow fields were irrigated by a single "channel" of split-bamboo pipes laid from the mountain streams. Thus, households in Sarayama never formed exclusive groups for the control of water, and friction over the allocation of water has generally been avoided.

Third, apart from agriculture, the way in which water is channeled to work the clay crushers does not affect downstream potter households. In the production of pottery, there is no critical period, such as exists in the agricultural cycle, when a household *must* have water. In wet-rice agriculture, when water is scarce, there is a shortage for everyone; when it is abundant, there is plenty for everyone, regardless of whether a household has its clay crushers upstream or downstream.

CLAY PREPARATION AND COMMUNITY EXPANSION

Since the founding of the community in 1705, potters have had their local, hard clay powdered by water-powered clay crushers, known as *karausu* (literally "Chinese pestle"). These clay crushers are usually in groups of twos and threes and line both streams running through Sarayama. Water is channeled so that it flows into the hollowed out scoop at the end of each crusher; the weight of the water makes the crusher seesaw down, empty the water from its scoop, and fall back with a thud onto a mound of clay placed under its far end.

The clay crushers have always fascinated visitors to Sarayama, and those involved in the folk craft movement have not failed to mention the crushers in their descriptions of Onta pottery. The following passage is by no means atypical and illustrates the way in which the method of clay preparation is given some responsibility for the beauty of the pottery made in Sarayama:

> As you come down from the mountain pass into the valley, you first hear the echo of the water-powered *karausu* used to pound the clay.

The silence between each echoing thud is terribly long. Only a little wa-ter trickles along the channel from the river to the crusher. There is no need for things to be done in any rush, however, and it seems as though it is only our hearts that find it hard to wait. But it is because there is this gentle rhythmic sound that the village exists. If some busy-sound-ing machinery were to be introduced, the whole place would fall into disarray. This is something written about by Yanagi in *Hita no Sara-yama*. It is probably unnecessary to reappraise Onta's pots when there is such a beautiful collection of crocks and jars in the Folk Craft Muse-um in Tokyo. But I still had to see these pots in Sarayama itself where they listen to the sound of the clay crushers. (Matsukata 1955:15–16)

Some people have considered the *karausu* to be extremely rare (Koyama 1967:101), but this is not actually so. There are two varieties of crusher to be found in Japan. One is water-powered and is general-ly known as *battari* or *sakontaro*; the other is foot-powered and is widely distributed over southeast Asia. Both kinds of crusher have, however, generally been used to pound rice and cereals, and the un-usual thing about the crushers in Sarayama is that they have been adapted to pound clay.[2]

The question of interest to students of the structure of the Japanese hamlet is: how has the fact that clay crushers can only be used in limit-ed number affected community expansion? Answering this question, I should make it clear that the description given here of community ex-pansion is ideal in that market considerations are *not* taken into ac-count. Thus, during the Meiji period (1868–1912), there were probably very few newly-established branch-household heads who wanted to take up pottery, since it was hardly an occupation that reaped much—if any—economic reward. Whether branch households actually took up pottery immediately upon being formed, or waited until later, is not known. Chikara, of Irisai (the last potting branch-household to be es-tablished), suggests that his household may not have started pottery for some twenty years, until market conditions had improved.

In Sarayama (Onta), all pottery is made from a local clay which is

---

2. I have come across foot-powered crushers being used for pounding clay in a pot-tery village in northern Thailand, and for pounding paint materials in an umbrella vil-lage nearby. A photograph in the June 1977 edtion of the magazine *Aruku Miru Kiku* shows that clay in Shigaraki, Japan, was also prepared by a foot-powered crusher of the *battari* type during the Meiji period (Cort 1977:18). The clay in Shigaraki and in the pottery village referred to in northern Thailand is in fact softer than that used in Onta, where anything other than a heavy water-powered crusher would not be effective.

rich in iron content and can be obtained from the mountain land in the immediate neighborhood of the community.[3] As was noted above, this clay is extremely hard, and it can be used for throwing at the wheel only if it is first powdered, then sifted and left to settle in tanks of water, before being dried.

The rock-like substance of the clay requires something really heavy to break it up into tiny granules and give the clay the plasticity the potter requires. In the days before modern machinery was devised to pound the clay (and adopted now in the neighboring village of Koishiwara), water-powered clay crushers provided the only means by which clay could be properly powdered.

Each crusher must be about fourteen feet long, and in order to see-saw properly, it must pivot at a point about one-and-a-half to two meters from the tip of the hollowed-out scoop into which the river water pours. Each crusher, therefore, must be set at about the same distance above the bed of the stream from which it takes its water. As a result, there must be a drop between each crusher or set of crushers. This effectively limits the branching of households, because (1) access to either of Sarayama's two streams depends on land ownership; (2) such access should be within reasonable distance (say, 200 meters) of a potter's workshop; and (3) the total drop of the stream between the cultivated land at the top and the bottom of the community is fixed. The last factor limits the *total* number of farming households able to take up pottery in Sarayama; the first two factors make *specific* limitations on which households take up pottery.

At present, the total drop of the two streams will not permit the further introduction of clay crushers within the residential confines of Sarayama. Land immediately above and below the community on the Sarayama stream and to the north along the Gōshiki stream is being used to grow rice.[4] Both streams flow in a series of stepped dams through the community. These dams are called *ize* and allow the *kara-usu* to seesaw effectively. Each household builds a dam above its clay

---

3. Sarayama clay is a form of propylite which is found in an area north of Hita City, stretching from Oku-Yabakei to Iwaya. A further pocket of similar clay may be found around the pottery community of Sarayama (Koishiwara). The mountains were formed geologically in the early Pleistocene era; propylite itself derives from hornblende and andesite (*anzangan*) (cf. T. Matsumoto 1961:82-86).

4. Fields owned by Kaneyo in the Gōshiki valley and by Yamamasu at the bottom of Sarayama are still being farmed. Yamaichi also grew rice in his fields immediately above the community, but gave up farming in 1979. This makes it possible for the community to expand up the mountainside toward Ikenzuru.

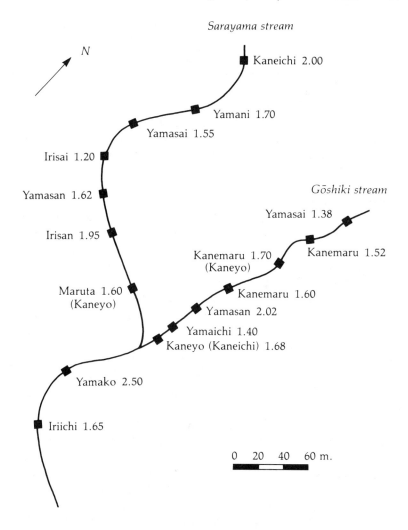

NOTE: Names in parentheses show the original owners of the dams.

FIGURE 9. *Ownership and height (in meters) of dams (ize) above clay crushers along the Sarayama and Gōshiki streams*

crushers; it is ownership of land for the crushers, and the fall of the river between these crushers and the crushers of the household immediately upstream, which in the end determine whether a household will or will not take up pottery (fig. 9).

In the past, dams were made from large stones. They were frail constructions that were almost inevitably washed away every June by floods that occurred during the rainy season. However, during the past ten years or so, almost all of the dams have been concreted and their heights established once and for all. Only along the upper stretches of the Gōshiki stream, where the flow of water is never strong, are the dams still made of stone.

The building of each dam originally required the permission of the household that owned land alongside the stream above, since the downstream household's dam would determine the upstream water level. The dams had to be rebuilt after the rainy season every year, and arguments sometimes broke out. An upstream household might complain that the dam downstream had been built too high and that its clay crushers had been adversely affected by the raised water level. Now that the dams have been concreted, conflict between potting households rarely occurs.

The relation between dam heights, water levels, and clay crushers has to some extent affected the siting of branch households during the forming of the community. *Bunke* have generally been placed *downstream* of their main households when they were to take up pottery as well as farming. In this way, the establishment of a new dam would affect only the main house forming the *bunke* (see fig. 10).

There was never any particular rule about the formation of potter households in Saramaya. However, it can be seen that those households which were established early in the nineteenth century had residences and dams located at a considerable distance from their main households. As more and more branch houses were formed, access to the streams became more difficult and pottery *bunke* could only be established with their dams immediately below the clay crushers of their main households (cf., for example, Yamasai/Irisai and Yamaichi/Kaneichi). Actual residences, however, were at times placed at some distance from *honke* because of a shortage of land space (e.g., Yamaichi/Kaneichi).[5]

---

5. There is some difficulty in establishing the origins of Yamako and Kaneyo. It is possible that Yamako branched from Yamasai and Kaneyo from Yamako. The marriage of the daughter of the founding ancestor of Kaneyo to the head of Yamako would ap-

If we look at the estimated dates of branching of households within Sarayama, we can see that almost all potting households were in fact early *bunke* (table 1). There are exceptions, of course. Maruta, for example, was formed because a first son did not want to take up pottery in the main household of Kaneyo, whereas Irisai was able to take up pottery—despite late branching—because its land bordered the Sarayama stream. However, its dam has the lowest drop of all, and clay crushers do not function efficiently when the level of the water is raised by heavy rains.

Once Irisai was established as a potter household, the drop of the beds of both streams running through Sarayama was completely uti-

TABLE 1   *Estimated Dates of Household Branching, Together With the Occupation of the Branch Household*

MAIN HOUSEHOLD	BRANCH HOUSEHOLD	DATE	OCCUPATION
Yamasai	Kaneyo	1810	Potter/farmer
Yamasai	Yamako	1810	Potter/farmer
Sakamoto *honke*	Yamaichi	1820	Potter/farmer
Yamasan	Irisan	1855	Potter/farmer
Sakamoto *honke*	Yamani	1865	Potter/farmer
Kaneyo	Kanemaru	1866	Potter/farmer
Kaneyo	Maruta	1870	Farmer/retired
Yamaichi	Iriichi	1872	Potter/farmer
Yamaichi	Kaneichi	1875	Potter/farmer
Kanemaru	Kanemaruichi*	1878	Farmer/retired
Sakamoto *honke*	Yamajō*	1880	Retired
Yamasai	Irisai	1895	Potter/farmer
Yamani	Yamamaru	1897	Farmer/*tatami*-maker
Yamaichi	Marumoto*	1905	Farmer/*kimono*-salesman
Yamako	Yamamasu	1906	Farmer/carpenter
Kaneichi	Yamau*	1907	Farmer/plasterer
Iriichi	Irika*	1924	Farmer/stonemason

*Household now nonexistent.

pear to support this view. However, memorial tablets (*ihai*) include only three Kurogi names in the Yamako household, and these suggest that Yamako and Kaneyo branched at about the same time. Therefore, I have applied the principle of downstream branching to the determination of when and from where Yamako and Kaneyo were formed.

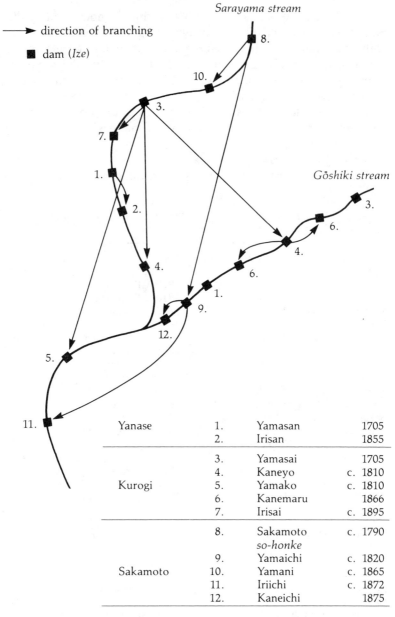

Yanase	1.	Yamasan	1705
	2.	Irisan	1855
	3.	Yamasai	1705
	4.	Kaneyo	c. 1810
Kurogi	5.	Yamako	c. 1810
	6.	Kanemaru	1866
	7.	Irisai	c. 1895
	8.	Sakamoto so-honke	c. 1790
	9.	Yamaichi	c. 1820
Sakamoto	10.	Yamani	c. 1865
	11.	Iriichi	c. 1872
	12.	Kaneichi	1875

FIGURE 10. *Location of dams (ize) showing relationships between main house and branch house*

lized by dams and clay crushers. Consequently, branch households formed after 1895 were unable to take up pottery. They did not have access to water, for clay crushers could by this time be placed only at the very top or the very bottom of the community. If further crushers had been established along either of the two streams, they would have encroached on agricultural land. But this land, of course, provided households with vital food supplies. The fact that Sarayama was a self-sufficient closed community relying on agriculture prevented the number of pottery households from increasing. It may therefore be argued that the development of the community of Sarayama has been limited by the twin problems of access to water and to land. Not only has the establishment of branch houses depended on the availability of irrigated rice paddy, but the number of households engaged in the production of pottery has been limited by the necessity of their using crushers to pound the local clay.

It should be pointed out that over the years there have been exchanges of land adjacent to two dams and that these have affected households' "rights" to take up potting in Sarayama. When Kaneichi gave up potting in 1910, its clay-crusher land below that belonging to Yamaichi was not returned to the latter (Kaneichi's main house), but was given or sold—for reasons unknown—to Maruta. This meant that Maruta, if it wanted to, could take up pottery, but Kaneichi could not. However, when Osamu, the present head of Maruta, decided to start a noodle shop some ten years ago, he arranged to exchange the plot of land acquired from Kaneichi for that belonging to his main house, Kaneyo, since the latter was adjacent to his residence.

This exchange meant that, should Maruta—which was not originally a potting household—decide at some stage in the future that it wants to take up pottery, it still has the dam required for clay crushers to be activated, and these crushers would be situated on the full-flowing Sarayama stream. Kaneyo, on the other hand, which gave up pottery in 1928 owing to the illness of the present household head, Shigeyoshi, would be able to set up only one or two crushers on its plot of land below Yamaichi's crushers on the Gōshiki stream. Moreover, matters are complicated by the fact that according to official maps there is no access to this land except through Yamaichi's land. Permission would have to be obtained from the latter should Kaneyo express a desire to restart potting. The fact that Kaneyo sold its other crusher land to Kanemaru some years ago now would make it extremely difficult for the former to powder enough clay to restart full-time pottery production.[6]

My second point about the method of clay preparation and Sarayama's social organization concerns the composition of each potter household. The work-rate of every clay crusher, or set of crushers, is determined by the actual flow of water from the stream into the hollowed out scoop at one end of the *karausu*. The more water flows through the Sarayama and Gōshiki streams, the more frequently the crushers rise and fall; the more frequently they seesaw up and down, the more clay is prepared.

Households have on average three or four crushers each, and these are lined along the Sarayama and Gōshiki streams, as was described. During the rainy season in June, these can be seesawing seven or eight times a minute. By early August, however, the crushers will have dropped their work-rate by half, and by the end of the autumn, when there has been little rain for some months, they will pound only once or twice a minute. Thus the clay prepared in late summer and autumn takes longer than that prepared in May and June (although the added sunshine in the later months helps compensate for the lack of river water when it comes to drying the prepared clay). The worst time of all is winter, when the flow of the streams tends to be slow (except following a thaw) and the crushers are so weighted down by icicles that they freeze in their sockets and fail to pivot at all!

There is also a considerable difference in the flow of the two streams, which means that Yamako, for example, whose crushers are powered by the combined flows of the Sarayama and Gōshiki streams, can prepare almost twice as much clay as Yamaichi, whose crushers are situated on the Gōshiki stream only. But the important point here is that *no* potter household is able to prepare more clay than can comfortably be used by two men working full time at the wheel. In other words, the nature of the clay and the method used to

---

6. Kaneichi, which decided to take up potting again quite recently, was able to do so because the Sakamoto *sō-honke* had left Sarayama, making one *ize* dam available for use, and the increased demand for pottery had made it possible for potters to give up agriculture. Both land and water at the top of the hamlet have become available for community expansion.

prepare it determine the composition of each potter household, in that the household head and only one son may work full time at throwing pots. The number of crushers owned by each household has been increased by one or two to meet the increased demand for pottery and enable the potters to turn to full-time production. No more crushers can be introduced, and they are now working at maximum capacity. And because the crushers are unable to prepare more clay, Sarayama households cannot employ either apprentices or throwers to boost production. The expansion of the community as a whole into a larger pottery-producing complex is very difficult so long as the potters continue to throw with Onta clay and maintain the *karausu* to prepare it for the wheel.

CONCLUSION

I have here outlined the way in which the nature of the clay used to make Onta pottery has affected the social structure of Sarayama. One point to be emphasized is that in neither pottery nor agriculture has the way in which water has been used given rise to a hierarchical form of relationships among households in the community. So far as agriculture is concerned, there has been neither a shortage of water nor an extensive system of irrigation. Irrigation water has generally been taken directly from a number of mountain streams that flow abundantly throughout the year. Every household has had free access to water, and there has been no need to form irigation unions. Moreover, in pottery, the way in which water has been used to work the clay crushers is such that households can draw water independently of one another. If there is a shortage of water, it affects *every* household's clay crushers, regardless of whether they are located up or downstream. Neither in agriculture nor in pottery has the question of "privilege" or "rights" to the use of irrigation water arisen in Sarayama.

Land has also been important to the kind of relationship existing among households. In Sarayama there have never been any landlord-tenant relations. All households have had a small but adequate amount of agricultural land on which to make a living, and it has not been necessary for branch households to depend on their main houses for a supply of capital and land in exchange for labor services.

Honke and *bunke* have maintained equal rather than hierarchical relations.

The egalitarian nature of such household relationships may also be seen in the manner in which branch households have been formed. I have pointed out that many of the *bunke* in Sarayama have been retirement houses (*inkyoya*) for elderly household heads. Although, in theory, the main house should keep its capital intact for the most part, in fact the house formed by a retiring head, accompanied by one of his sons, very often received an unusually large share of land and property (T. C. Smith 1959:41). Nakane (1967:14–16) suggests that the *inkyo* system prevails where there is, among other things, reasonably equal economic standing among the households of a village.

This point is important to my argument for, although I have shown that land holdings are fairly evenly distributed among households in Sarayama, I have not yet discussed how the production of pottery might lead to some households becoming considerably wealthier than others. So far, I have deliberately omitted market considerations from my argument. The question arises then, are households of a reasonably equal economic standing; and if so, why? The short answer to this is yes, because the potters have shared a cooperatively fired kiln. The cooperative kiln has had an extremely important influence, not only on the economic standing of households, but on forms of labor cooperation among them—the subject of the next chapter.

General view of Sarayama Onta.

Two aspects of the production of Onta pottery have important consequences for the social organization of the community of Sarayama. One is the way in which potters have persevered in using water-powered clay crushers to prepare their clay; the other is their continued use of a cooperative kiln to fire their wares (see chapter 5).

After clay has been dug from the mountainside above Sarayama, it is left to weather. Then, because it is very hard, it is pounded into small lumps by hammer before being placed under the *karausu* clay crushers.

The clay is left under the *karausu* for four to twenty days, depending on how much water is flowing through the stream lined by the crushers. During this time the clay is usually turned over every morning and evening and heaped up anew for the crusher to pound.

   Once the clay has been powdered, it is taken from the *karausu* and poured into a mixing tank (*fune*). Here it is mixed with water and stirred vigorously with a long paddle a number of times before being sieved and left to settle in the settling tanks (*sotobune*). In this way, all the grit and sand are removed from the raw clay body.

When enough clay has accumulated in the settling tanks, water is drained off and the liquid clay is ladled out onto straw-matted drying frames (*oro*). There it is left to drain in the sunshine. The frames are covered at night and in bad weather.

After about a week, when the clay is of a soft ice-cream texture, it is scooped out of the drying frames and placed in large porous planters (*moribachi*), or on the top of a clay-drying kiln, where it is left until it is hard enough to be used at the potter's wheel. Sometimes potters sharing the cooperative kiln will place semi-dry clay on the arched roof of each chamber after the kiln has been fired. Preparation of clay takes about a month from the time it is put under the clay crushers until it is taken into the potter's workshop.

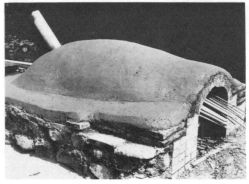

During the past three or four years, a number of potters have built clay drying kilns (*tsuchihoshi-gama*). They use these during the winter months when frost and snow make it practically impossible for the potters to dry their clay by the method described above. The kilns are heated very slowly and clay is slapped down onto their upper surface to warm and dry out for three or four days. If it is dried more quickly, the clay will lose its plasticity.

5

Labor Cooperation

We have seen the various ways in which Sarayama households are formally linked, mainly by kinship and residential ties. Let us now examine how these links have been reenforced and new ties created through projects involving labor cooperation. The description here is again idealized, in that it is valid for Sarayama only as it was at the time Bernard Leach visited it in 1954, before the folk craft movement seriously affected community life. Later I will describe changes in social organization that have occurred as a result of the folk craft movement and will contrast the "model" given here with life in Sarayama twenty-five years later. Thus I hope to offer a guideline by which community solidarity and the emergence of individualism may be measured.

One trend in critical thought among those living in advanced industrialized societies has been a nostalgia for "community," as I noted earlier. People frequently hark back to the concept of community when they find their society going through a period of radical social change. In this chapter I will deal with what is generally termed by people living in Sarayama as *mukashi*, "the past"—a verbal concept to which I shall return later. I wish to make clear that the "model" presented here is not just my analytical construct; the kinds of social organization described are part of an ideal of the past, as presented by potters and others living in Sarayama. Although there is some evidence that the individual did not always subordinate his interests to those of the community, the ideal of the past denies this and says that the community has always been more important than the individual. In other words, the model of the past becomes a model *for* the present. The kinds of social organization described in this chapter form a set of rules according to which people used to behave and should still behave in Sarayama.

I have described the Japanese household (*ie*) as a ritual, political, and economic unit that continues through time. The *ie* system may be said to have evolved around the intensive cultivation of wet rice paddy. In a society where modern technology is either unavailable or not taken advantage of, a family or a household finds that its work force cannot cope with certain aspects of production on its own. It is then obliged to cooperate with other families or households. The forms that such cooperation takes in Japanese rural society have been noted by students of the social organization of farming hamlets, and I shall describe the composition of household groups for such activities as transplanting rice and growing mountain crops, since Sarayama households have been partly engaged in agriculture. However, most households have also made pottery, and it is the forms of labor cooperation resulting from this occupation that have not been documented in sociological studies. The combination of these two occupations of farming and pottery has meant that households in Sarayama have been more closely linked through forms of labor cooperation than is usual for rural communities.

POTTERY PRODUCTION

Before we consider the way in which households have cooperated in the digging of clay, in the acquisition of glaze materials, and in the firing of their kilns, we should see how pots are made in Sarayama (see Fig. 11).

The single indispensable ingredient of all pottery is, of course, clay. A potter's ball clay should have three characteristics: plasticity for shaping; the ability to retain its shape during firing; and a rock-like hardness after firing at a suitable temperature. Four distinct processes are involved in turning raw clay into a finished pot: (1) the clay is dug from a clay deposit and *prepared* into a plastic clay body; (2) an object of clay is *formed* by pinching, modeling, squeezing, coil or ring building, using slabs or molds, or by "throwing" on the wheel; (3) the finished pot must be completely *dried*; and (4) it must be *fired*.

In Sarayama, raw clay was customarily dug out by the potters with pickaxes, but in the past few years a bulldozer has been contracted to do the job. In the space of a few days, the bulldozer can extract

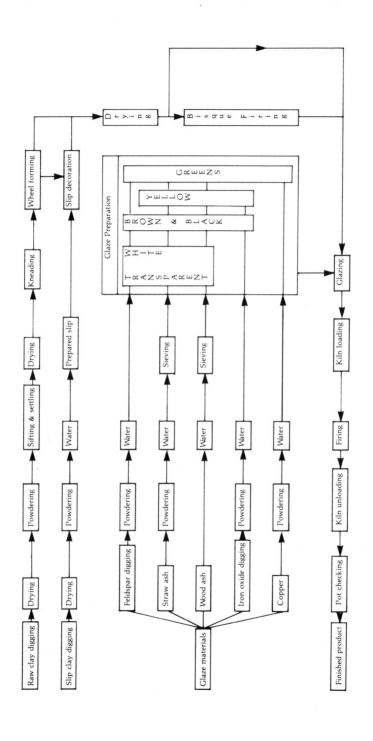

FIGURE 11. *Process of pottery production in Sarayama (Onta)*

enough clay for all the potters to work with for the following three years. Although no precise measurements have ever been taken, potters estimate that they use between two and three tons of clay per household every year.

Once the clay has been dug for the deposit, it must be prepared into a plastic body, a job usually undertaken by the potter's wife, mother, or daughter-in-law. First of all, as was explained earlier, because the clay is extremely hard, it has to be pounded by crushers. After the clay has been powdered, it is carried in baskets to mixing and settling tanks, where it is stirred, sieved, and left to settle. Water in the tanks is drained off, and the clay is then ladled out onto straw-matted frames where it is left to dry in the sunshine. After about a week, when the clay is of a soft ice-cream texture, it is scooped from the drying frames and placed in large porous planters or on a clay-drying kiln; there it is left to harden until it can be used on the potter's wheel. On average, the time taken for any one piece of clay to be powdered, sieved, and dried is about a month.

The next step is the forming of pottery. Although several means were cited above whereby an object of clay may be formed, in Onta pots are almost always thrown by men on the wheel. One or two women occasionally model chopstick rests, and Shigeki's wife in Yamaichi makes about a hundred slab-molded radish graters for every kiln firing, but pottery forming is primarily a man's job. A potter will sit at his wheel from about eight o'clock in the morning, and throw pots continuously all day, with only an hour's break at lunch. If he is trying to meet an order deadline and fire his kiln quickly, he may well continue making pots until ten or eleven at night. During an average day's work, an experienced potter will make more than 350 teacups or their equivalent.

Once pots have been formed on the wheel, they are placed on boards or bats and put out to dry. Drying can take from two days to two weeks, depending on the size of the pot and the season of the year. When they are leather hard, most smaller items, such as plates, bowls, and tea and sake cups, are trimmed and foot-rims formed. It is at this stage of drying, too, that parts are applied and handles and spouts are fixed to the bodies of coffee cups, teapots, pitchers, and other pouring vessels.

Potters also decorate their work with a slip clay and overglazes. Although they now purchase the slip clay from Arita, they used to dig it from a deposit close to Sarayama. When the pots are completely dry and ready to go into the kiln to be fired, they are glazed. All potters use the same ingredients to prepare their glazes: feldspar, iron oxide, copper, wood ash, and rice-straw ash. All of these have to be prepared—by clay crusher, mortar and pestle, or mixing and settling tanks. Women do these jobs and generally try to prepare enough glaze bases to last two firings at a time. As with the preparation of clay, glaze materials have to be sifted a long time before they can be mixed in the quantities required to obtain the desired colors—transparent, brown, greens, black, white, and yellow. It is usually the potters themselves who make the final decision as to how much of each ingredient should be mixed into the recipe. They will then glaze the bigger pots and leave their womenfolk to glaze the smaller ones.

Pots can be fired either before or after glazing, when they are almost completely dry. Until about 1962, glazes were always applied to unfired pots, but recently, smaller items have been fired to a low temperature (about 800°C.) for about twelve hours in a small (generally updraught) kiln. This process is known as bisque firing, and it has been adopted in Sarayama because bisquing helps the clay body accept thicker glazes.

Before firing, however, kilns have to be loaded. This is done by the potters while the women are glazing. Kiln loading can take as long as three days, as pots are taken from the workshop to the kiln and carefully stacked in each chamber. Some pots are piled on top of each other, and it is the women who carefully wipe off the glaze at the point of contact between the pots to prevent them from sticking together. All potters fire their pots in climbing kilns, which have from four to eight chambers each and take between 24 and 42 hours to reach a temperature of about 1250°C.[1]

The kilns are almost invariably lit early in the morning (5–6 A.M.), so that potters need spend only one night without sleep. Climbing kilns are fired at the main mouth for about twelve hours before potters start feeding wood into the single side mouth of each chamber, working upwards. It usually takes about three hours to complete the firing of a chamber. When the first chamber (for example) has reached the maturing temperature, the second chamber will already have reached about 850°C. and the third chamber 450°C. from the hea' overflow from the first chamber. The firing is generally done by men,

---

1. Potters measure the temperature of the kiln chamber by eye, rather than by Seger or Orton pyrometric cones, or by color-check test pieces.

but in a household where a potter is working without the help of his son, he will be aided by his wife. Once all chambers have been fired to the desired temperature, the kiln is shut down and not opened for two or more days.

Kilns are fired with wood,[2] which is brought up to Sarayama from lumber yards in and around the town of Hita. The side mouths of the kiln are fired with two-meter strips of cedar. As this wood is too thin to be of practical use in the firing of the main mouth of the kiln, potters have also arranged to have old, demolished houses brought up to the community. Thick beams are sawn up by potters (or by hired labor) into suitable lengths and used in the firing of the main mouth of the climbing kiln.

When pots have been fired, they are left in the kiln for two to three days before being unloaded and sorted. Broken pots or seconds are put on one side, while well-fired pots are placed on trays ready for sale. The potter puts aside special items that have been ordered (on average, between 40 and 60 percent of a kiln firing).

Almost all pots are sold in and around the town of Hita, although orders are filled from places as far afield as Sendai and Sapporo in the north of Japan. Buyers are generally aware of when a potter is likely to be firing his kiln, and they ask him, some days before, when they may be allowed to view a kiln's contents. Potters like to have at least one day in which to unload and sort a kiln firing, but buyers tend to come to Sarayama a day early (i.e., on the day on which the kiln is being unloaded) in order to get the pick of the good pots. They wander round the workshop and outbuildings, selecting and putting aside pots that they like. The potter's bill is generally paid in cash, either on the spot (if the merchant is taking the pots with him) or on delivery. One or two dealers pay potters at the time of the following kiln opening.

Once the buyers have left—leaving the workshop looking much like the carcass of a zebra that has been eaten by vultures—the potter packs up those pots that are to be sent away—to private individuals or to folk craft shops in cities like Tokyo and Osaka. He also packs pots to be delivered to Hita shop owners, and takes these down in boxes sometime during the day or two following a kiln unloading. A few pots that are left over are placed on shelves outside the workshop

---

2. There is one exception: Chikara of Irisai fires the main mouth of his kiln with oil for five hours. He claims that this is a temporary measure only.

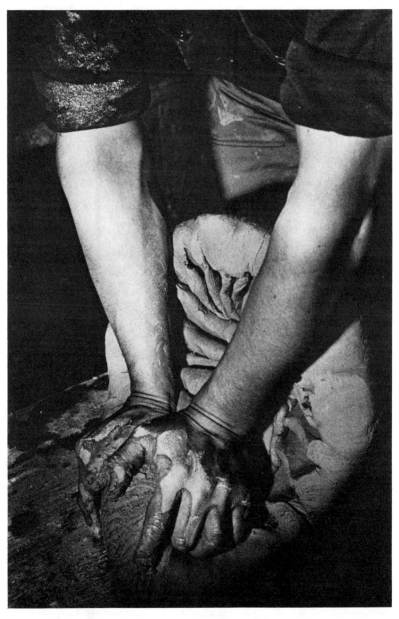

Prior to throwing at the wheel, the potter has to wedge his clay. In Sarayama, as in most potteries in Japan, the *kikumomi*, or chrysanthemum pattern, style of clay wedging is used.

In Sarayama, pots are thrown on a kick-wheel, which is generally turned counterclockwise by direct contact with the foot. This is unusual in that in most potteries in Japan the wheel is turned clockwise, and the fact that Onta potters kick the wheel counterclockwise may be a result of their Korean origins. Three types of throwing methods are used, and of these the oldest is that known as the coil-and-throw method (*himozukuri* or *nerizuke*). In the past, the coil-and-throw method was used for all pots, regardless of size. Nowadays it is used only for larger wares.

With the *himozukuri* method of throwing, a lump of clay is placed on the wheel-head and beated with a wooden paddle to form the base of the pot. Then the potter rolls more clay between the palms of his hands to form a long rope (*himo*). This is coiled on to the base of the pot, with the potter holding the clay in his right hand and pressing it down and out from the inside against the flattened palm of his left hand. The wheel is slowly turned clockwise as the clay is coiled to form the wall of the pot. When enough clay has been coiled for the size of the pot to be made, the potter kicks the wheel counterclockwise and draws the clay up before throwing it to the shape he wants. Very large pots are thrown in two sections: the lower half is first thrown and left to dry for about a day until it is strong enough to take the weight of more clay. Then the potter coils clay onto the lower half of the pot and throws the upper half. In this case, he has to make allowances for shrinkage when determining the final shape of the pot.

Onta potters have recently adopted the *hikizukuri* method of throwing off the hump for their smaller wares. This method has come to be used in particular since 1962 when, at the suggestion of Hamada Shōji, potters brought in a one-quarter horsepower electric motor. This is attached to the kick-wheel by a belt that drives the wheel at a constant speed. This method is only suitable for small pots, such as rice bowls, sake cups, teapot spouts, and lids.

Kurogi Toshiyasu throwing a large plate (early stages).

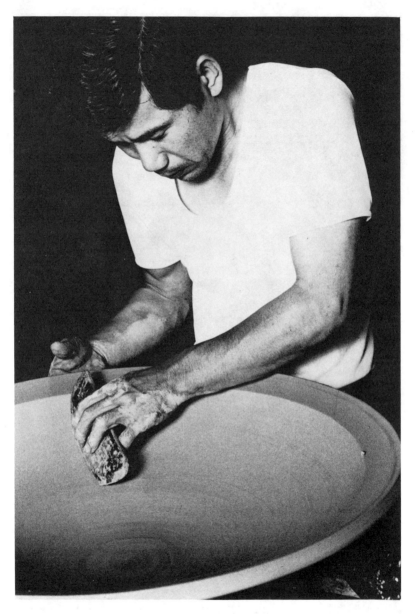

Sakamoto Kazuo throwing a large plate (late stages).

Sakamoto Haruzō throwing an umbrella stand.

Sakamoto Yoshitaka throwing a bottle form.

Yanase Mitsusaburō throwing a large vase.

Kurogi Chikara trimming a teacup.

Sakamoto Shigeki working alone in his workshop.

and are bought over the next few weeks by tourists visiting the community. Potters expect to sell almost *all* pots that come out of a firing unscathed.[3]

From this outline of the way in which pottery is produced in Sarayama we can see that it is virtually impossible for an individual to prepare clay and glazes and make and fire pots by himself. He has to rely on his wife and mother or daughter-in-law to help with the clay and glaze preparation, and his job is made considerably easier if he has an able-bodied father or a son who can help him throw pots at the wheel, and load and fire his kiln. A large family greatly contributes toward efficient production—one reason why the idea of the household is so important to people living in Sarayama.

Without doubt, the most important form of cooperation found in Sarayama is potters' use of the cooperative kiln. Not only do many of the alliances between potter households (described below) derive from their membership of the cooperative kiln, but the fact that potters have fired their pots together in a kiln whose chamber space is equally distributed has meant that the economic standing of each household has remained similar. I am not suggesting that every household had exactly the same income; nor that one or two households were unable to control others for a short period because of *relatively* greater wealth. However, it has not been possible for those living in Sarayama to rank households categorically according to wealth. I believe that the lack of a household ranking system has made it easier for those living in Sarayama to identify with the community *as a whole*, rather than with selected households of similar status within the community. The cooperative kiln has been responsible not only for cooperation among households, but for the egalitarian nature of that cooperation; ultimately, it has given those living in Sarayama a remarkable sense of community solidarity.

There are various kinds of kiln suitable for firing stoneware. Until recently, most potters in Japan have relied upon multichambered climbing kilns in which to fire their pots. In some communities, such

---

3. Estimates regarding breakages during firing vary wildly, since potters are intent on defeating the intentions of the local tax authorities. The number of broken and faulty pots, however, would appear to average about 20-30 percent.

as Onta, Koishiwara, and Naeshirogawa, where a number of households have lived and worked together, potters have chosen to fire
their pots in the same kiln. Such communally fired kilns are known as
kyōdōgama (cooperative kilns), and cooperation in Onta extended in
the past to *all* potter households, which shared the labor and expense
of building, firing, and repairing the kiln.

There are three methods by which a kiln may be cooperatively
fired. Either households will take it in turns to fire the whole kiln (as
used to be the case in Koishiwara) or they will combine to fire an allotted number of chambers in the kiln. It is also possible, though un-
usual, for households to load their pots into the same chamber and
share the firing of that chamber.

In Sarayama (Onta), the cooperative kiln has almost always been
fired according to the second of the methods cited above. In certain
circumstances, however, when potters wished to complete a firing
somewhat earlier than their usual schedule allowed for, all households would combine to share kiln chambers, with one household
taking the far side and another the near side of a chamber. This method of firing is known as *hazamayaki*, and used to take place just before
the ancestral *o-bon* and new year festivities, since potters considered it
their duty to fire before these important household events.

The first cooperative kiln is said to have consisted of four chambers. Since 1847, however, the *kyōdōgama* has always been rebuilt
with eight chambers (cf. Terakawa 1975:100). These have been
shared by as many as ten households.[4] From 1935 to 1948, however,
the cooperative kiln was worked by eight households, and from 1949
to 1952, by seven households. These were divided into two groups of
four households and of four and three households respectively, their
composition being fixed by lot at the beginning of every year. When
nine households were firing the cooperative kiln, those participating
were divided into groups of four and five. While lots were again
drawn to decide who would fire in which group, potters made sure
that they rotated fairly evenly between the four- and five-household
combinations.

---

4. Ten households shared the cooperative kiln when Kaneyo was still potting and
Irisai had not as yet built his private kiln (prior to 1927), thereafter nine households
till Irisai's breakaway in about 1935. Since Irisai was established as a branch household in 1895, and Kaneichi continued potting until 1910, it is possible that at one
period between these dates eleven households were sharing the *kyōdōgama* (provided
that Irisai did take up pottery immediately upon branching).

Having fixed household firing groups, potters then had to arrange who would fire which chambers. Since chambers near the top of the kiln tended to be larger than those at the bottom, chamber combinations were fixed according to size, in order to give each household as nearly equal a distribution of kiln space as possible. Further lots were then drawn to decide which household in each group would fire which (combination of) chamber(s). Households would rotate through these combinations, taking different chambers with each successive firing throughout the year (fig. 12).

The fact that households sharing the cooperative kiln had to fire together meant that ultimately they were all tied to a similar work pattern—from clay digging and preparation of materials, through wheel throwing to loading and firing of the kiln. At the same time,

Household number	Group	Chamber 1 2 3 4 5 6 7 8	Firing	Date
10	5×2	a b c c b d e a e a b b a c d e d e a a e b c d c d e e d a b c b c d d c e a b	1st, 6th 2nd, (7th) 3rd 4th 5th	1910–1927
9	5×1	see above 5 household gp		1927–1935
	4×1	see below 4 household gp		
8	4×2	a b c d d c a b d a b c c b d a c d a b b a c d b c d a a d b c	1st, 5th 2nd, 6th 3rd, (7th) 4th	1935–1948
7	4×1	see above 4 household gp		1949–1962
	3×1	a b b a c b c a c a a c b a b c b c c b a c a b	1st, 4th, 7th 2nd, 5th 3rd, 6th	
6	3×2	see above 3 household gp		1962–1971
5	3×1	see above 3 household gp		1971–
	2×1	a b b a a b a b b a a b b a b a	1st, 3rd, 5th 2nd, 4th, 6th	

FIGURE 12. *Allotment of chambers to households sharing cooperative kiln*

households were engaged in wet-rice farming, so that those with more active members used to finish their work earlier than those short of labor. Thus households which had two men working at the wheel tended to finish the quota of pots that allotted kiln space allowed them some time in advance of those households in which only one potter was throwing. In such cases, it was customary for the former to give a few days' free labor in the latter's workshop.

TYPES OF LABOR COOPERATION

Five kinds of labor cooperation may be distinguished in Sarayama: (1) *moyai*, or cooperative labor, whereby households form cooperating groups to work on a project of common interest; (2) *temagēshi*, or reciprocal labor, where labor given by one party is returned equally by the recipient and applied to the same task;[5] (3) *kō*, or group labor, in which all or selected households of the community combine to work together for a specified time for the benefit of one of their number. Each household takes it in turn to receive this labor given by other households in the association;[6] (4) *kasei*, or casual work, in which labor is freely given by one party, with the recipient returning the favor at some later, unspecified time and occasion; and (5) *yatoi*, or hired labor, whereby labor is given in exchange for a cash payment for services (table 2).

Moyai

All households in Sarayama used to practice wet-rice agriculture, with each family farming an average holding of between three and four *tan* (1 *tan*=.245 acre). Rice yields were low, being approxi-

5. Many of the terms used by residents of Sarayama are not standard throughout Japan. Nakane (1967:144), for example, refers to *temagēshi* as *yui*, and R. J. Smith (1956:16), as *tema-gae*. Embree (1939:134-136) talks of *kattari* for his village in nearby Kumamoto Prefecture. Much of Embree's valuable description of rural life in prewar Japan is still valid for Sarayama. Since Japanese scholars already regarded Sue Mura as "retarded beyond the average for Japan" (Norbeck 1977:196, fn. 2) in 1935–1936, one wonders what they may think of this description of Sarayama.

6. More frequently, however, the *kō* acted as "cooperative credit clubs" (cf. Embree 1939:138-153; Fukutake 1967:106-107; Yoneyama 1967b:316-317), and Sarayama households banded together to purchase such items as *futon* bedding, watches, and so on.

TABLE 2   *Types of Labor Cooperation for Various Aspects of Farming and Pottery Production*

TYPE OF COOPERATION	FARMING	POTTERY
moyai	Mountain Cultivation	Clay digging Slip-clay digging Feldspar digging Iron-oxide digging
temagēshi	Transplanting Weeding Harvesting Threshing	Glaze preparation
kō	Roof thatching	—

kasei	Building repair
	  & construction
	General jobs
		Wheel work
		Kiln loading and
		  unloading
		General jobs

yatoi	—	—

mately two *koku* (360 liters) per *tan*, but harvests were sufficient to provide a household with enough rice to feed its members for a year. Every household also grew its own garden vegetables and various kinds of beans, sweet potatoes, and buckwheat in the mountains. It was for the latter tasks in particular that households used to form *moyai*, or cooperative labor groups.

In 1954 (and until about 1965), it was customary for households in Sarayama to grow buckwheat, soy beans, red *azuki* beans, wheat, yams, and sweet potatoes on mountain land that had recently been cleared of trees. Between two and four households often formed cooperative labor groups known as *moyai*. Each household would provide a stipulated number of workers (generally three), and on an agreed day all households would gather together before going to work in the mountains.

First of all, the area in which trees had been felled would be cleared of roots and remaining pieces of wood. A suitably sized strip of mountainside was then burned. The ash, which served as an excellent fertilizer, was dug into the earth as the soil was prepared for sowing. Buckwheat (*soba*) was always planted first, and this crop was followed by varieties of beans (*azuki* or *daizu*), and finally by sweet potatoes (*imo*). It was possible to use the same strip of land for approximately five years, after which reforestation made cultivation impossible.

The sowing of each crop would take at least a week's work, and later on considerable time and labor were required for the harvesting of crops, when wheat had to be humped back down the mountainside to Sarayama—sometimes a distance of several kilometers. Buckwheat and beans had to be dried up in the mountains before being carried down by the men of the participating households. Women would beat, husk, and sieve the grains. The produce would be evenly distributed among participating households.

Household labor groups were not fixed, and allowed for cooperation along other than household or personal kinship ties. Thus we find that Yamaichi, for example, formed *moyai* with both Yamamaru and Yamamasu, two households with which it was not normally linked by kinship or residential ties.

Although there were some households, such as Yamaichi, that actively participated in mountain cultivation and went so far as to rent an area from outside landowners in such neighboring communities as Ichigi or Koda, other households, like Yamasai, very often did not bother to cultivate mountain land that had been cleared of timber. There appears to have been one principle often underlying the formation of *moyai*—common ownership of mountain land. Thus Kanemaru, Yamani, Yamako, and Kaneichi formed one cooperative labor group for slash and burn cultivation, not because they were related by kinship ties so much as because they shared ownership of certain areas of land.

Moyai cooperative groups were formed not only for mountain cultivation but in order to obtain the raw materials needed for the production of pottery: clay, slip clay, feldspar, and iron oxide.

First, let us consider the preparation of clay. So far as anyone in the community can remember, there have been two kinds of cooperatives for the digging of the raw clay from deposits in and around Sarayama. The earlier period (prior to 1952) involved households in small cooperating groups which were linked primarily by kinship ties; the later period (1952–1964), which covers the date at which this "model" of social organization of the community has been set, brought all potter households together into one group.

Note here that the switch from several small cooperating groups to a single large one was brought by *internal*, not *external*, causes. The fundamental principles on which such cooperative grouping of households was based did not alter until external forces, such as communications and technical knowledge, made an alternative means of clay digging possible (to be discussed more fully later).

In the early part of this century, potter households took their clay from various sources around the community. Three areas in particular were favored: one was above Irisai's present kiln site, another behind Yamaichi (both on privately owned land), and the third in community-owned land above Yamako. The first area was owned by Irisai, and clay was dug by this household, together with Yamasai and Kanemaru. The second deposit belonged to Kaneyo, which was then potting, and dug by this household in cooperation with Yamasan and Irisan. The remaining households dug from community-owned land, although on occasion each took clay from its own private land. Clay in the privately owned deposits was considered of superior quality to that in the hamlet-owned deposit.

When Kaneyo stopped potting in 1927, Yamasan and Irisan were forced to get their clay from the community-owned deposit. The Irisai-Yamasai-Kanemaru combination, however, continued to work as a separate group. In the community-owned deposit itself, households tended to work together in groups of twos and threes, since extremely cramped conditions at the work-face of the deposit did not allow more than a few men to dig at any one time.

As was mentioned above, some households also dug clay from privately owned land, and this led to the formation of a single clay-digging group in 1952 by all potting households. The problem started when the road just above where Yamako was taking its clay crumbled away because of undermining, and became impassable. Potters decided that clay should henceforth be dug cooperatively from the point which Yamako had penetrated (which was deemed to be community-owned land!), and the work-face was widened to facilitate working conditions. Three or four times a year, each potter household would send one man and one woman to do the laborious task of clay digging. For four or five days, the men would work with picks and shovels at the clay face, while the women would carry the clay in woven bamboo panniers (*tsuchimego*) down to the path below Yamako, where eight even piles of clay were made. A ninth pile was taken directly to Yamako's clay-crusher shed. At the end of each day's work, lots were drawn by the remaining eight households to decide who would get which pile of clay, and the clay was then removed to each household's crusher shed or drying yard.

Other cooperative groups were formed for the acquisition of such other materials as slip, feldspar, and iron oxide. Deposits of slip clay existed in the Kitanamizu area, about a kilometer and a half to the north of the community, up the Gōshiki valley. Until the mid-1950s, potters used to dig from this deposit. Because of the extreme difficulty of access (the deposits are located at the top of a 1:3 incline) and the limited area in which the work was possible, two or three houses would combine to work for a couple of days on the deposit, digging when a common need arose. Two days were needed to clear away fallen topsoil and get down to the pure veins of white slip, after which four or five days were spent digging about one year's supply of slip clay. When the face of the deposit became dangerous to work in (a trench as deep as three meters would sometimes be cut out), all nine pottery households would combine to clear away earth and clay.

Groups also cooperated to get their supplies of feldspar and iron oxide as they needed it. Feldspar, which takes its name (*akadani*, red valley) from the place where it is dug, has always been obtained some fifteen kilometers away from Sarayama. This hillside has probably been used from very early on by potters of both Onta and Koishiwara, but sometime during the Meiji period (1868–1912), the landowner complained, and potters from both communities joined together to purchase the land in which the deposits were located.

Until the mid-1950s there was no form of motorized transport, and potters used to leave Sarayama before sunrise, leading their draft cows across the mountains for two or three hours before reaching Akadani. There they would hack away at the work-face, clearing away loose earth and material of poor quality, before loading their animals with good feldspar and returning home late at night. Potters tended to go together because the long day's trip made companionship desirable. Working conditions were (and still are) poor, for the feldspar seams were not broad enough to permit more than two or three men to work together with pickaxes.

Iron oxide used to be taken from a disused mine in Fukakura some twelve kilometers away. Potters would take their draft cows with them as far as Iwaya, before tethering them and walking over the mountains for another hour and a half. As the path was often difficult to follow, the potters usually took a guide (a woodcutter who knew the mountains well). The mountainside where the mine was located was privately owned, so that the potters used to dig without permission. The iron oxide was chipped with a hammer and chisel from the roof of the disused mine, a long shaft that ran several tens of meters into the mountainside. Only two or three people could work at any one time in the confined space, and this was why only a limited number of households formed any one cooperative group. Potters would take only as much iron oxide as each man could carry on his back down the mountain path to where he had left his draft cow tethered.

Temagēshi

A second type of labor cooperation adopted by households in Sarayama was that of reciprocal labor (*temagēshi*), for such activities as the transplanting, harvesting, and threshing of rice and also for the weeding of paddy fields. Such groups often formed because of—and thereby reenforced—kinship ties (e.g., Yamako-Yamamasu; Kaneichi-Yamani-Yamamaru). But there was another principle that brought households together and that did not involve kinship ties: households reciprocated labor with households whose paddy fields lay close to their own. For example, Yamani, Yamamaru, Yamaichi, Iriichi, and Kaneichi joined together in various agricultural tasks because they farmed fields in the valley immediately above Sarayama, *not* because they were related by kinship ties (cf. Cornell 1963:113).

Potter households also used to exchange labor to prepare glaze materials, particularly straw ash. Straw ash is usually very rough in texture and must be pounded fine if it is to produce good glaze colorings. The clay crushers are much too heavy for this task, so the ash has usually been pounded by wooden mallets before being trodden down into barrels. The preparation of glaze materials is a woman's job, and in the past households worked in pairs to prepare their straw ash in this way (e.g., Yamako-Iriichi).

Kō

Another form of labor cooperation, very similar to the *moyai* described above, was the *kō*, or "mutual credit association" (Fukutake 1967:106–107). This kind of group existed primarily to facilitate re-thatching of house and outbuilding roofs. On March 1 every year, two members from each household in the community assembled to cut

thatch grass (*kaya*) from the community-owned mountain behind Yamako. For the following three days, the grass was cut by the men and
carried down to Sarayama by the women. One face of the roof of two
or three houses was rethatched every year. The decision as to whose
turn it was to benefit from the *kaya-kō* each year was made on the
basis of need (cf. Johnson 1967:164). However, the *kō* generally rotated in fairly strict order, unless someone else's roof was seriously leak-
ing or in otherwise poor condition and would not keep until his turn
for repair came round.

Kasei

Another kind of cooperation was *kasei*, or casual work, which
was by far the most frequent form of labor exchange. *Kasei* involves
assistance without financial reward, and assistance received does not
in theory have to be returned. However, in practice, of course, anyone
who had been helped out by another household in this way was expected to repay that help at a later date when so requested.

Kasei was the most pervasive form of labor exchange in the community, overriding kinship or residential groups, even though it was those
most closely related and living nearby who would be commandeered
for such tasks as the construction and repair of buildings, thatching, or
simply the lifting of a heavy object. In particular, such informal exchanges of labor took place among potters. Saihito of Yamasai, for example, recalls that after his grandfather died, leaving him at eighteen
years of age as the sole surviving household breadwinner, he was not
yet skilled enough to make large pots. So Shigeki of Yamaichi, Asao of
Irisan, or Chikara of Irisai would come and throw the required shapes
and sizes for him in his workshop, while Saihito himself went and
made small pots in their workshops in exchange. Similarly, when Shigeki was taken to the hospital with acute appendicitis, Mitsusaburō,
Asao, and Saihito came to finish off half-completed pots for him. Such
labor exchanges were to a large extent based on personal friendships,
but when asked who they were helped by in the past, potters unani-
mously reply that they were helped by *everyone* in the community.

Yatoi

In 1954, so far as I could discover, there were no instances of
households hiring labor within the community in exchange for a daily

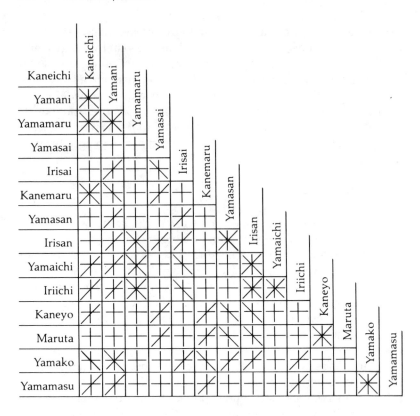

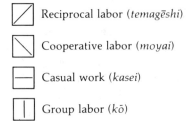

Reciprocal labor (*temagēshi*)

Cooperative labor (*moyai*)

Casual work (*kasei*)

Group labor (*kō*)

FIGURE 13. *Linking of households through all forms of labor cooperation (1960)*

wage. All labor exchange was expected to be repaid in kind and not in cash. Some idea of the pervasiveness of the labor exchange groups hitherto discussed may be gathered from figure 13.

Finally, it should be mentioned that on any day during which one of the forms of labor cooperation occurred, participating households invariably shared an evening meal following the day's work (cf. Dore 1978:105; Embree 1939:137), with the household that benefited from the labor providing the feast.[7] When potters were firing the cooperative kiln together, they would also share the midday meal (provided by the household whose turn it was to fire the first chamber, *anko*). On occasions when *hazamayaki* took place, with all households sharing kiln space in the bottom chamber,[8] there tended to be fairly prolonged drinking sessions during firing. These often resulted in less-inebriated potters firing the next chamber or two on behalf of their slumbering companions.[9] Without doubt, exchanges of food and drink, together with the song and dance that inevitably accompanied such festivities, strengthened community solidarity.

CONCLUSION

In this chapter I have described various means by which households have exchanged labor in agricultural and pottery tasks. I have suggested that cooperation in farming did not depend on kinship ties so much as on territorial factors; in pottery, households worked together to dig raw and slip clays, feldspar, and iron oxide, not just because they found it difficult to do the work successfully on their own, but because their production schedule was determined by the existence of the cooperative kiln. Potters were given an equal amount of kiln space; they therefore fired more or less the same number of pots every year and consequently used approximately the same amount of clay and glaze materials.

The cooperative kiln served another important function in the

---

7. When labor was performed for mutual benefit, as in *moyai*, participating households took it in turns to act as hosts.

8. All households shared the bottom chamber of the cooperative kiln, because the risk of breakage was extremely high.

9. Some potters are known to have taken advantage of codes of etiquette that forbade a man, out of politeness, from waking a sleeping comrade, and to have purposely feigned drowsiness in order to get others to fire their chambers for them.

community: it helped to regulate the distribution of wealth. If each potting household was allotted an equal amount of kiln space and fired the cooperative kiln the same number of times each year, potters were likely to sell about the same number of pots. Although income from pottery was barely sufficient to buy those essentials which a household could not otherwise produce, this money was equally distributed among all potter households. Nonpotting households derived a similar, small cash income from such jobs as stone masonry or tatami-mat making.

As I have said, this description of community cooperation has been to some extent idealized—valid for 1954 when Bernard Leach first stayed in Sarayama and before the folk craft "boom" had begun to affect market demand for Onta pottery. The time has come to see how Sarayama has changed over the past twenty-five years. Some of these changes have been noted in passing: the fact that clay is now dug by a bulldozer, for example, or that the cooperative kiln is now shared by only five potter households. Now I want to concentrate on the way in which technological advances and economic improvements have led to the breakdown of community solidarity and to the rise of individualism.

While the model presented in this chapter is an ideal of the past as seen by the potters, it is also an ideal espoused by leaders of the folk craft movement. There are two things about the production of pottery in Sarayama that are selected for special praise by scholars and critics. One is the fact that potters rely on natural methods of preparing clay and of making and firing pots; the other is that they work together as a group.

It will be remembered that Yanagi Muneyoshi emphasized that if folk crafts were to be really beautiful, they had to be made in a spirit of cooperation and the craftsman had to surrender his self to nature. Onta potters share a cooperative kiln; they are known to help one another with all kinds of work; *therefore*, in the critics' opinion, their pots are beautiful. Hamada Shōji, for example, commented on the marvelous quality of Onta's pots at one of the annual autumn exhibitions in the Folk Craft Museum: "The thing that is particularly striking about the way Onta potters work is the fact that the more skillful potters always help out those who are not so advanced. This makes me really happy. . . . As a result everyone's work gets better and better, and it is hard to know which pots to pick out for special praise" (in *Mingei* 276:13).

Critics realize that cooperation among potters stems primarily from the fact that they are close to nature. "The hamlet's solidarity is really unflinching, and its heart-felt desire to preserve its tradition is stronger than any other pottery kiln's. One might almost say that this attitude has been decreed by the providence of nature" (Tanaka Takashi 1969:44). Nature, cooperation, tradition—these are the three ingredients of folk craft beauty (Yanagi 1955a:220–221). The fact that Onta pottery is made with natural materials in a traditional manner is what makes it beautiful (Noma 1955:6). "Whatever pottery you go to, you will find beautiful and ugly pots mixed up together, but not in Onta. Surprisingly, every pot has good glaze colorings and there isn't a single ugly pot to be found. I suppose it must be because tradition has not been destroyed" (Yanagi 1947:253).

The traditional way of life is seen to derive entirely from nature. At the same time, nature affects a man's character and *thereby* the quality of his pots. Leach is quoted as saying of Onta: "It is the purity of the link between man and nature that these potters have not lost. This purity gives them a warmth that is reflected in the beauty of their pots" (Noma 1965:16).

So, leaders of the folk craft movement have praised Sarayama because they see the potters living in a kind of ecological equilibrium, in harmony with nature and with themselves. It is this which makes their pottery so beautiful. Yet this is where a paradox arises: because Onta pottery is seen to be beautiful and truly *mingei,* many people suddenly want to buy it. But it is this growth in market demand that has been responsible for changes in the potters' social organization. Potters find that they can now sell whatever they make. The less time they spend preparing their materials, the more pots they can throw; the more they throw, the greater their income. Farming ceases to be economically viable, and cooperation breaks down; considerations of status based on wealth and talent develop; community solidarity is effectively undermined. But precisely because potters adopt technological innovations and stop working together, precisely because they begin to make a lot of money and their individual talent is recognized, folk craft leaders claim that the quality of Onta's pottery is rapidly deteriorating. I shall now deal with this paradox.

6

Environmental and Social Change

In my idealized description of the social structure and organization of the community of Sarayama, my argument has been that (1) community expansion has been limited by the way in which potter households have had to prepare clay for their wheels; (2) the individual worked in a multigeneration household group because environmental factors did not permit him to farm his land or produce pottery on his own; and (3) each household combined with other households because of these environmental factors and because it fired its pots in a cooperative kiln. In outlining the way in which households were linked by various forms of labor cooperation, I presented a "model" of hamlet organization as it existed at the time of Bernard Leach's stay there in 1954.

This model of Sarayama's social organization is in fact the way that the community's residents now view what they call the "good old days." The model emphasizes that there were no permanent divisions within Sarayama's social organization. All fourteen households formed a closed community, tightly knit by kinship relations and various kinds of communal activities. While a resident retained primary loyalty to his or her household group, he or she simultaneously acted as a member of the community and in many cases subordinated household interests to those of the community.

There is, of course, no way of showing that the people's model reflects the true state of affairs in Sarayama a quarter of a century ago. To a certain extent it is idealized. However, I believe that the model is by and large, a fair reflection of community life, and that Sarayama residents did, as they say, form a community and put group before individual interests.

In fact, the ideal of loyalty to the community is still upheld, and Onta potters are quick to point out to visitors of all kinds that they do everything together and everyone is the same. Clay is dug together, they say; glaze compositions and materials are the same from one household to the next; prices are fixed; tax payments have, until 1975, been paid by the potters' cooperative as a whole rather than by individual households therein; even the pottery is uniform, hardly differing in shape, color, or design from one workshop to another. "All together" is the motto with which the community faces the outside world. But *do* potters still do everything together? *Is* everyone the same? Nowadays, the community's social philosophy is, I think, only an ideal which is not practiced, mainly because of changes brought about by improvements in communications, technology, and the market.

Fundamentally, of course, it is the general improvement in Japan's economy and the large demand for folk crafts in particular that have led to the breakdown of Sarayama's sense of community solidarity. But market demand as such is difficult to describe. Its impact can be guessed, perhaps, from the way in which local tourism more than doubled during a ten-year period between the mid-1960s and 70s (see table 3), and I shall discuss the financial implications of the demand, mainly tourist, for Onta pottery, in the following chapter. Here we will look at

TABLE 3   *Tourism Statistics for Sarayama, Hita, and Oita Prefecture, 1967–1976*

	1967	1968	1969	1970
Sarayama	37,220	39,340	43,840	50,000
Hita	691,490	765,420	885,850	1,327,877
Oita	728,710	804,780	929,410	1,377,897

	1972	1974	1976
Sarayama	65,140	55,310	81,010
Hita	1,564,990	1,327,870	1,444,300
Oita	1,630,130	1,383,180	1,525,310

Note: Statistics for Sarayama, as supplied by the Hita City Office, are not reliable, but do give some indication of the increase in visitors to the community. Statistics prior to 1967 are not available.

some of the more obvious ways in which market demand has affected potters' lives. How do the decline of social cooperation and the economic independence of each potting household affect folk craft leaders' appraisal of Onta pottery? How do potters adapt to such changes in the institutional framework of the community? Can the community as such survive the pressures put on it by the outside world?

TECHNOLOGICAL INNOVATIONS

This discussion of social change begins with an account of the way in which labor cooperation has broken down in Sarayama. In the preceding chapter, I enumerated five types of such cooperation. Of these five, two have disappeared entirely, and one is now practiced by nonpotting households only. One other form of cooperation, which was formerly not found in the community, is now quite widespread. Superficially, the breakdown of cooperation among households may be said to have resulted from technological innovations and from an improvement in communications between Sarayama and the outside world. Both of these have affected the way in which the community hitherto adapted to its natural environment. They may in this sense, therefore, be seen as "ecological" changes.

I will start, and finish, with the cooperative kiln. The cooperative kiln in Onta consisted of eight chambers. Each of these had a sloping, sandy floor on which pots were placed to be fired. They could not be stacked very high, and most of the available space in a chamber was wasted. In the 1950s, the technique of manufacturing strong, heat-resistant kiln shelving was developed in the ceramic complexes of Arita and Seto. In 1957–1958, in an attempt to increase the number of pots they could fire at any one time, potters in the neighboring pottery village of Koishiwara decided to buy shelves for their kilns. The innovation proved successful. Shizuma, the half-brother of Kazuo of Iriichi, was at that time working in Koishiwara, and he soon told his father, Jinichi, about what was going on. The following year, Jinichi fitted his allotted chambers in the cooperative kiln with shelves.

The use of shelving meant two things: first, the *whole*, and not just one-third, of a chamber could be stacked with pots, without fear of their falling over; second, it allowed the firing of a large quantity of *small* pots, which in Onta had not hitherto been made. The economic advantages of Iriichi's decision to buy shelves were not lost on the other potters. The two potters firing their own kilns and then all the other households sharing the cooperative kiln agreed to put shelving into their rebuilt or newly built kilns. By 1962 all potters in Sarayama had switched from the old, sand-sloped chambers to chambers fitted with shelves.

The adoption of kiln shelving had an important effect on the community's social organization in that it induced potters to spend their time on pottery rather than on agriculture. Admittedly, they were already devoting more time than before to wheel work, because there was considerable demand for smaller pots and they were being asked to fill orders by stipulated dates. However, so long as they kept using the old-style sand-sloped kilns, there was a limit to the number of pots that could be made and fired at any one time. It did not make economic sense to fill each chamber with small pots only and increase the number of firings, because the old methods of kiln loading gave a very low yield for small items. The problem was solved by kiln shelving, which permitted smaller pots to be fired in very large quantities. At the same time, it meant that potters had to spend five or six times longer working at the wheel if they were to meet orders and continue to fire their kilns at the same rate as before.

The adoption of kiln shelving affected the distribution of labor within any one pottery household, in that from the early 1960s, both father *and* son began to devote their time fully to wheel work rather than farming. Women were left to prepare clay and glazes and attend to the rice paddies and vegetable patches; men came to their aid only during the really busy seasons of transplanting, harvesting, and so on.[1]

This is not to say that *all* pottery labor was devoted to wheel work. A lot of time was spent in the gathering and preparation of materials for clays, glazes, and firing. As I shall show, the content of pottery labor itself was about to change considerably. But another decision about how much time to give to what task had an even greater effect on social organization. In the 1960s, the Japanese government adopted a rice-curtailment policy (*gentan seisaku*). Because people in Sarayama were not growing rice for cash and because potters found that,

---

1. Unlike other communities, household labor organization in Sarayama was not affected by mechanization and technological innovation in agricultural methods (cf. Shimpo 1976:46ff.).

thanks to the introduction of kiln shelving, they could satisfy a continually increasing market demand, they decided to give up wet-rice agriculture.[2] Those households that were short of manpower, Yamasai and Irisai, were the first to stop in 1966–1967. They were soon followed by all other potting households except for Yamaichi, whose head, Shigeki, clung to the *mingei*-inspired philosophy of farming and pottery production (*hannō-hantō*) until the autumn of 1978.

Once potter households gave up farming, the kind of labor exchange known as *temagēshi* came to an end. Osamu of Maruta also stopped farming in order to run a noodle shop and to retail Onta pottery, so the only households to continue exchanging their labor were Yamamaru, Yamaichi, Kaneyo, and Yamamasu. With Shigeki's decision to stop growing rice from 1979, *temagēshi* was continued by only three of Sarayama's fourteen households.

In 1971 five potters purchased electric ball mills in order to help prepare some of their glaze materials. This decision has brought an end to the informal labor exchange groups which used to be formed to pound straw ash. Those households which do not possess these ball mills either prepare the materials on their own or hire labor (*yatoi*) for help. They never ask to borrow the use of a ball mill.

IMPROVEMENT IN COMMUNICATIONS

The social organization of households in Sarayama has also changed as a result of better communications. Since 1954 existing country roads have been widened and metaled, and methods of transportation have greatly improved. By the late 1950s, potters were able to go to places like Akadani and Koishiwara by car or three-wheeled vehicle. Instead of walking across the mountains with their cows, they drove and loaded up their cars with feldspar from the Akadani deposit. They acquired their supplies of white slip clay from Koishiwara, since it was simpler to drive the forty kilometers there and back than to struggle for several days on end climbing the steep

---

2. Another reason cited by potters for their giving up farming is that their rice paddy was often ravaged by wild boar. People from nonpotting households point out, however, that the wild boar started coming out into the fields from the thickly wooded mountains only when the potters had stopped farming (i.e., from the mid-1970s). For a description of some of the economic problems arising from the curtailment policy, see R. J. Smith (1978:96–130).

slope to the Kitanamizu deposit and humping the heavy clay back down to the hamlet. Potters also claim that there is not enough slip clay in Kitanamizu to justify further digging there.[3]

Once it had become easier to travel by car, potters stopped going on foot to get their iron oxide from the mine shaft at Fukakura. Fukakura was still inaccessible by road, but new deposits were discovered in Sujiu, which could be reached by car, and so potters have been going there since the mid-1960s. Whereas, in the old days, several potter households had always banded together to go and get their supplies of feldspar, slip clay, and iron oxide, they now tend to go singly.

Improved road conditions between Sarayama and Hita in particular, together with a rapidly expanding local lumber industry, have led to three other important changes in labor cooperation. These concern the preparation of fuel for firing the kilns, the practice of *yamasaku* slash-and-burn mountain cultivation, and the rethatching of house roofs in the community.

Preparing enough wood to fire a kiln involved a lot of work, as we have seen. Potter households used to spend at least a week collecting wood from the mountains and then splitting and drying it before each firing. After the Pacific War, local government authorities tried to alleviate unemployment by creating job opportunities in forestry. Government land was reforested, and cedar plantations were greatly increased throughout Oita Prefecture. Cedar was a fairly fast-growing tree, whose wood could be put to a variety of uses, from craftwork to house building. By the late 1950s, interest in cedar plantations had spread to the private sector of the lumber market. There was a big increase in planting between 1958 and 1962, and landowners round Sarayama tried to make the most of the potential economic value of their land by replacing deciduous trees with cedar.

Local government policy seriously affected household labor patterns,[4] since cedar was replacing the hardwoods which the potters had hitherto used for their kilns. Because the mountains around the

---

3. It is generally agreed that the quality of the Kitanamizu clay is far superior to that of any other slip, as was painfully brought home to potters when they had to obtain supplies of slip clay from Arita in the 1970s. There has been talk—but no action yet—of going back to the Kitanamizu deposit.

4. It is ironical that decisions about forestry made by one group of local government officials should go right against the concept of "tradition" so dearly held by those in another department of the town hall who were more concerned with promoting Hita's tourism.

community were being reforested with cedar, all the undergrowth died out. It was not just the wild undergrowth that was affected, but households' cultivated crops of beans and potatoes, which they had been growing on cleared strips of land. The cedar grew too fast to make it worthwhile for any household to go to the trouble of preparing land for its *yamasaku* vegetables, and so the old custom of *moyai* cooperative labor came to an end. I am not suggesting that the potters were sad about this: after all, it was mostly *their* land on which *they* had planted the cedar. By the early 1960s, considerations of the economic advantages to be gained from cedar-forested land and from fuller production of pottery far outweighed any possible nostalgia for a sense of "togetherness" resulting from a lot of toil for little concrete gain.

But the potters' decision to plant their land with cedar in the first place was made easier by the fact that they had found a new means of procuring fuel for their kilns. The road up to Sarayama had been improved soon after Leach's visit to the community in 1954, so that heavy vehicles were able to come up the valley. Consequently, potters had only to order their wood from the lumber yards down in the Ono valley or in Hita, and great truckloads would be brought up to Sarayama. One phone call saved the potters a week's hard work cutting felled trees to suitable lengths for their kilns. The cost of having the wood brought up from the valley was more than covered by the additional time potters could thereby spend at the wheel. They were also able to invest in the planting of cedar on their mountain land.

At about the same time, two or three potting households replaced their thatched roofs with prestigious tiles. This meant that not only were they reluctant to participate in the *kaya-kō*, roof-thatching association, but they also began to suggest that the community-owned land on which the thatch grass grew be converted to cedar plantations. In the mid-1960s, potters found that the *mingei* boom was making it financially possible for them to rebuild their homes. As more and more new tiled houses were put up, fewer and fewer people were prepared to participate in the *kaya-kō*. Moreover, once potters stopped farming, they no longer required their draft cows; fodder became unnecessary, so community-owned land was finally replanted with cedar at the beginning of the 1970s. The handful of residents who had not yet tiled their houses were thereby deprived of a last source of thatch, and the *kaya-kō* came to an end.[5]

---

5. Cf. Shimpo (1976:103) for the breakdown of the roof-thatching association in

Improved communications led to one more change which affected the way in which potter households once worked together. In 1963 the go-ahead was given for a completely new road to be built between Sarayama and the neighboring hamlet of Koda, in Tsurugimachi. This made access to Ōtsuru and Fukuoka much easier, and also saved the potters a roundabout trip down the Ōtsuru valley via the hamlet of Onta, which was the only way they had previously been able to travel westward (see map 2). When the Sarayama–Koda road was first opened up, deposits of raw clay were discovered along the mountainside to the southwest of the hamlet near where Irisai, Yamasai, and Kanemaru had once dug their clay. It seemed much more sensible to the potters to take their clay from these new deposits, rather than continue working in the extremely cramped conditions of the community-owned clay pit behind Yamako. Since the newly found clay was right by the roadside, access was easy. So in 1964, potters arranged with two of their number, who owned the land on which the clay had been found (Yamako and Irisai), to allow them to dig there. A sum of ¥10,000 per annum was agreed upon, to be paid by each potter household in exchange for the right to take clay from the new deposits.

For the first few years after the road had been opened up, households continued to cooperate in the way that was described earlier in the model of social organization. Each household provided two of its members, one male and one female, when they were needed; a three-wheeled vehicle took the clay from the deposits to each household's drying yard or crusher shed. In due course, however, the potters began to look for new, less time-consuming methods of getting the clay out of the deposits. First, they tried to dynamite the clay from the mountainside, but this was not successful, and they gave it up after a couple of years. Then, in 1972, they found that a bulldozer could be brought up to Sarayama by heavy truck, and they hired one to shovel out the clay. One day's bulldozing supplied all the potters with enough clay to last them the next three years! It cost them ¥50,000 to hire, but it saved them the effort of two or three weeks' annual work together in the clay pits.

All of this means that not only have various forms of labor cooper-

---

Shiwa with the adoption of tiles. In Sarayama, improved economic conditions made it unnecessary for households to participate in *kō* to buy bedding, watches, and so on. Expensive items were now purchased outright or through credit or on hire-purchase terms. For further instances of *kō* which, in most parts of Japan came to an end before the Pacific War, see Cornell (1956:149) and R. J. Smith (1956:16).

ation come to an end, but the amount of time devoted to the acquisition and preparation of pottery materials has been drastically reduced (table 4). The time saved is now spent working at the wheel.

MARKET DEMAND

Leach came to Sarayama in 1954; the *mingei* boom started three or four years later. Many of the changes in social cooperation in Sarayama came about as a result of potters' readaptation to the environment, in response to technological innovations and an improvement in communications, as outlined above. But it was the demand for folk craft pottery that was the underlying force behind these changes. Potters adopted kiln shelving and purchased ball mills; they

TABLE 4   *Annual Number of Labor Days Devoted to the Acquisition and Preparation of Pottery Materials by One Household (Yamaichi) in 1960 and 1977*

	1960			1977		
ACTIVITY	*F*	*M*	*TOTAL*	*F*	*M*	*TOTAL*
Clay digging	18	18	36	0	1	1
Slip digging	10	7	17	0	0	0
Wood cutting and drying	45	40	85	30	0	30
Feldspar digging	0	2	2	1	1	2
Iron-oxide digging	0	2	2	1	1	2
Straw-ash preparation	4	0	4	4	0	4
Wood-ash preparation	5	0	5	5	0	5
Totals	82	69	151	41	3	44

hired a bulldozer to dig their clay; they bought their slip and telephoned orders for wood for their kilns. All of these changes suggest that potters thought it worthwhile to alter their methods of production. It was no longer necessary to continue farming, because there was market demand for their pottery.

Two things happened as a result of the demand for folk craft pottery. First, potters became extremely wealthy. Within the space of a few years, they found that they had more money than they needed for their everyday living costs. For the first time, perhaps, they were able to make use of the principle of investment: that a little money, wisely used now, could in due course generate more wealth. So they used their extra money to pay for the kiln shelves, for example, that increased the number of pots that could be fired, and hence the total income yielded by each firing. At the same time, they learned that cash could be converted into other forms of wealth—into new land, for example, into the saplings that would eventually grow into giant cedar trees, into stocks and shares, or into bars of gold.

Second, potters began to rely on the use of money to conduct their everyday affairs. In the old days, labor was the community's wealth, and land, the household's. People had to work together, and they had to own agricultural land (or be able to work it) if they were to survive. Land provided people with rice and vegetables on which they could subsist; it gave them wood with which to build their homes, grass with which to thatch their roofs; it gave the potters clay for their pots, materials for their glazes, and fuel for their kilns. If potters sold their wares, they would use the money to buy things they could not produce on their land—a piece of fish, or cloth, or even salt. But they never had enough money to buy more than this. Household land, and the people who helped work the land, were more important to a man than money.

However, once potters started earning much more as a result of the folk craft boom, they began to place more emphasis on the use of money than on working the land together. In other words, the use of cash gave rise to impersonal relations. By deciding to buy the wood for their kilns, potters were able to give more time to work at the wheel and get more money for their pots. But by using the extra cash to plant their land with cedar, potters stopped working together to cultivate mountain crops. After all, more than a supply of vegetables could be bought with the results of the time that had been saved and spent making pots instead. Thus the acquisition of money as an end in itself became more important than working on the land; people ceased to matter so much.

It is hardly surprising to find that by the mid-1960s some potters had decided to stop farming. It made economic sense to use one's energies in the workshop rather than in the rice fields. It was cheaper to buy rice than to grow it—the government's requisition policy had seen to that. And since people were being paid *not* to plant rice in their fields, *moyai* labor cooperation came to an end and *temagēshi* labor exchange was confined to Sarayama's three farming households. This left only two forms of labor cooperation available to households, *kasei* and *yatoi*. People still give labor to their neighbors or relatives when it comes to building a new house; but building is a rare occasion, and *kasei* is now limited to minor tasks. The main method by which labor is recruited is by hiring people to help. One or two potters now employ women from Ikenzuru or nonpotting households in Sarayama to help sift and settle clay, stack wood, or load and unload kilns; men are hired to saw up wood and to build or repair kilns and clay crushers, and so on. The free exchange of labor, so frequently and wistfully referred to by people talking of the past, has now almost come to an end.

Another way in which market demand affected cooperation among potter households was in the running of the cooperative kiln. In 1954 the kiln was shared by seven households, while Irisai and Yamako fired independently. By 1978 only five households remained members of the cooperative kiln; five others fired their own private kilns.[6]

The cooperative kiln has always been of great importance to Sarayama community life. This may be seen clearly in the mysterious circumstances surrounding the building of the first independent kiln by Hamakichi of Irisai. The story goes that there was a doctor living in nearby Ōtsuru who was very fond of pottery, in particular of the pots made by Chikara's grandfather, Hamakichi. The doctor apparently gave Hamakichi a sum of money with which to build "an experimental kiln" and fire pots glazed with a certain type of red glaze (*shinsha*) that he especially liked. It is said that the experimental kiln was originally intended for the whole community; certainly, all the potters

---

6. This apparent anomaly in figures stems from the fact that Kaneichi stopped potting in 1910, and then started its own kiln in 1970 after the demand for Onta ware had boomed.

helped to build it. But once they had completed it, Hamakichi claimed the kiln as his own. He was immediately ostracized by his co-potters, and there was a rift between the old man and his adopted son, Chikara's father, with the latter eventually choosing to leave the hamlet entirely. Although, eventually, Hamakichi was permitted to participate once more in community life, the kiln has remained in the possession of the Irisai household to this day.

Once one potter had separated from the cooperative kiln, it became easier for others to do so. In 1948 Yōzō of Yamako, a household situated at the bottom of the hamlet, asked permission to build his own kiln; the cooperative kiln was too far, he said, and it was impractical to carry pots two hundred meters up the road from Yamako's workshop to the kiln and then back again after every firing. Permission was granted then and again twelve years later when Haruzō of Yamani used the same pretext to build himself a private kiln in 1962. Certainly, Yamani's workshop was some distance from the cooperative kiln, but it was clear that Haruzō hoped to—and in fact did—benefit from the increased demand for Onta pots by being able to fire as often as his work-rate permitted. With his own private kiln, Haruzō was no longer held back by potters who did not have sufficient manpower to keep up with his fast schedule.

It is significant, therefore, that when Yoshitaka of Kaneichi decided to take up potting again after a sixty-year interval, he did not apply to be taken into the cooperative kiln (which he had the right to fire), but built his own private kiln at the top of the community. Finally, in 1971, for completely different reasons, Shigeki of Yamaichi left the cooperative kiln. He was working on his own and found that he was neither prepared nor able to keep up with other households in his firing group. The cooperative kiln is now shared by just five households.

All in all there is now very little formal cooperation between households in Sarayama (fig. 14). Only Kaneyo, Yamamaru, and Yamamasu combine for reciprocal labor in agriculture; none of the potter households practice *temagēshi* in either pottery or farming. The custom of *moyai* cooperative labor has disappeared entirely, as has the *kō*, group labor or "mutual credit association." The only way in which households in the community cooperate, regardless of occupation, is informally in the exchange of *kasei* casual work (cf. fig 13).

Yet there is a paradox in the way market demand has affected patterns of cooperation among households in the community as a whole,

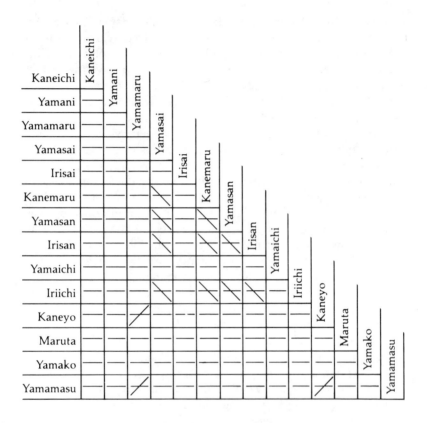

	Reciprocal labor (*temagēshi*)
	Cooperative kiln
	Casual work (*kasei*)

FIGURE 14. *Linking of households through forms of labor cooperation (1979)*

for potters have been made more aware of themselves as a group. Although the number of potters sharing the cooperative kiln has decreased, and although the potters do not exchange labor as frequently as they used to, the potters' cooperative (*dōgyō kumiai*) as a whole has begun to play an important part in their lives. This is precisely because of market demand and the renown of Onta pottery throughout Japan. The cooperative is frequently approached by local government officials concerning promotional exhibitions of pottery (linked with tourism in Oita Prefecture and Hita City); folk craft leaders contact the cooperative whenever they want something from Onta; the media do the same when they want to make a television film or a radio program or write a magazine or newspaper article about the pottery community. Potters therefore find themselves called together to discuss what are essentially administrative matters. For the most part they find these matters extremely irksome. There is no doubt, however, that the attention given the potters serves to unite them as a group. Community solidarity may have been weakened, but not necessarily the occupational solidarity of the potters, a point to which I shall return.

CONCLUSION

In this chapter, I have discussed environmental and social changes in Sarayama over the past twenty-five years, particularly the way in which various forms of labor cooperation have been affected by improvements in technology and communications and by an increase in market demand. I have suggested that the adoption of kiln shelving directly influenced the potters' decision to stop wet-rice agriculture, and indirectly led to the breakdown of the cooperative kiln. Improved transportation facilities between the community and the outside world brought an end to households working together to get their raw materials; they also induced potters to buy wood for their kilns, instead of preparing it for themselves. Potters and other local landowners replanted mountain land with cedar rather than deciduous trees because of a burgeoning lumber industry in Hita. Because of the new plantations, thatching became difficult and mountain cultivation impossible. Thus the *kō* and *moyai* forms of labor cooperation also came to an end.

Such changes radically altered not only the way in which each household allocated its labor, but also how it viewed its priorities in production. As Embree (1939:306) has pointed out elsewhere, an increase in cash income has led to reliance on hired help, rather than on neighbors' cooperation, so that nowadays almost all households in Sarayama contract rather than exchange labor. There is consequently very little cooperation among households in their day-to-day living. Even informal labor exchanges have been affected. For instance, when Chikara of Irisai broke a bone in his wrist playing softball in 1978, nobody offered to help him out by making pots or by finishing off ones that had already been made but not turned or decorated. Instead, a small gift of money was made. Cash has become the medium by which one man expresses his feeling for another.

I have tried to show that environmental, technological, and social variables are systematically interconnected. T. C. Smith (1959:101) has written of a previous era: "Innovations rarely if ever came simply; they hung together in clusters by a kind of inner logic; one innovation brought others in its train, and often could not be adopted independently of them." Social changes have not been *determined* by environmental changes; causality should be seen not as unilinear but as circular, or reciprocal (Friedman 1974:44; Netting 1965:95).

But the environmental changes described in this chapter are not purely "social," for potters are involved in an aesthetic movement. Japanese folk craft leaders have a very clear perception of what the craftsman's relations with his environment ought to be, and any discrepancy between this "cognized" model and the actual "operational" model (Rappaport 1971:247) leads to severe criticism. In general, folk craft beauty has been seen to disappear with the onslaught of Western civilization. Almost all *mingei* kilns have been "ruined" by material changes that upset man's relation to "nature"; for example, the substitution of charcoal for wood in the firing of kilns, the forming of pots in plaster molds instead of on the wheel, and the inclusion of chemical substances instead of natural materials in glaze compositions (Mizuo 1966:83).

It is not surprising, therefore, to find that, because of the social changes that have occurred in Sarayama, Onta pottery is to some extent criticized by leaders of the folk craft movement. Tanaka Toyotarō, until 1978 director of the Folk Craft Association, has written:

> Recently people have begun to be more receptive to conventional beauty in form, colour and decoration. Whether it is because of the sudden changes that have occurred or not, I don't know, but it seems to me that the quality of the work of potters in Onta has deteriorated, as it has done in other potteries. (1961:8)

This remark is echoed by the potter Hamada (1965:9): "It is a shame how their work is gradually deteriorating," and he goes on to comment on a warning given by Yanagi (1961:5) on the dangers to Onta presented by local government authorities. It is they who, for a short period, prevailed upon the potters to make use of a mechanical waterwheel to step up the process of clay preparation. As a result, the quality of their pots deteriorated significantly, and it was a triumph for "nature"—and for the beauty of folk crafts—when the potters went back to the old rhythm of life thudded out by the *karausu* clay crushers (Tonomura 1965:10). In fact, the potters rejected the waterwheel, not because of their desire to adhere to *mingei* ideals so much as because the wheel was technically inefficient and kept on breaking down.

Although potters may have discarded this innovation fairly quickly, they have not done the same with kiln shelving. Tanaka Yōko of the Folk Craft Museum has pointed out (1965:24) that the change in kiln-chamber loading methods has brought about poorer results with Onta slipware; she also suggests that the change in wood ash, which has come to be bought from local lumber yards, may be affecting the glazes.

Potters would probably agree in part with both these criticisms. Kiln shelving does affect the way in which flames reach the pots during firing; the new wood-ash is not as good as the old, mainly because the lumberyard people tend to burn polythene bags and plastic containers along with the wood. Potters are also aware of the fact that the slip clay that they now get from Arita is inferior to that which they used to dig from Kitanamizu.

They might well object, however, to the criticism that their work has deteriorated because they have stopped farming. "Onta potters were originally half potters and half farmers; if they give up farming, it will mean that they will forget the very essence of folk craft" (Miyake in *Nihon no Mingei* 190:7). They also have to contend with the argument that because a bus has started plying between Hita and Sarayama, their pots are getting worse (Hamada 1965:9; B. Leach in conversation). Tourism is seen to make the potters produce such poor work; visitors look for cheap pots; folk craft dealers only buy things that are superficially beautiful (Tanaka Takashi 1969:47). Onta pots are seen to be "polluted" (Mizuo 1968:110).

7

The Economic Development of a Potting Household

In his discussion of a Japanese fishing village in the Seto Inland Sea, Norbeck (1954:207) attributes social structural change to the rise of a money economy. Once people start using cash for transactions, he says, cooperation breaks down and "individualism" emerges. I have described a similar situation: the richer potters have become as a result of demand for their work, the less interested they appear to be in cooperating with others in the community. Ultimately, I shall be concerned with whether the ideal of individualism exists in Sarayama. First, however, it is necessary to give an outline of the way in which Onta pottery is retailed and, by tracing the economic development of a pottery household, to find out just how wealthy potters have been made by the folk craft boom.

Onta pottery is currently retailed all over Japan, from Hokkaido in the north to Kyushu in the south. Some pots are ordered by post or by telephone, and are sent directly to the person or shop concerned; others pass through one or more distributors before reaching the retail market. By far the greatest number of pots is bought direct from Sarayama by dealers who visit each potter's workshop after a kiln firing. One of these dealers comes from as far away as Kamakura, near Tokyo; the majority of them have shops in and around the town of Hita, less than twenty kilometers away.

At least fifteen buyers from Hita regularly purchase pottery worth between ¥700,000 and ¥8 million (averaging just over ¥2 million) from Sarayama potters every year. Two of them are distributors who forward pots to shops whose owners cannot make the trip to Sarayama or who do not have the personal introduction necessary to start business with a potter. The other buyers from Hita sell varying quantities of Onta pottery, which may be found in the tourist centers of Yufuin, Beppu, and Oita, as well as in the northern Kyushu industrial complex of Tobata, Yahata, and Kokura.

Onta pottery sells particularly well to the many people visiting Kyushu on holiday from all parts of Japan, and especially from the Kansai and Kanto regions. The number of tourists to Oita prefecture and the town of Hita doubled between 1967 and 1975, although it has remained fairly steady since 1970. As a result of tourist demand for souvenirs, many of the buyers from Hita have only recently started dealing in Onta pottery. It is because *ontayaki* is considered by many people to be a medium of gift exchange, rather than simply a folk craft, that several problems concerning "individualism" among potters arise. I shall come back to this point in the following two chapters.

INCOME AND EXPENDITURES OF A POTTING HOUSEHOLD

The folk craft boom lasted about fifteen years altogether, starting in the late 1950s and finishing in the early 1970s. Although the boom as such may be said to be over, folk crafts still sell well. Pottery in particular has been in great demand, and potters in Onta are able to dispose of all firsts coming out of each kiln firing. More than 90 percent of these pots are sold immediately to buyers in the trade; the rest are bought by visiting tourists. The latter buy misshapen and blistered seconds to some extent, but not as much, apparently, as they used to at the height of the boom.

The vital question is this: What did the boom mean in terms of hard cash? The answer is not simple, and has required some calculated guessing. Money is not an easy topic to discuss with anyone, unless you happen to know him or her very well. In Sarayama the subject was made more difficult by the fact that potters have been underreporting annual incomes in their tax returns by as much as 300 percent. When I somewhat innocently began enquiring about kiln capacities, and how many pots could be stacked into each firing, I re-

ceived evasive answers or what I later realized were outrageously un-
derestimated figures. By the second year of my fieldwork in the community, potters had come to realize that I was not an agent of the tax
office. Nevertheless, questions about income and costs, capital expenditure, investments, and so on were met with silence or embarrassed
laughter. Fortunately, Shigeki of Yamaichi let me have full access to
his household accounts for 1976–1978, and Shigeoyoshi of Kaneyo let
me have his account books for 1967 and 1975. I was then favored
with the kind of luck that every anthropologist dreams of. Shigeki's
sister-in-law was clearing out her room one day and came across a
diary written by her father-in-law in 1962. In this diary was written
down every single item of expenditure and income for that year.
These sources have enabled me to gauge the effect of the folk craft
boom on potter households in Sarayama.

In 1962 Yamaichi's total annual income came to ¥716,348, and expenditure to ¥713,003 (table 5). Of this income, only ¥457,344, or
63.9 percent of the total, came from sales of pottery; the rest came
from sales of land and timber, from pensions, gifts, and so on.

In 1962 Shigeki fired his allotted chambers in the cooperative kiln
six times; his average income from pottery was therefore about
¥76,000 per firing. In May of that year the cooperative kiln was rebuilt, and shelves were put into each chamber. Shigeki fired twice before and four times after the kiln's rebuilding, but the deferment of
payments by buyers makes it difficult to judge exactly the differences
in incomes from the old and new methods of loading the kiln chambers. Also Shigeki admits that he was unable to fill his chambers completely after the adoption of shelving, since his father made very few
pots. Thus the following figures do not support a potter's estimate
quoted earlier, that kiln capacity was increased five or six times by the
introduction of shelving. In 1962 Shigeki's first two firings averaged
¥68,070 (pottery income from January to May inclusive); the last
four came to ¥80,301. This gives an 18 percent increase in income per
firing.

Expenditure for the same year gives a fairly accurate picture of the
way in which pottery gave each household a source of cash income.
The year 1962 was exceptional in that capital outlay on the rebuilding
of the cooperative kiln and the purchase of shelving was extremely
high (¥36,000 and ¥16,020 respectively), coming to 43.55 percent of
total pottery expenditure for that year. Moreover, in November a new
clay-crusher shed had to be built at a cost of ¥21,150. All these items

TABLE 5　*Statement of Income and Expenditure (in yen) for Yamaichi During the Calendar Year 1962*

INCOME			EXPENDITURE		
SOURCE	TOTAL	%	ITEM	TOTAL	%
Farming	15,009	2.1	Farming	29,210	4.0
Pottery	457,344	63.9	Pottery	119,455	16.6
Land/timber	159,255	22.2	Household	128,166	17.9
Pensions/			Food/clothing	152,238	21.2
insurance	73,000	10.2	Medical/dental	16,659	2.2
Labor*	1,800	0.2	Communications	24,613	3.3
Gifts	8,050	1.1	Insurance	60,224	8.3
Other	1,890	0.3	Taxes/dues	55,773	7.7
Totals	716,348	100.0	Labor*	14,880	2.0
			Ceremonies/		
			fees/gifts	42,670	5.9
			Relatives	40,580	5.7
			Recreation	10,415	1.4
			Other	28,120	3.8
			Totals	713,003	100.0

*Labor was hired (*yatoi*) from outside the community for thatching in April, with two Sarayama households giving free labor (*kasei*). People from outside the community were hired in May to repair the walls of a rice paddy, and in June to help transplant rice. Income under the item of "labor" came from work contracted outside Sarayama.

were to last Yamaichi at least ten years. The average annual pottery expenditure for 1960–1965, therefore, was probably about ¥50,000. The cooperative kiln would also have been fired more than six times from 1963, since rebuilding interfered with the potters' schedules in 1962. More than ¥15,000 had to be spent on rice paddy repairs as well, so that Yamaichi decided to sell a lot of cedar in July to pay for the extra expenditure incurred. In a more normal year, one would have expected the household to make a modest profit of about ¥50,000, assuming that land did not yield any income apart from that gained from farming.

Income and expenditure figures belie, in my opinion, the importance of farming to potters. According to a census made in 1960, official agricultural income for all households in Sarayama was estimated at under ¥100,000 per annum. The cash return on Yamaichi's farm-

TABLE 6   *Statement of Annual Income and Expenditure (in yen) for Yamaichi During the Calendar Years 1976 and 1977*

INCOME

SOURCE	1976	%	1977	%
Pottery	4,652,220	86.9	4,414,430	83.0
Land	300,000	5.6	372,812	7.0
Gifts	0	0.0	450,000	8.5
Loans	300,000	5.6	0	0.0
Interest	104,298	1.9	79,178	1.5
Totals	5,356,518	100.0	5,316,420	100.0

EXPENDITURE

ITEM	1976	%	1977	%
Living expenses	2,103,000	39.0	1,970,000	42.1
Farm expenses	20,505	0.4	19,607	0.4
Pottery expenses	797,703	14.8	474,365	10.1
Pottery fees	233,000	4.3	231,000	4.9
Pottery labor	108,000	2.0	73,200	1.6
Car purchase	613,950	11.4	0	0.0
Communications	215,075	4.0	390,790	8.4
Electricity	63,682	1.2	78,895	1.7
Insurance	483,979	9.0	628,095	13.4
Taxes	128,600	2.3	168,995	3.6
Loan repayments	102,645	1.9	188,909	4.0
Ceremonies/gifts	0	0.0	360,000	7.7
Recreation	516,500	9.6	96,000	2.1
Totals	5,386,639	100.0	4,679,856	100.0

Note: Figures under the heading "gifts" for both income and expenditure result from the death of, and funeral arrangements for, Shigeki's father in March 1977.

ing activities for 1962 was only ¥15,009. This sum does not show, however, the amount of money the household was saved in the purchase of foodstuffs through the consumption of home-produced rice, beans, various kinds of potatoes, and other vegetables.

By 1976 both income and expenditure had increased by seven or eight times. Yamaichi's income came to ¥5,356,518, of which more than 85 percent derived from pottery sales. Land sales and loans feature in the accounts, mainly made to meet recreational expenses incurred in the construction of a hamlet softball ground above the community, and in the purchase of a new car (table 6). Pottery expenditure in 1976 is again unusually high because of the rebuilding of the clay-crusher shed once more and of the purchase of a new set of kiln shelves. The 1977 accounts give a somewhat more balanced picture of annual pottery expenditure. Income in 1977 comes to less than that for the previous year, but Shigeki admitted to underestimation for the purpose of tax returns. The figure for pottery sales alone (from six firings in 1977, as opposed to five in 1976) should come to ¥5,500,000, putting total income at about ¥6.5 million. Shigeki also has deposit accounts in the Agricultural Cooperative and a local bank, amounting to ¥12 million.[1]

By 1976–1977 Yamaichi had no cash income from farming, although some vegetables and rice were grown for domestic consumption. In neither case, however, were crops sufficient to feed the household for more than six months of the year.

With such high income over the past few years, Shigeki (like almost all other potters in Sarayama) has been able to rebuild his home and workshop, pay for the construction of his private kiln, and more recently have it fitted with a chimney. Washing machines, television sets, and cars have been bought (each item three times over the years) since Leach's stay in the community. The bathroom has been renovated, and water has been taken from underground springs by pump rather than from mountain streams as of old. Expenditure of this sort may be considered to be fairly typical of potting households (table 7), for where Yamaichi has laid out capital on a new kiln, other potters have preferred to purchase trucks, build drying kilns and woodsheds (often necessitating bulldozing away mountain land), and have their water bored from deep underground (table 8).

Although figures are not available for a nonpotting household for exactly the same years (1962 and 1976–1978), household accounts for Kaneyo in 1968 and 1975 give some indication of the difference in income levels between the poorest of the potting and nonpotting households in Sarayama. Kaneyo's total income in the above specified years (including withdrawals from savings) was ¥519,931 and ¥2,256,368; expenditure amounted to ¥776,836 and ¥3,216,857 respectively. Kaneyo's 1968 income does not even come up to Yama-

---

1. Compare this sum with figures quoted by R. J. Smith (1978:118) for his village of Kurusu, where the average household savings are quoted as ¥328,812 (ranging from ¥5,792 to ¥1,235,471) for July 1975.

TABLE 7   *Summary of Capital Expenditure for One Household, Yamaichi, Over the Ten-Year Period 1967–1977*

House and workshop	¥4,300,000
House furnishings	¥ 700,000
Outbuildings	¥1,000,000
Kiln	¥1,400,000
Kiln equipment	¥ 257,000
Clay crushers	¥ 95,000
Kiln chimney	¥ 700,000
Cars	¥ 900,000
Total	¥9,352,000

TABLE 8   *Capital Expenditure and Running Costs for a Pottery Household (Yamaichi) in 1962 and 1976*

CAPITAL EXPENDITURE	1962	%	1976	%
Clay-crusher parts	455	0.4	95,000	8.3
Clay-crusher shed	21,150	17.7	95,500	8.4
Clay-drying planters	5,150	4.3	0	0.0
Motor, purchase of	6,150	5.1	0	0.0
Drying trays	0	0.0	10,000	0.9
Kiln rebuilding	25,000	20.9	0	0.0
Kiln fire bricks	20,000	16.7	31,800	2.8
Kiln shelves	16,020	13.5	150,000	13.2
Hake brushes	0	0.0	28,100	2.5
Other	0	0.0	6,990	0.6
Subtotals	93,925	78.6	417,390	36.7
Running costs				
Raw clay	1,900	1.6	10,000	0.9
Slip clay	0	0.0	36,833	3.2
Feldspar	1,750	1.5	5,000	0.4
Wood	12,600	10.6	150,780	13.2
Packaging costs	1,350	1.1	161,200	14.2
Freight costs	7,930	6.6	17,500	1.5
Cooperative fees	0	0.0	120,000	10.5
Autumn festival fees	0	0.0	33,000	2.9
Auditor's fees	0	0.0	60,000	5.3
Mingei seminar fees	0	0.0	15,000	1.3
Mingei exhibition fees	0	0.0	4,000	0.4
Hired labor	0	0.0	108,000	9.5
Subtotals	25,530	21.4	721,313	63.3
Totals	119,455	100.0	1,138,703	100.0

ichi's 1962 income, and by 1975 there is a difference of more than ¥2 million when Kaneyo's income is compared with Yamaichi's sales from pottery alone.

It can be seen, therefore, that there is a considerable difference in income levels between potting and nonpotting households in Sarayama. However, it must also be pointed out that potters' incomes vary immensely. Shigeki has a four-chamber kiln, which he fires five times one year and six times the next, each firing yielding on average ¥900,000–¥1,000,000. The capacity of Yamaichi's kiln, however, is only 10.35 cubic meters, the second smallest in the community (table 9). Because he is often in a hurry to complete an order on time, he does not make as much use of available kiln space as do other potters, who very often take the greatest advantage possible of piling pots in and on one another.

By anthropological sleuthing and the measurement of kiln-chamber capacities, I have made an estimate as to each potting household's income (table 10). Potters with private kilns, and with sons working with them at the wheel (Yamani and Yamako), fire between seven and nine times a year. Those working on their own (Yamaichi, Irisai, and Kaneichi) fire five or six times a year. The cooperative kiln, it will be remembered, is split into two and three household groups. On average, the former fires six and the latter eight times a year. Those potters with sons working with them (Yamasan, Kanemaru, and Iriichi [father]) tend to concentrate on a greater number of smaller pots, since to some extent they have to bide their time waiting for single potters (Yamasai and Irisan) to complete their schedules. The former's in-

TABLE 9   *Capacity (in cubic meters) of the Cooperative and Private Kilns in Sarayama*

CHAMBER NO.	1	2	3	4	5	6	7	8	TOTAL
Cooperative Kiln	1.79	2.37	2.54	3.10	3.32	3.63	3.53	3.31	23.59
Private kilns									
Kaneichi	2.26	2.20	2.25	2.59					9.30
Yamani	2.75	2.89	3.33	3.43	1.50				13.90
Irisai	2.67	3.04	3.59	3.38					12.68
Yamaichi	2.07	2.80	3.05	2.43					10.35
Yamako	1.97	2.23	2.89	3.41	3.22	1.29			15.01

comes are probably, therefore, slightly higher than the latter's, but this difference has been ignored in calculations.

These figures would appear to be fairly accurate. The total amount of traced sales of Onta pottery came to ¥74,300,000 per annum. If we subtract the wholesaler's markup to three retail outlets, the figure for ex-kiln sales comes to ¥63,750,000. If allowances are made for Yamani's sales out of Hita, one kiln per potter household being sold at the Mintōsai pottery festival every October, and general retail sales amounting to about 7 percent of total kiln contents, the final figure is not too far from the estimated annual income given here.[2]

All potters have spent a lot of money rebuilding their homes, kilns, outhouses, and so on, in much the same way as Shigeki has done. However, the latter's expenditure of just under four and a half million yen is modest in comparison with the sums spent by other potters in Sarayama, which frequently amount to two or three times that figure. Many of them have also invested their accumulated profits in land holdings, and all but two potters have increased their holdings of mountain land over the past twenty years or so (the two exceptions, Shigeki of Yamaichi and Yoshitaka of Kaneichi, having recently had to lay out capital on the building of independent kilns). At least three potters now own more than fifty thousand square meters of forested mountain land.

Not all potters, however, invest in land. Some prefer to buy gold or purchase shares in a local silk factory, for example, or in a national automobile manufacturing corporation. That the potters have money to spare can be seen in the way each household spent ¥850,000 in 1975 on the leveling of mountain land and its preparation into a softball ground for the hamlet of Sarayama (including Ikenzuru).[3]

---

2. I made my estimates of kiln capacity when I helped unload, and thereby could count, the total contents of firings by Kaneichi, Yamasai, and Yamani. Before seconds had been discarded, these firings came to ¥833,840, ¥1,667,830, and ¥2,161,010 respectively (calculated at wholesale prices). Yūki of Yamako admitted to me while under the influence of sake that he earned at least ¥2 million per firing, a figure admitted by his brother Haruzō of Yamani in an unguarded moment when sober. Kazuo of Iriichi also became more forthright as my fieldwork progressed, and one day he confided that each chamber of the cooperative kiln yielded an average of ¥350,000. I have taken this figure for my calculations in table 10. Both Kazuo and Shigeki agreed, independently, with my suggestion that Chikara of Irisai earned about ¥1,600,000 per firing.

3. Other hamlet households contributed ¥100,000 each. To allay the suspicions of the Hita tax authorities, potters agreed to pay only ¥350,000 in cash and to borrow the remainder from local banks, thereby making it appear as if they had no ready cash.

The prosperity of the community in general may be gauged perhaps from the hamlet accounts. These show that, on average, each
Sarayama household spent, each year, six or seven times more than
families living in the village of Shinohata, studied by Dore
(1978:208). More remarkable, perhaps, are the annual accounts for
the potters' cooperative. Here, annual expenditure for the ten potting
households amounted to ¥1,406,220 in 1977. Entertainment alone
amounted to approximately one-third of this figure.

CONCLUSION

In this chapter I have given details of the way in which potters' incomes have increased as a result of the folk craft boom. I concentrated in particular on the economic development of one potting
household, Yamaichi, and showed how the demand for pottery had
enabled its head, Shigeki, to pay for extensive renovations of his
house and workshop, build a brand new kiln, and buy cars and other
expensive items.

But Yamaichi's income is by no means the highest among Sarayama's potting households. Because of the potters' decision to specialize
in the production of pottery, considerable variation in incomes has occurred. On the one hand, potters now earn far more than nonpotting
households; on the other hand, increases among potters themselves
differ greatly because of (1) ownership of private kilns, and (2) the
composition of household labor. Economic differentiation within the
community has only really started with the decision to stop farming.

But potters' increased incomes from the folk craft boom have also
led to further criticism of Onta pottery. The folk craft leaders' attitude
to consumerism in general may be summarized in the following passage from Mizuo Hiroshi's series of articles on handicrafts, where
people and things are seen to exist for one another:

> Someone who uses crafts also "brings them up." Although everyday
> articles are destined to be used in our lives and eventually to become
> too old or worn-out for use, handicrafts should not be seen simply as
> consumer items. People have to put their hearts into using things, to
> look after them and to make sure that they do not get damaged in any
> way; they have to give things as long a life as possible. Obviously, one
> cannot deny that there is some economic reasoning behind this idea,
> but in the old days there was a seriousness about the way people used

handicrafts that could not be neatly categorized as "economic." People did not treat things as material objects so much as things with life that needed their love. So were people at one with the objects they used. (Mizuo 1974:6)

This extract shows quite clearly that critics do not blame the crafts-man entirely for any deterioration in his work. Yanagi himself has dis-tinguished between what he calls the "first" and "after" lives of a craft, between its production and its final use (Yanagi 1932), and pres-ent leaders of the folk craft movement emphasize that it is the meth-ods of marketing—in particular of wholesaling—that adversely affect the quality of handicrafts. After all, how can potters have a chance to look at their work and see how bad many of their pots are when deal-ers come up to Sarayama and take away all the pots while they are still hot from firing (Tanaka Takashi 1969:45)?

But ultimately, the fault lies with the potters, for it is they who al-low the dealers to take away their pots, they who are ready to sell anything and everything. People in all walks of life frequently inti-mated to me during fieldwork that the richer potters became, the more their work deteriorated. Potters are seen to put profit before quality in their hierarchy of values, and this can only lead to "pollu-tion" in their work (Mizuo 1971:61; cf. Yanagi 1955a:130).[4]

That demand for pottery should increase and the kiln flourish is ex-cellent. That people should appreciate Onta pots and flock to buy them is not in itself particularly bad. However, once there is too much de-mand and commercialism gets the upper hand, the quality of the pot-tery produced has to be affected for the worse. This is precisely the evil afflicting Onta. (Mizuo 1972:106)

With the increase in demand for folk crafts, Onta pottery has been seen to be losing its qualities of "craftsmanship" and "healthy pricing." It is moving away from the essential charac-

---

4. *Mingei* critics are not the only ones to suggest that artistic standards de-cline as a result of the rise of industrial capitalism. Coomaraswamy (1943:26), for instance, no doubt influenced by William Morris's hatred for "commercial-ism and profit-mongering," argued that good crafts could not be created by in-dustry where the love of work no longer existed. Indeed, there would appear to be a pervasive idea among art critics and anthropologists all over the world that art is above such base considerations as money (Read 1936:2; Duvignaud 1972:37; Haselberger 1961:351).

teristics of *mingei*, which no longer exists in its original "beauty" and "honesty." Those craftsmen who survive have to make the choice between two evils: whether to become individual artists or to merely turn out souvenir items (Mizuo 1966:84–85).

Which choice have the potters in Sarayama made? Have they decided to ignore Yanagi's ideals entirely and turn out kitsch? Or have they opted to be artist-craftsmen, and if so, what has happened to the ideal of community solidarity? What sort of pressures from outside are forcing potters to adopt one option rather than the other, and how do these pressures ultimately affect the potters' vision of Sarayama as a community? I shall try to answer these questions in the following chapters.

8

The Decline of Community Solidarity

Thus far I have argued that economic development, along with improvements in technology and communication, has been largely responsible for the breakdown of social cooperation in Sarayama. I have inferred that the ideal of the "community" is no longer as important as it once was, and that there has been a gradual decrease of what may be termed "community solidarity." People in Sarayama may say that they do everything together, but in practice they do not. In this chapter, I will describe the kind of arguments that have broken out among people living in the community. I will show in particular that dissension has occurred in Sarayama along two main axes: (1) between potting and nonpotting households (i.e., between occupational groups); and (2) between older and younger men, thereby upsetting the age-grade seniority system. Such dissension has been caused by (1) an unequal accumulation of wealth as a result of the folk craft boom; and (2) the external appraisal of Onta pottery. Within the context of the community, the first serves to differentiate one *household* from its neighbor; the second, one *individual* from his fellow.

ECONOMIC DIFFERENTIATION AMONG POTTING HOUSEHOLDS

Earlier, I argued that, *ideally*, economic equality among potter households in Sarayama derived from their use of the cooperative kiln. I have now shown that in practice potters have recently become very wealthy and that there is a considerable difference in income levels between potting and nonpotting households. I suggested that there was also some diversity of income levels among the potters themselves. There are several reasons for this variation in wealth: the main one is the sudden, sustained increase in demand for folk craft pottery; others include the potters' decision to specialize full time in pottery production, and the composition of each potter's household labor force at the beginning of the folk craft boom.

Nevertheless, there would not have been such a difference in income levels among the potters if they had continued to fire the cooperative kiln all together. It is because five potters have separated from the cooperative kiln and now fire independently that the increase in market demand and the decision to specialize in pottery full time take on such importance with regard to community organization.

In 1962, during the early stages of the folk craft boom, there was still not much difference in income levels among those firing the cooperative kiln and those firing independently. Shigeki of Yamaichi reckons that Haruzō of Yamani, who had just built his own private kiln and to whom Shigeki was himself apprenticed from 1952 to 1954 averaged only ¥20,000 more per firing than his own household's ¥60,000–¥80,000.

So long as potters did not specialize in pottery, income levels among households in the community remained fairly standard. What really upset the financial equilibrium was their decision to give up agriculture. Potters were able to earn far more than those not potting— especially those potters who had sons working with them, for they were able to make and sell more than those working on their own or with aging fathers. Yamani and Yamako were the first to step up production in the mid-1960s; Kanemaru and Yamasan followed them a few years later.[1] Other potters sharing the cooperative kiln and working on their own found themselves being asked to fire the moment one household had completed its quota of pots. Whereas, in the past, the schedule of the cooperative kiln had been geared to the pace of the slowest working household, it now proceeded at that of the fastest.

Once the operation of the cooperative kiln changed in this way, Shigeki of Yamaichi decided to separate and build his own private kiln in 1971; he could not maintain the speed with which the other

---

1. Haruzō's father (Yamani) made no pots at all, and Yūki's adopting father (Yamako) made very few. Both potters had been working more or less on their own until about 1965. Although Irisai had had its own kiln for several decades by the time of the folk craft boom, Chikara had also been working entirely on his own, since his father had left the community before he was born.

TABLE 10   *Estimated Annual Income (in yen) of all Potting Households for the Calendar Year 1977*

HOUSEHOLD	TOTAL KILN YIELD	HOUSEHOLD SHARE	FIRINGS P.A.	TOTAL ANNUAL INCOME
Yamani	2,000,000		8	16,000,000
Yamako	2,250,000		7	15,750,000
Yamasai	2,800,000	1,400,000	6	8,400,000
Iriichi	2,800,000	1,400,000	6	8,400,000
Irisai	1,600,000		5	8,000,000
Yamasan	2,800,000	1,050,000	8	7,700,000*
Kanemaru	2,800,000	1,050,000	8	7,350,000*
Irisan	2,800,000	700,000	8	7,350,000*
Yamaichi	900,000		6	5,400,000
Kaneichi	800,000		5	4,000,000
Total annual income for all potting households				88,350,000

*In 1977, in the first three-household firing of the cooperative kiln, Yamasan fired chambers 1, 4, 8, Kanemaru 2, 3, 6, and Irisan 5 and 7. I have estimated the total annual income for these households on the basis of this order of rotation, whereby Irisan and Kanemaru thrice and Yamasan twice fired the two-chamber combination.

potters worked. This left five households firing the cooperative kiln together. As I showed in the preceding chapter, the incomes of these five households (Yamasai, Yamasan, Kanemaru, Irisan, and Iriichi) are fairly evenly balanced. There is, however, a wide variety of income levels among those firing independently (see table 10). The cooperative kiln once effectively limited and standardized all potters' incomes and gave rise to financial equality in the community. Now that half the potters have built their own kilns and fire independently, they have widely varying incomes. Market demand also gives all potters incomes far exceeding those on nonpotting households.

The breakdown of the cooperative kiln has affected community solidarity in a less obvious manner. In the past, many households shared certain tasks precisely because they were working to the same schedule; now that they are firing independently, there is no need for them to continue such cooperation. A potter nowadays can start firing his kiln without the knowledge of other people in Sarayama; this would have been unthinkable a quarter of a century ago. The cooperative kiln was not just the potters' but the community's kiln. Every working man or woman in the hamlet would make some contribution toward a firing, by preparing wood or by carrying pots back and forth as the kiln was loaded or unloaded. This is no longer the case.

The economic differentiation among potting households has been aided in minor ways by potters' methods of wholesaling and filling in tax returns. Until the early 1960s, ex-kiln prices were fixed for the most part by the buyers who purchased from Sarayama potters. The folk craft boom, however, created a demand that could not be satisfied by existing methods of production. Instead of buyers paying potters one-third the retail price of each pot, potters found themselves in the position of being able to ask for higher prices as they saw fit. Yamani, Yamako, and Yamasan took advantage of this newfound freedom and began charging much more than others in the community. Eventually, in 1970, when they realized the amount of money that these three households were making, Chikara of Irisai and Shigeki of Yamaichi suggested that all potters fix a standard ex-kiln price for each type and size of pot. This proposal was met with approval by the majority of potters, and prices were accordingly fixed. Over the past decade, therefore, Chikara and Shigeki have been to same extent successful in checking the extremes of economic differentiation that occurred among potter households in the mid and late 1960s.[2]

As tor the matter of taxation, until 1975 the potters' cooperative as a whole, rather than the individual households therein, was taxed each year. It was argued—mainly by Haruzō, who was leader of the potters' cooperative—that potters were not making much money, that they helped one another out with unfinished work, and that this *kasei* could not be reckoned in financial terms. This argument was accepted by the Hita tax authorities, who would proceed to bargain with the potters over the sum to be paid by the cooperative that particular year. The tax office in Fukuoka, however, insisted that there *had* to be economic differences between households, so that the Hita tax authorities told the potters to work out slightly differing income levels within the total revenue assigned the cooperative, before sending in their household tax returns.

In theory this was fine. Once potters got together, however, they found that it was impossible to fix income levels to everyone's satisfaction. This led to considerable resentment and friction among the heads of potting households. The major problem was that Haruzō of

---

2. My inquiries among retailers, however, revealed that Yamani and Yamasan still tend to price their pots higher than other households.

Yamani and Yūki of Yamako were earning by far the most and yet wanted to report incomes that were the same as those firing the cooperative kiln. It was pointed out that their incomes were in fact very much higher, but Haruzō took advantage of authority conferred by his position as leader of the potters' cooperative to ensure each year that one of the households firing the cooperative kiln reported the same annual income as his own fabricated figure. Haruzō fixed a kind of rotation system among households so that each potter would come out at the top of the income bracket every five or six years. However, even then, it is said, people like Haruzō or Toshiyasu of Kanemaru, underreported the income they had been assigned.[3] Shigeki and Chikara once more insisted that they were going to keep proper household acounts so that they could present individual tax returns from 1975. Once two people refused to participate in the system, everybody else was obliged to send in his own tax returns. Until the tax office decides to investigate these returns, however, there is little likelihood that Haruzō, Yūki, and others will be more honest about their incomes. Economic differentiation among potter households continues at that much greater a pace.

POTTING AND NONPOTTING HOUSEHOLDS

Economic differentiation has led to a greater concern with household than with community affairs. An indication of this is the frequency with which arguments break out between households. Saihito, for example, laid plastic pipes to his clay crushers after his water channel caved in under the road through Sarayama and the prefectural authorities refused to let him unblock it. In order to get the water to flow through the newly laid plastic pipes, Saihito had to raise the level of the dam above his crushers by about fifteen centimeters. Haruzō, whose clay crushers lay immediately upstream of the dam, immediately objected that the higher water level had stopped his crushers from working properly. Potters quickly pointed out that this was not so at all, and public opinion ruled in favor of Saihito.

Saihito was also involved in another petty quarrel of this sort. There is a tiny patch of land in front of Irisai, which belongs to the

---

3. Either this part of the story is sour grapes on the part of the loser, or the tax office did not notice, or decided to ignore, the fact that underreporting failed to meet the overall income agreed between the tax office and the potters' cooperative.

main household, Yamasai. Chikara of Irisai had long wanted to buy the land from his nephew, Saihito, in order to extend his drying yard. Even though the latter knew this, he decided to build a woodshed on part of the land, thereby denying his uncle the extra space he required and, incidentally, spoiling the view from the front window of Chikara's house.

Other arguments affect not just two, but all potting households. Yūki of Yamako, for example, incurred the wrath of all when he arranged for several extra truckloads of clay to be taken down from the clay deposit to his workshop one day, without bothering to ask the permission of any of his fellow potters. He thereby broke the rule that clay should always be shared equally.

One of the more violent rows among potting households occurred over access to clay deposits situated in private land. It will be remembered that when the road between Sarayama and Koda was opened up, new deposits of raw clay were discovered and potters decided to dig from these rather than from the less accessible clay pits in the community-owned land behind Yamako. At first, they dug from land above the road, owned by Yamako and Irisan, but gradually moved away from Yamako's land into Irisan's. After the bulldozer had finished digging out another three years' supply of clay in 1975, the Koda road was asphalted by the city authorities. According to local government regulations, however, bulldozers are not allowed to operate directly from a metaled road, so that in 1978 it was necessary for some of Irisan's or Yamasan's land along the roadside to be cleared away, if potters were to go on supplying themselves with clay from this area.

A few months before the bulldozer was to be hired, however, the two heads of Irisan and Yamasan, Kingo and Mitsusaburō, quarreled over the use of a strip of land on the other side of the road. Kingo claimed that Mitsusaburō was drying wood on his household land; he asked him to remove the wood, but Mitsusaburō refused. Kingo then retaliated by saying that he would not let his main house, Yamasan, have any clay from the deposit that he owned. This meant that *all* potters would have to get their clay from elsewhere.

After several arguments and considerable behind-the-scenes negotiating, Saihito of Yamasai was persuaded to let potters take clay from his land adjoining Irisan's. However, to gain access to these clay pits, the bulldozer had to cross the small strip of land along the roadside, owned by Yamasan.

Of course, the potters say, Mitsusaburō knew that his land would have been needed for the bulldozer to work from—even if Kingo had not refused to let potters have any more clay from his household's land. And yet Mitsusaburō went to the expense of clearing away a flat space and building a woodshed just where the bulldozer would have to maneuver. The simplest thing, perhaps, would have been for the potters' cooperative to have bought Yamasan's strip of land, but people were annoyed at the thought of having to pay out half a million yen extra to cover the cost of a woodshed that need never have been built in the first place. As it was, potters rented the land and pulled down the woodshed to make room for the bulldozer to pass into Yamasai's clay deposits. In a week or two the trees on Saihito's land were cleared, and the topsoil was removed and deposited, for a sum, on a piece of Yamani's land.

When the bulldozer had finished, Mitsusaburō began talking about rebuilding his woodshed. The potters objected. Were they going to have to pull down a woodshed every time they wanted to dig out clay? Mitsusaburō was adamant; he needed a shed for his cardboard boxes. In the end, potters were forced to rent land nearby from a resident of Koda, so that Mitsusaburō could build his shed elsewhere. Costs for digging clay that year come to almost three-quarters of a million yen.

Much of the bickering that goes on is limited to potter households, but sometimes it affect the whole community. When this happens, potters often band together against the remaining nonpotting households in Sarayama. The argument over clay digging described above illustrates the way in which the community can be divided into two factions.

When the bulldozer was hired to dig from Yamasai's land, it was discovered that it would have to maneuver, not just across Yamasan's strip with the woodshed on it, but on another, even smaller area of land owned by the whole community and on which one of the guardian deities, Kompira-sama, was housed. The potters decided that it would be best to buy the community-owned piece of land outright. They therefore called a meeting of the heads of all households in Sarayama to discuss the matter. The argument that followed was extremely confused. Shigeyoshi, of Kaneyo, which is not now a potting household, wanted the potters to pay the hamlet annually for digging rights. The potters retorted that in the past community-owned land had always been freely used, for thatch, fodder, wood, and clay; why should they now pay to rent the land? They were, however, prepared to buy it.

Most of the potters reckoned that Shigeyoshi was trying to thwart them by keeping the Kompira-sama land in the name of the community, in case he ever tried to take up pottery again. If clay were then being dug from community-owned land, he would have an automatic right of admission to the potters' cooperative; if, on the other hand, clay were being taken from privately owned land, his position would be considerably weaker. Eventually, Shigeyoshi gave in and said that the land could be sold provided that the money was used for some community project. However, potters offered what nonpotting households thought was a minimum price for the land. Haruzō and Mitsusaburō, who were negotiating for the potters, wanted to protect their own interests; they felt that if they offered too much for land from which clay could be dug, then Saihito of Yamasai might ask for more than the fixed annual sum of ¥100,000 for the clay taken from his land. Osamu and Moriyuki, negotiating for the nonpotting households, felt that if the potters were going to disturb community-owned land for the sake of their pottery, they ought to pay the going rate for the amount of clay in the piece of land. In the end, after a violent row, the nonpotting households gave ground, and the land was bought by the potters' cooperative for ¥150,000. The story does have a happier ending, however. A few months later, potting and nonpotting households saw the wisdom of exchanging this piece of land for another, on which the Kompira deity was then rehoused.

Those households that do not pot—Yamamaru, Kaneyo, Maruta, and Yamamasu—all complain that potters behave high-handedly: they do what they like, how they like, and when they like to. Those who do not fire kilns are "idiots." And yet, if ever one of the nonpotting households makes any attempt at starting pottery, potters protest bitterly. They have for the most part been successful in preventing an increase in their number. Although Osamu of Maruta began learning pottery from Yamasan, he stopped within a year. Nobuyuki's father in Yamamasu is said to have wanted to build a kiln some time ago, but was quickly dissuaded by his main house, Yamako. Shigeyoshi of Kaneyo has been prevented from potting because of illness, but now that a healthy son-in-law has married into the house, he is seriously thinking of taking up pottery once more. The only successful household has been Kaneichi, whose head, Satoshi, drove a hard bargain when the potters tried to buy his land for a car park for the tourists.

Yes, he would willingly sell them his land, but only if his son were allowed to take up pottery once more. Since Kaneichi had made pots in the past, the potters decided to let the household do so again, and a deal was made. Shigeki of Yamaichi (Kaneichi's main house) sold Satoshi one of his rice fields so that the latter could install his clay crushers and build mixing and settling tanks for clay preparation.

But it is not just the nonpotting households in Sarayama that regard the potters as "big headed." People in the surrounding hamlets have the same opinion of them. These farmers may resent the fact that urban society pays such attention to a group of rural potters *simply because* they produce a kind of "art" (cf. Graburn 1976:23). More probably, they may resent the way potters have come into the money; certainly, they dislike the way in which, in regional matters, potters always put what appear to be the interests of their community first.

But, in fact, potters' own interests are often put forward as "community" interests. This is what makes the nonpotting households in Sarayama so unhappy. While they are out at work—sometimes as far away as Fukuoka—the potters can assemble at a moment's notice to make decisions that frequently affect the whole community. Potters were able to commandeer ¥150,000 from community funds to help pay for netting to be hung round the softball ground, and not one nonpotting household was represented at the meeting. When potters decided to hold a ceremony for Kompira-sama when it was moved to its new sanctuary after the clay-digging episode, nonpotting households were given only a few hours notice of this theoretically important community event. Potters arranged to have the road widened along the ascent from the Ono valley to Sarayama. Sometimes, as in the last instance, the fact that the potters are a tourist attraction gives them a tool with which to turn the wheels of bureaucracy somewhat faster. Since communities down the valley have been waiting a decade to get a road put in and asphalted, the widening of an already existing metaled road up to Sarayama is a luxury which, in their opinion, the potters do not deserve. Nonpotting households in Sarayama did not object to the widening of the road; they objected to the fact that potters did not consult them before the decision was made. Although, theoretically, everyone is supposed to do things together, in fact the principle of cooperation by all households had once again been ignored.

It should be stressed that the division between potting and nonpotting households in not an unbreachable rift of the kind described for

Kurusu by R. J. Smith (1978:229–248). All fourteen households in Sarayama do participate in all sorts of activities together. However, potters all do the same work, they have the same technical problems with production, and they deal with the same buyers. They have to employ extra police to control traffic during their annual pottery festival, are asked by local authorities to contribute to exhibitions, and discuss their financial affairs together with the tax office. To repay favors done for them in business, they must entertain these groups, playing softball and drinking sake. So the potters have their own softball team, and they all spend a night out on the town together from time to time. People from nonpotting households cannot participate in all these activities, hence they are very much aware of the differences between themselves and the potters.

Because potters produce a folk craft and folk crafts are a national tradition, folk craft groups, television crews, and newspaper reporters spend a lot of time talking about Onta pottery and Onta potters; often they do not realize that the community of Sarayama actually contains four households that do not fire kilns. The newly appointed head of the Folk Craft Museum, Yanagi Munemichi, publicly expressed his earnest wish that "everyone in Onta" would rally together, when he was in fact referring only to the potters' cooperative. The Japan Broadcasting Corporation (NHK) put out a radio program in the series "Country Villages of Japan" [Nihon no furusato]; but the announcer limited his discussion to pottery and talked only to potters; when he staged a party to get the community together, only potters were invited. The potters did not take it upon themselves to ask nonpotting households to go to the party with them, which suggests that they put their own group interests before those of the community as a whole.

THE APPRECIATION OF INDIVIDUAL TALENT

In addition to the way in which an individual household or a group of households will put its own interests before those of the community as a whole, community solidarity is being weakened in another way: by the appreciation of pottery by outsiders. Methods of retail pricing, of promoting potters' names, and of exhibiting pottery all serve to emphasize the individual as a human being, rather than simply as a member of a small group such as a household or a community.

Shop owners and dealers fix their prices according to the quality of the pots that they hope to sell; they must also take current market considerations into account. However, when a buyer decides that one pot is better than another, he is in fact suggesting that one potter may be better than another. Any differentiation in price becomes a differentiation in individual talent.

Buyers are interested in good pots because they are made by good potters. Buyers' profits can be increased if they are able to "sell" the potter. They therefore encourage customers to buy the work of certain potters whose individual names they do their best to promote. What buyers do not realize, and what potters theoretically cannot accept, is that within the sphere of the hamlet group all households must be more or less equal. If one potter is consistently picked out for what outsiders see as "good" work, he and his household will gain status and thus destroy the nonranking equilibrium of all households in Sarayama. By promoting the individual names of certain potters, and by pricing their work higher wherever possible, buyers are threatening the solidarity of the community. Thus, within Sarayama, individual talent has to be denied unless it reflects upon the community as a whole. One of the reasons for potters' banding together to fix a standard wholesale price, therefore, was to provide some measure from within the community to counter the chaos of retail pricing in many Hita craft shops. Potters were in effect telling the outside world: "You can retail pots at whatever prices you feel like setting. But here in Sarayama we don't admit to exceptional individual talent. Every potter is as good as another here."

Onta pottery is generally marketed as such (*ontayaki*), and in theory at least, none of the potters in Sarayama signs any of his work with his individual name. Over the past decade or two, however, buyers have encouraged potters to use special names for their tea ceremony bowls, since it is a "name" that enables a tea bowl to be sold at a high price. The potters have been given "tea names," and most of them sign their tea bowls with these names. They also comply—albeit unwillingly—with requests to write calligraphy on wooden boxes for these bowls.

But is not just a potter's "tea name" that buyers now try to sell. Many people ask for all pots to be signed in some way or other. Most of them want to give "personalized" presents: one man, for example, orders fifty signed flower vases to be given to guests at his daughter's wedding; another wants signed plates for distribution by his company to customers; even the Onta prefectural authorities, who are in theory supposed to preserve the "tradition" of Onta pottery, have been known to make orders through Osamu of Maruta, asking to have the name of the maker of each pot written in pencil on its box. The authorities then arrange to have the craftsman's name written on the box in beautiful calligraphy in order to enchance the value of the gift.

The Japanese are concerned with what they call "name value." Onta pottery has value in itself as a name, but in the past few years there have been indications that the pottery-buying public has become more interested in individuals working in Sarayama than in Onta pottery as such. To some extent, buyers encourage the signing of pottery by individual potters in order to increase their profits. They are also trying to safeguard their own interests, however, and make potters responsible for their work. At present, if a complaint is made about a pot by a dissatisfied customer, the buyer cannot return the pot to the man who made it, since the latter will almost invariably deny that the work is his own. If potters did sign their work, they would have to take responsibility for its quality. This is the primary reason for the suggestion made by Miyake of the Folk Craft Society that potters use household marks (*yagō*) on all their pots. Potters have refused to do this, even though they realize that some of their number are getting away with poor quality work. They see the signing of names in any form whatever as endangering the community as a whole. Buyers would connect household marks with individual potters; but each potter acts as a member of his household, and each household is closely tied to the community of Sarayama. Yet, by not putting his name on his work in some form or other, a potter avoids responsibility, and this can and does lead to the deterioration of the reputation of the community as a whole. This is a paradox that permanently bothers the more serious-minded potters in Sarayama.

Ironically, in view of the fact that folk crafts are supposed to be made by "nameless craftsmen," the folk craft associations themselves have been largely responsible for the publicizing of Onta potters' names, although the media have tended also to make "artists" out of craftsmen. The Japan Folk Craft Association holds an annual autumn exhibition at its museum in Tokyo, and Onta potters are asked to send in their pots. Although the Onta Potters' Cooperative as a whole was awarded the Museum Prize in 1968, potters have generally been invited to contribute as individuals and not as members of the cooperative. Prizes have been awarded to individuals rather than to the cooperative as a whole. The Japan Folk Craft Society has given prizes only to individual Onta potters, never to the potters' cooperative.

In 1973 Onta potters were encouraged by the Folk Craft Association to contribute to a biannual national exhibition known as the Japan Ceramics Exhibition (Nihon Tōgeiten) and sponsored by the Mainichi Newspaper Company. Exhibition regulations stated that only two pots could be contributed by any one individual or group. This meant that potters either contributed as individuals or chose two pots from among all their works and contributed as the Onta Potters' Cooperative. It is doubtful whether all potters were seriously interested in the exhibition; but the thought of having to decide whose work from ten households was good enough to be sent in to the exhibition was enough to stop the potters from contributing as a group. Instead, two of them, Shigeki of Yamaichi and Asao of Irisan, contributed as individuals. Both had pots accepted, and Shigeki was awarded one of the four major prizes at the exhibition (the Foreign Minister's Award, plus half a million yen).

The news of Shigeki's success astonished everyone. The immediate reaction of the older potters was that his prize-winning lidded jar could have been made by any one of the other potters in Sarayama. The award was theirs as much as it was Shigeki's (cf. Nakane 1970:83). In other words, they denied an individual's talent as recognized by the outside world. What was worse, however, so far as the older potters were concerned, was that the media paid so much attention to Shigeki that his name became extremely well known among those interested in pottery and folk crafts. He was soon bombarded with requests to make this or that kind of pot, and anyone who had a query about Onta's history, its annual pottery festival, community life, the acquisition of materials, and so on tended to ask Shigeki instead of the cooperative leader.

OLDER AND YOUNGER POTTERS

The attention Shigeki received because of his award highlights a further aspect of the way in which community solidarity has been affected in Sarayama. There was some resentment among his fellow potters because Shigeki was called upon by *outside* forces to act as spokesman for *internal* affairs when he was still a comparatively young man in his mid-thirties. But it will be remembered that the appointment of the potters' official spokesman, the cooperative leader, was based on seniority of age. Thus, public evaluation of a single pot not only led to the acclamation of the individual who had made that pot; it also conflicted with the seniority system prevalent in the community in which that individual was living. So far as older men like Haruzō and Mitsusaburō were concerned, Shigeki's position within the community had been strengthened and their own position weakened.

This was not the only occasion on which the Folk Craft Association's dealings with potters upset the community's gerontocracy. In 1962 one of the Folk Craft Museum employees, Miss Y., was sent to stay in Sarayama and give advice to potters concerning what was and was not "acceptable" *mingei* pottery. Over a period of ten years, Miss Y. came down from Tokyo, staying a few days at a time in Sarayama, talking to potters, and making suggestions concerning the shapes, decoration, and glazing of certain pots. Her advice culminated in the distribution of an album to each potter household with photographs of what were considered by the Folk Craft Association to be "old" and "authentic" shapes and designs of Onta pottery.[4]

Undoubtedly, Miss Y.'s visits helped many of the younger potters who had very little idea of what Onta pots made half a century earlier looked like. Unfortunately, some of the older potters began to resent her appearance in Sarayama, for she posed a threat to the hitherto unquestioned assumption that the way in which they taught their sons to pot was the best possible way. As a result, Miss Y. naturally found herself associating with those potters whose fathers were not working with them at the wheel—that is, with younger potters from Irisai, Yamaichi, Irisan, Yamasai, and Kaneichi. These men were able to look at their work more objectively, since they were not bound by loyalty to fathers who still oversaw their work.

Although Miss Y.'s consorting with younger potters was a natural result of the existence of Sarayama's household system, it led to the Folk Craft Association's public approval of the work of the younger Onta potters. This only annoyed the older potters more, since they sensed that their authority was gradually being whittled away. Younger potters appear to have been less conscious of the friction that Miss

---

4. Nelson Graburn has pointed out that the Folk Craft Museum's decision to distribute an album of what it considered to be "authentic" Onta pots is extraordinary and almost unparalleled in the ethnographic literature on folk art. He has documented one other case, for the Canadian Eskimos in the early 1950s (see Graburn 1976:55).

Y.'s visits generated, but the matter was recently taken up by the dealer Mr. T., who saw the elder potters' resentment as an opportunity for him to undermine Miss Y.'s position, both in the community and in the Folk Craft Museum itself. After all, she posed a threat to his own established position as general "expert" on Onta's potters and pottery. For the past three years or so Mr. T. has been proclaiming that Miss Y. has "broken up the community," that the potters are "divided into factions." "As in the *Tale of the Heike*, the proud must fall"; Onta's new found fame is but "a puff of smoke in the blistering winds of history," and "the greatness of its pottery is forever gone." Here we have another example of the way in which social changes are seen to affect pottery aesthetically.

But there is a further way in which Sarayama's gerontocracy has been weakened, and this goes back to the discussion of the economic differentiation of households. I argued earlier that an unequal distribution of wealth brought about by the folk craft boom led to a lessening of community solidarity and, in particular, to a division between potting and nonpotting households. It happens that the wealthiest households in Sarayama are mostly those whose heads are the oldest men: Haruzō of Yamani, Yūki of Yamako, Mitsusaburō of Yamasan, and Toshiyasu of Kanemaru. They were able to work with their sons soon after stopping agriculture and thus take advantage of the folk craft boom.

I have suggested that all households in Sarayama were of more or less equal economic standing, and this is indeed the ideal to which potters refer when they talk of the past. However, potters also admit that some richer households provided for the welfare of all and expected a certain measure of obedience in return. Those who did not have enough money to contribute to community affairs were not expected to express their opinions in public. Now, this rule no longer works effectively, because, although there are differences in income levels among potting households, the enormous increase in their wealth has been enough to put them on an equal footing with one another. (At the same time, potters' newly acquired wealth separates them from nonpotting households, which are expected to submit to potters' decisions.) In other words, there seems to be a minimal level of affluence above which everyone thinks he has a right to have a say in community affairs, and it is only since the folk craft boom that potter households have risen above this threshhold.

Because all potters have a lot of money, younger men such as Shigeki of Yamaichi and Chikara of Irisai can now express their opinions in front of others in the comunity. But the wealthiest and oldest men resent what they see as unnecessary outspokenness. They object to Shigeki and Chikara, not because the latter speak up when they are not as wealthy as themselves, but because the two men are much *younger*. It is on the basis of this logic that people like Haruzō and Yūki now refuse to give liberally on behalf of the whole community. Instead, they insist that all households should contribute money equally, proclaiming that things should be done together "democratically." The ideal of "everyone together" is thereby given a neat little twist. When it comes to such contributions as netting for the softball ground, Haruzō and Yūki refuse to give any more than other households. This leads younger potters with lower incomes to claim that if Haruzō and the others were really thinking of the good of the community they would arrange for those with higher incomes to pay more and those with lower incomes less. This would help redress the imbalance in income levels, and is the way in which things are done in many other communities.[5]

COMMUNITY SOLIDARITY, "TRADITION," AND "THE PAST"

It can be seen that community solidarity has been threatened in various ways. First, within Sarayama a differentiation in wealth has led to the breakup of the cooperative kiln and to household individuation. Second, people are becoming increasingly conscious of the existence of two groups within the community: one, the majority, consists of potting households; the other, of nonpotting households. Third, the appreciation of pottery by outsiders has tended to emphasize individual potters. Fourth, the increased wealth of potter households and the external recognition of individual talent have been interpreted by some within the community as a threat to the seniority system of authority.

I would argue that it is precisely because community solidarity is thus being weakened that two concepts are much referred to by residents. One of these—*mukashi*, the past—concerns the community as a whole; the other—*dentō*, or tradition—affects potters in particular.

---

5. In Sue Mura, contributions made by parents for musical instruments to be used in a primary school and for a piano in a middle school were worked out according to income levels. Those who earned more made larger contributions (Tsuchiya 1965:45, 50).

The first is unconsciously aimed at uniting all households within the community and hence stemming the possible flood of resentment between potting and nonpotting households. The second results from recognition of individual talent and is an attempt to bring all potters together and standardize their work so that they market a readily recognizable product known as *ontayaki*. Both are, in my opinion, direct or indirect assumptions that the way in which things used to be done was best.

The idea of *mukashi*, on which my "model" of social organization was based, is probably prevalent throughout much of rural Japanese society. Dore (1978:65), for example, has commented on the way in which villagers of Shinohata frequently reminisce about the past. The themes are the same: the poverty of the past and the comparative luxury of the present. In Sarayama, anyone speaking to an outsider tends to talk of the way in which people used to lead their lives, of the hard times they had when there was not enough money to buy food or clothes, of the exhaustion of working in the fields and mountains. At the same time, the old way of life is viewed with a certain nostalgia, for villagers know that the "good old days" of cooperation have gone forever. *Mukashi* is, in my opinion, an important concept that is called upon, first, to remind fellow residents of how things used to be and should be, and second, to present a united front to the outside world.

I would argue similarly that the concept of "tradition" is also designed to maintain not just unity within the community, but the unity of the community as a whole vis-à-vis the outside world. Potters discourage one another, and are discouraged by leaders of the folk craft movement, from experimenting with clay texture, glazes, and designs. Onta potters all use the same glazes with more or less frequency; they all decorate their pots in almost identical manner, limiting the number of designs. There is a remarkable unity about Onta pottery that is not found in other folk potteries, such as Koishiwara, Tamba, or Mashiko.

Some potters want to experiment with new designs or glazes, but they realize that, if they do so, they would be accused, during the next drinking session of "betraying the community." On the purely technical level, Chikara has pointed out that one way of preventing bloating (a common trouble that comes from firing clay too quickly) would be to mix some grog into the raw clay and so raise its heat resistance. Every potter knows this; and yet nobody does it, because mixing clay with grog is considered to go against the grain of what constitutes "Onta pottery." From the point of view of design, Shigeki has remarked that in the past potters used to make a simple, white slipped rice bowl; nowadays they spend all their time decorating rice bowls with chattering, combing, or slip brushing. If Shigeki does make a simple white bowl, he is accused of imitation of other pottery kilns— not only by potters, but by the dealer, Mr. T., who, if he is the "expert" he pretends to be, ought, in Shigeki's opinion, to know better.[6]

"Tradition" would appear to have been adopted as a concept aimed at maintaining order within the community. It is unlikely that Onta potters had any understanding of what tradition meant until the term was used by others, who could see in Sarayama's social organization and methods of pottery production a stability that was lacking in other sections of Japanese society. I suspect that the potters were made very much aware of the word when the techniques by which Onta pottery was made were designated an "intangible cultural property" in 1970.[7] Nevertheless, I would also argue that the idea of "tradition" came into its own only when community solidarity began to break down, following contact with the outside world. Tradition is called upon precisely because the community is in many ways no longer traditional. It has become vital for potters to maintain a tradition in pottery, despite the number of minor innovations in methods of production, since this serves to reinforce an otherwise rapidly fading sense of community solidarity.

At the same time, it should be pointed out that Sarayama potters— and only potters—can all recognize one another's work and can tell with fair ease who made what pot. In other words, potters are keenly aware of the stylistic differences among themselves, differences that they feel could be exploited by outsiders and be seen in terms of indi-

---

6. Onta's self-imposed restriction is remarkable, and nothing similar exists in potteries such as Koishiwara, for example, where "anything goes."

7. The system of "intangible cultural properties" was instituted in 1952 by the Agency for Cultural Affairs, Ministry of Education, primarily to protect Japan's traditional arts. Two years later, a Committee for the Protection of Cultural Properties made the following revisions. First, a very few craftsmen (including the *mingei* potters Tomimoto Kenkichi and Hamada Shōji) were selected as being the holders of "important intangible cultural properties" and received an annual stipend from the ministry. It is these men who are popularly referred to as "national treasures." Second, the committee simultaneously designated certain individuals and groups of craftsmen as the holders of "intangible cultural properties." Although the general public tends to confuse the two groups, it should be made clear that the latter designation is far inferior to that of the "national treasures." Holders of the title of "intangible cultural properties," among whom Onta potters are included, receive no stipend from the Agency for Cultural Affairs.

Onta potters rely almost entirely on the use of a white slip clay to decorate their wares. Two forms of decoration—the *hakeme* and the *tobiganna*—are particularly famous. With the *hakeme* the body of the pot is brushed with slip immediately after it has been thrown. Turning the wheel very slowly clockwise with his left hand, the potter then taps his brush (*hake*) rapidly up and down the slipped surface of the pot, to leave a series of eyes (*me*) radiating out from the center of a plate or bowl.

With the *tobiganna*, or chattering, method of decoration, the pot is first slipped and then left to dry until it is leather hard. It is then placed on the wheel head and turned fairly fast. The potter holds a thin piece of metal (called a *kanna*), hooked at one end, against the pot. This vibrates over the leather-hard surface of the clay and leaves a trail of raindrop-like chips in the body of the pot.

Another form of slip decoration commonly used in conjunction with the *hakeme* on larger wares is combing (*kushime*). This is generally, but not always, done in wet slip.

Finger wiping (*yubigaki*) is a further form of wet slip decoration used on water jars, *unsuke* pouring vessels, and large plates.

The *uchikake* form of glaze splashing is used either with slip on the leather-hard body of a pot, or as an overglaze—in copper green and translucent brown. Another method of overglazing is that of the *nagashi* trailing, where either slip or glaze is poured in vertical lines with a slip trailer from the rims of large plates and bowls, or from the shoulder of lidded jars, umbrella stands, and water containers.

After pots have been thrown, they must be dried. During the night or in bad weather, they are placed under the eaves of the house and the first thing that potters do on a sunny morning is carry out trays of pots. They place these on transverse logs of wood in the drying yards in front of their workshops. This photograph shows a fairly typical layout of a potter's household—with living quarters to the left and above the workshop, clay-drying frame in the right foreground, with a corrugated-iron-roofed clay-drying kiln just behind it.

Potters keep turning their pots round while they are drying. This ensures that pots are evenly dried and prevents them from warping. Plates are placed rim to rim when they are fairly hard to keep them in shape.

When pots are leather hard, they may have parts—handles, lugs, or spouts—applied to them. This is done almost invariably by women, who have to fix handles and spouts to dozens of side-handled teapots (*kyūusu*) and to the famous green glazed Onta teapots (*dobin*).

vidual talent. I would suggest, therefore, that potters try to cover up their differences by stressing to the outside world that they all make the same traditional pots.

In many ways, pottery is the idiom in which social change is expressed. For example, when a potter is accused of not making a traditionally shaped teacup, he is really being accused of stepping out of line from the rest of the pottery households and attempting to go things alone. Again, a potter will explain that the potter's "character" will remain in a pot if he uses a kick-wheel, but that it will be lost should he decide to throw on an electric wheel. What is actually meant is that by continuing to use a kick-wheel a potter is affirming the existence of his community, which would fall into total disarray should machinery be imported and each household start competitive production, as in Koishiwara. Another potter says that if you start studying really hard, you end up changing the shapes of pottery entirely. He was referring to the problem of coffee-cup handles that either are too small or make the cup warp at the lip, and the potter concerned said that in the end one would have to buy a new mold from Arita. But once you bought one mold you would buy others for other pots—pitcher handles, teapot spouts, or flower-vase grips, and so on—and in this way *ontayaki* would "disintegrate."

Changes in methods of production almost inevitably—in the eyes of the potters—lead to social changes that affect the organization of their community. The adoption of molds would lead to the purchase of machinery for clay preparation, to the building of new types of kilns, and to the employment of apprentices or professional workmen. Ultimately, not only the community but the household system itself would be threatened. If a glut of Onta pots were brought about by overproduction, potters would have to sell their individual names or undercut one another in as many ways as possible in order to make a living. Sarayama as a community would no longer exist—at least not in the sense in which "community" has hitherto been used. The potters' decision not to mechanize shows the importance that they still attach to the community as a whole.

CONCLUSION

In this chapter I have given an account of ways in which community solidarity may be said to have lessened in Sarayama. I do not, however, wish to give the impression that solidarity has disappeared entirely and that people now invariably put their own self-interests before those of the community. The ideals of "harmony" and "all together" may not be lived up to all the time, but on the other hand, as Dore (1959:379) says, "Japanese villagers are not given to feuding as a pastime." Indeed Sarayama, unlike many of its neighboring hamlets, remains very much a "community," in contrast to a place where several dozen people happen to live in close proximity to one another but nothing more. People still share their lives; they still participate in communal events. Everyone turns out to help when it comes to building a new house, unlike—for example—the inhabitants of Kurusu (R. J. Smith 1978:142). They all gather for frequently held community festivals,[8] and the purchase of a new car, the completion of building projects, or a man's forty-first birthday, are occasions for all households in Sarayama to celebrate. Programs appear on each household's television screen by way of a common aerial. Although this might not seem to indicate "community solidarity," in fact three or four households have forfeited the pleasure of being able to watch six different television channels obtainable on their own individual rooftop aerials; instead, they share four channels with the remaining households, whose location in the narrow valley had not permitted more than the two NHK programs to come their way until a high antenna was erected on the top of the nearest mountain.

On their monthly day-off from work, all men participate in softball games or archery contests before getting down to some fairly serious drinking in the late afternoon and evening. The exchanges of sake cups that flow so fast and furious are an important form of communication and serve to unite one man with his neighbor; indeed, the intensity of the arguments that accompany drunkenness reveals, paradoxically, how much each man values the ideal of a "community" transcending the individual. The trouble is that one man's ideal is not necessarily another's.[9]

---

8. In Sarayama (Onta) deities that are specifically connected with the production or marketing of pottery—Akiyasama, the fire goddess (cf. Dore 1978:211), and Ebisu, the god of trade—are celebrated by the *whole* community. In Koishiwara such deities are celebrated by potting households only.

9. In his discussion of sake drinking in Sue Mura, Embree remarks that a quarrel rarely breaks out (1939:104). In Sarayama, sake drinking is used as an opportunity to air one's views quite openly; what is said is forgiven, but *not* forgotten, and community problems tend to be "discussed" with as much heat as is in a kiln chamber in mid-firing.

So what Fukutake (1967:95) wrote of Japanese rural society in 1964 is still true, for the present, of Sarayama: "The hamlet imposed on its members an ideal of hamlet unity and hamlet harmony as the highest possible good, and although that ideal is losing its power to suppress individuality, it has still by no means disappeared." There are cracks in the ideal, and without doubt the potters' vastly increased wealth is partly responsible for them. Higher income levels resulting from the decision to specialize in full-time pottery production have served to divide potting from nonpotting households within the community and, as Nakano and Brown (1970:201) have observed, "economic diversification with the emergence of specialized interest groups, also contributes to a decline in community solidarity."

In my early discussion of Japanese rural institutions, I said that the hamlet (*buraku*) was an occupational and residential group. The relation between occupation and residence is important to our understanding of modern Japanese society. Fukutake (1974:57) has suggested that the "community" does not necessarily depend on occupation; it depends, rather, on "neighborhood." I have shown that almost all forms of social cooperation (particularly in the exchange of labor) in Sarayama depended on ownership of land and similar work patterns. When potters decided to give up agriculture, occupation became more important than residence. It would seem to me, therefore, that ownership of land and neighborhood are only important to the hamlet as a community if all, or almost all, of its households are engaged in wet-rice agriculture. Once people start doing other kinds of work, or once they start specializing in different kinds of agriculture, the hamlet as such ceases to be either an occupational or a residential *group* (Johnson 1967:181). This is why Ariga (1956:25) stressed that one should examine the links between households forming an occupational group, rather than the hamlet itself, if one wants to understand the Japanese sense of community. The importance of occupation to the formation of a community may be seen in the way urban Japanese give precedence to their place of work (which lawyers in fact refer to as their "village," or *mura*) rather than to their local residential group (Nakane 1970:59-60).

Another point concerns individual and household status within the hamlet. In their discussions of hamlet organization, many scholars (cf. Fukutake 1967:138ff; Norbeck 1954:208) suggest that economic differences are primarily responsible for maintaining status differences. I suggested in my discussion of Sarayama's social organization that the age-grade system is important, for it provides an alternative to wealth in the determination of status. Seniority in age gives each individual (and household) authority in turn over other individuals (and households) junior to him. The system is ideally one of equilibrium in that a household retains its authority over other households only as long as its head is senior, but not senile. Once he is replaced by his son, his house will lose authority. In theory, therefore, every household in the community has the opportunity to rise to the top of the status system.

But the system of gerontocracy has recently been upset. I have shown that considerable conflict between older and younger potters has arisen from the accumulation of wealth and the public appreciation of their pottery. Although most older potters quickly observe that the "artist" potter is a one-generation phenomenon, the appreciation of individual talent does offer an opportunity for one household that manages to produce successive generations of publicly acclaimed potters to rise above, and hence perhaps rule over, other households whose potters remain very much run-of-the-mill. Whether this will happen in Sarayama remains to be seen, but it can be seen that talent is an alternative criterion to wealth and seniority in the determination of household status within the community.

The kind of data provided in this chapter as support for my thesis that community solidarity has been seriously undermined by the folk craft boom is not wholly new. Other scholars have commented on the household's disengagement from the social sphere of the hamlet. What is special about Sarayama is that not only the household but the individual as well is affected by the appraisal of Onta pottery. By concentrating on the way in which the appreciation of individual talent affects household relations, I have, I believe, presented a new angle from which the subject of community solidarity may be viewed.

Individual talent is an ideal to which the primary group in Japanese society appears to have some trouble adjusting. Shimpo (1976:104) has shown in his description of a village volleyball tournament that the group takes the credit for any of its members' successes. In the neighboring pottery village of Koishiwara, a case occurred in 1958 which was remarkably similar to that described above about Shigeki's national award. A young potter, Ōta Kumao, had his work selected by Yanagi Muneyoshi and sent to the Brussels Exposition, where it won the *grand prix*. Other potters in the community claimed that the prize belonged to all Koishiwara potters as a group and not to

Kumao, since the pot had been exhibited, not under his own name, but under that of Koishiwara. The fact that *only* Kumao's work had been exhibited did not appear to worry anybody in Koishiwara except Kumao himself.

I have argued that the appreciation of talent endangers the community, which cannot *ideally* function as an egalitarian group if one of its members is consistently picked out for special praise. This point may be illustrated further, I think, by a weaving community in Amami Ōshima, an island situated south of Kyushu. Hatae (1970:6) has noted that in theory these *tsumugi* weavers should be designated, like Onta potters, an "intangible cultural property" for the tradition with which their work is done. However, opposition comes from the weavers themselves, who fear that one or two of their number might consequently become "national treasures" and collar the "art" market. Other, less-talented weavers would have to mechanize and shift to mass production in order not to go out of business; but by doing this, they would put an end to social organization in the community as it now exists.

The problem of talent in the craft world is by no means limited to Japanese society. D'Azevedo (1973:141) has noted that woodcarvers among the Gola of western Liberia "claim that any special talent is looked upon with jealousy by others as a potential threat to the family in its efforts to develop loyal and dependable members." It is not surprising, therefore, to find that Zuñi Pueblo Indian potters, like the potters in Onta, also claimed to be able to distinguish the works of their fellow potters (Bunzel 1972:64-65). Of course, the recognition of individual style does not have to be connected with the relationship between individual talent and the group, which I have discussed above. In communities like Sarayama there can be little anonymity, and "most people would know the details of style, the aesthetic choices, and even the tool marks of their contemporaries" (Graburn 1976:21) as a matter of course.

"Anonymity" suggests the related problem of an individual craftsman's signing his name on his work. Graburn has argued (1976) that it was precisely to offset the growing lack of individuality in large-scale societies that the signing of art work was developed. In his book on tourist arts, we find middlemen and buyers doing their utmost to promote the name of individual artists, whether they are Seri woodcarvers, Navajo weavers, Pueblo potters, or Eskimo soapstone sculptors. Similarly, Dockstader (1973:119) mentions that the identification or hallmarking of their work by American Indian artists has been brought about primarily by the Indian Arts and Crafts Board. Onta potters may well be confused about whether to sign their pots or not. At least, they have not so far reached the stage where, like some pottery vendors in central Mexico, they put fake names on their work in the belief that any name is better than none at all (Charlton 1976:142).

It is clear that Sarayama's problems are by no means unique, and that the potters living there face the same difficulties as other craftsmen throughout the world. Local government authorities and the Folk Craft Association have tried to "help" potters over the years by sketching designs, commenting on shapes and glazes, and even providing them with a book of photographs of old Onta pots. Bunzel (1972:88) has remarked on the mutation of style of Pueblo Indian pottery caused by the outside influence of white people, and Graburn's book (1976) has numerous examples of the way in which folk crafts all over the world have been "interfered with" at the design level— for example, Hopi weaving and the Museum of North Arizona (p. 93), Navajo weaving and trading posts (p. 96), Aborigine bark paintings and a Methodist mission station (p. 274), and Yoruba dyeing and a representative from the Peace Corps (p. 309-310).

Sometimes, "help" is not limited to stylistic change, but includes complete innovations. Such "ethnic" arts as Eskimo soapstone carving and printmaking were introduced by a Canadian artist in the late 1940s and 1950s (Graburn 1976:42-43), and various forms of "traditional" Indian art have been introduced in recent times by traders and curio makers (Dockstader 1973:116). It is thus not surprising to find people claiming that there is very little "traditional" art being produced in the world today (Graburn 1969:458).

Comparatively speaking, Onta pottery's reputation for being traditional is perhaps fair. To a certain extent, potters embrace folk crafts aesthetic ideals by not experimenting with shapes and glazes. They turn down the numerous requests for this or that kind of shape, design, or color combination, as buyers attempt to satisfy the demand for something different, something new. Potters do not experiment, because they know that Onta pottery would thereby lose its distinctiveness and, more serious, Sarayama would lose its consciousness of being a "special" community that retains its distinctiveness precisely through its pottery. As with Pueblo Indian potters, Maori or Aboriginal "artists," "the survival of the craft indicates the survival of the people" (Brody 1976:76; cf. Mead 1976:291; N. Williams 1976:284). Like many makers of what Graburn calls "Fourth World arts," Onta potters "carry the message: 'we exist; we are different; we can do something that we are proud of; we have something that is uniquely ours!'" (Graburn 1976:26).

Finally, let us turn to the relation between aesthetic criticism and social change. I have commented earlier on the way in which Onta pottery has been seen by folk craft leaders to "deteriorate" when production moves away from "natural" methods that make use of local materials and when social cooperation breaks down as potters seek to benefit financially from the increase in market demand. I have remarked on how the Folk Craft Association in particular has been responsible for some of the problems that have occurred in the social organization of Sarayama as a community. It is perhaps of interest to note here that, despite earlier criticism of Onta pottery, the Folk Craft Association has also acclaimed Sarayama's pottery as "the best in Japan" (Tanaka Toyotarō 1966:11). Mizuo Hiroshi, who earlier wrote about Onta pottery's "pollution" (1968:110), later reevaluated his estimation and decided that pots had been bad only during the period immediately following Leach's visit to Sarayama, from about 1955 to 1962. By 1970 they were really quite good (Mizuo 1972:106-107). He indirectly attributes this improvement to Miss Y.'s visits to Sarayama, which were instigated by the Folk Craft Association in 1962 (p. 111). The cooperative nature of the potters' work is emphasized by Mizuo, along with their reliance on natural materials (p. 113). Nevertheless, he makes the general point that the accumulation of wealth leads to ugliness in crafts, and most *mingei* critics cannot accept the fact that Sarayama's potters are making a lot of money (cf. Tanaka Takashi 1971:24). At the same time, consumer emphasis on individual names and the signing of work in pottery has meant that potters are no longer the "unknown craftsmen" that Yanagi advocated they should be.

Hitherto I have discussed the folk craft movement as it has affected the social organization of Sarayama, and tried to show how the critical appraisal of this pottery is closely linked to the *way* in which potters work, rather than to the pottery itself. While I have given examples of what folk craft leaders and critics have had to say about Sarayama's potters, I have not given any details of what the potters themselves think about *mingei* and Yanagi's ideals. Do they agree with what Yanagi said about beauty and direct perception? Do they understand his moral philosophizing? To what extent do they accept his arguments concerning the beauty of local materials, of nature, of cooperation and self-surrender? Have the potters read any of Yanagi's works? Do they even know who he is? I shall now deal with these questions before going on to show how potters, buyers, and critics differ in their attitudes to the appreciation of pottery itself.

9

Theory and Practice in Japanese Folk Crafts

In chapter 1 I sketched the historical background to the Japanese folk craft movement and then described the main details of *mingei* ideology as put forward by the movement's founder, Yanagi Muneyoshi. I made a rough classification of Yanagi's thought into what I termed its "moral" and "utilitarian" aspects, and argued that Yanagi was more concerned with how folk crafts were made (the moral aspect) than with folk crafts as objects in themselves (the utilitarian aspect). I made it clear that I did not regard the Japanese folk craft movement as an "aesthetic" so much as a "spiritual" movement. I showed how the critical appraisal of this pottery is based on the fact that ideally potters in Sarayama use methods of production that closely accord with Yanagi's theory: they use local materials for their clays and glazes; they do not rely on modern machinery, but are close to "nature;" they are "unknown craftsmen" who work in a spirit of cooperation with one another, without incentive for profit and personal gain.

With the recent sustained demand for folk crafts, however, potters have begun buying some of their materials from nonlocal sources; they have taken advantage of technological advances in the ceramics industry to purchase kiln shelving, ball mills, and belt-drive engines for their kick-wheels; they have made a considerable amount of money; they have stopped cooperating with one another; and they are beginning to be well known throughout Japan. As a result of these changes, their work has for a period been criticized by leaders of the folk craft movement. However, because social organization and the method of making pottery in Sarayama have remained relatively unchanged, compared with such other potteries as Tamba or Koishiwara, Onta potters' work is still seen to be the best in Japan.

Now I should like to examine what the potters in the community think about the whole idea of *mingei*, and how they react to comments about their work by people who usually know little if anything about the problems involved in pottery production. I will also discuss what pottery dealers have to say about folk crafts in general and Onta pottery in particular. I will be especially concerned with the relation between production and marketing requirements vis-á-vis the theoretical concept of *mingei*.

Of interest to me as an anthropoligist is the question whether "universal aesthetic standards" may be said to exist. Many would appear to aver with Read (1961:127) that "essential aesthetic qualities" are "universal and everywhere identical." If by "essential aesthetic qualities" Read means that all human beings have some kind of aesthetic sense of beauty, from the evidence of my fieldwork data I would not disagree. The problem is, do potters, buyers, and folk craft leaders all have the *same* aesthetic values? If not, why not? These are questions that I shall now try to resolve. Only by examining the "total art processes" (Silbermann 1968:583) surrounding the production, marketing, and aesthetic appraisal of Onta pottery will I be able to consider how the notion of "folk art" or its equivalent relates to society as a whole.

MINGEI THEORY: POTTERS' AND BUYERS' VIEWS

The Japan Folk Craft Association has published ten volumes of Yanagi's *Selected Works*, in which many, though not all, of his essays have been published. There are also numerous articles in folk craft and other literary magazines about various aspects of *mingei*. There is a wealth of lesser material in newspapers and popular magazines, which deals mostly with particular places renowned for a folk craft style of production.

During my stay in Sarayama, I talked with all the potters about problems arising from the existence of the folk craft movement. I also interviewed twelve dealers who bought and sold Onta pottery. Two of these men were from Tokyo, one from Kumamoto, one from Oita, and the rest from the local town of Hita. Three of these dealers sold Onta pottery as a full-time profession; the others ran their businesses as a sideline (cf. Yoshino 1971:14). Some of these retailers began to buy Onta pottery because they liked pottery as such; others because they

All Onta pottery is glazed, and all potters use the same ingredients in preparing their glazes: feldspar, iron oxide, copper, wood ash, and rice-straw ash. Feldspar and iron oxide are powdered by the clay crushers; straw ash is pounded by mallet and later placed in a ball mill until it is finely mined. Glaze colors are produced not so much by the actual mixing of the ingredients as by their careful preparation.

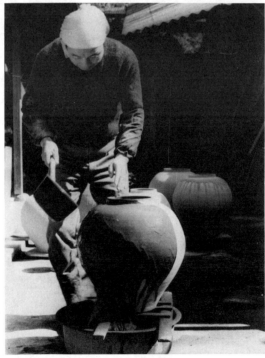

Small pots are frequently bisqued so that thicker applications of glaze may be made. Larger pots are raw glazed. Each household takes two to three days to glaze all its pots prior to firing. Small pots are glazed by women, large pots by men.

Kilns are loaded first by the men and later, when they have finished glazing, by the women of each household. The largest pots are stacked on the top shelves and the smaller ones between the lower shelves of each chamber. Translucent honey-glazed wares are placed at the back of the shelves farthest from the firing flames, then transparent glazed pots, then green and black glazed wares with high melting temperatures right at the front of the kiln chamber.

All kilns in Sarayama are climbing kilns (*noborigama*). These are fired for twelve hours at the main mouth with large pieces of dry timber, generally sawn-up beams of old houses. After the first few hours, potters will often put small strips of wood into the side mouths of the upper chambers of each kiln. This is called *tsuyu-daki*, or "dew firing," and is designed to get rid of the humidity generated by the early stages of the main-mouth firing.

After firing the main mouth of the climbing kiln for twelve hours, potters move up to the first of the chambers in which the pots are stacked. They fire this from one side with long strips of cedar wood, and it generally takes between three and four hours to reach maturing temperature. Potters do not use Seger or Orton pyrometric cones, or color-test pieces, but judge the temperature entirely by eye.

When the last chamber has been fired, the kiln is shut down and left to cool for at least 48 hours. Then the whole family turns out to unpack the kiln, carrying fired pots from the kiln to the workshop, where they are checked and sorted.

Dealers come up to Sarayama and select the pots they want, almost before the kiln has been unpacked. They either take these pots away, or put them aside for the potter to deliver later. Pots that are to be sent far afield are packed in straw, put in boxes, and sent by freight.

were interested in the idea of folk crafts; yet others because they were already involved in Hita's tourist industry in other ways. Both potters and dealers were questioned about each of the main points of Yanagi's theory.

All of the potters in Sarayama knew of Yanagi by name, and all those born before 1945 had met the man on one of his visits to the community. Of the fifteen potters currently working at the wheel in Sarayama, five had not read one word written by Yanagi; eight had only glanced at the articles in which he wrote about Onta pottery in particular (Yanagi 1931; republished in booklet form, 1961). Two potters had read volume one of his *Selected Works, The Way of Crafts*. Although they found the style difficult, both potters thought the work educationally rewarding.

Although all potters receive copies of the monthly publications *Mingei* and *Nihon no Mingei*, only two claimed that they regularly looked at more than the photographs. Four potters said that they had read comments or articles by Hamada Shōji, the artist potter who was head of the Folk Craft Museum until just before his death in January 1978. Although Mizuo Hiroshi, editor of *Mingei*, has emerged as the movement's leading critic, not one of the potters expressed any great interest in his writings. Those who had tried to read Mizuo's work regarded his style as "academic" in the worst sense of the word; from hearing him speak, potters felt that Mizuo had nothing new to tell them about *mingei*; he was but parroting Yanagi's ideas.

Potters were not prepared to define the word *mingei* beyond calling it a "popular craft" (*minshūteki kōgei*). Even though they had not read much of Yanagi's works, they had learned enough about *mingei* from the movement's leaders over the years to realize that both the word and the thought behind its coinage were too difficult for them to express clearly and concisely. Chikara avoided the question by exclaiming: "Craft potters exist to make pots, not to understand theories." His grasp of this ideologically important point made one suspect that he, and several other of the younger potters, knew more about *mingei* than they were prepared to let on. Although all potters had come to accept that Sarayama had become a "folk craft kiln" (*mingeigama*), many of them would have preferred that the term not be used of the community; *mingei* had, in the potters' opinion, come to broaden and change in meaning since its original conception in the 1920s.

This view was shared by many of the dealers, who felt that the whole notion of folk crafts had been overused and that, consequently, Onta pottery should not be labeled *mingei*. Some even suggested that everyone would be better off if the whole idea of *mingei* was forgotten. Although potters did not themselves take this extreme view, they were aware that some of the pots that they regularly produced, such as flower vases and tea bowls, were not *mingei* items at all. This would suggest that they had a fairly clear understanding of what *mingei* was, so far as their pottery was concerned. Neither they, nor a majority of the dealers, professed to understand or to accept the spiritual aspect of Yanagi's thought.

Earlier, I explained that Yanagi was mainly interested in beauty and that, in his opinion, what he called "direct perception" was the only means of understanding "true" beauty. He argued that, in aesthetic appraisal, one had to put aside all concepts and allow a thing to be seen for itself. Direct perception gave rise to a *standard* of beauty which could be appreciated by *anyone*, regardless of education or upbringing.

The reaction of dealers and potters to Yanagi's concept of direct perception was extremely interesting. All of the dealers and many of the potters felt that direct perception was not simply an abstract, theoretical concept, but one which could be successfully practiced; they accepted the idea that one should try to see a pot for what it was, "directly." However, neither dealers nor potters were prepared to accept that direct perception could provide a *standard* of beauty. Their disagreement with Yanagi on this point stemmed from their own experience in selling pottery. Potters, for example, often found that work they regarded as excellent would be entirely ignored by dealers or the general public; and what they thought were rather poor pots were frequently the first to be sold after a kiln firing.

One potter even contended that ten people would give ten different opinions of any one pot; in ranking ten pots in order of merit, they would give ten very different rankings.[1] The general opinion of both potters and dealers was that there had to be, and was, individual interpretation in people's decisions as to what was and was not "beautiful." Many thought, therefore, that Yanagi's concept of direct perception was an ideal which only an enlightened few, such as Yanagi himself, Hamada, or Leach, could attain. For everyone else the appre-

---

1. Compare Osborne (1955:39) on literary criticism for a similar "relative" view: "You may in fact choose any writer you like, any dozen critics you like, and you will find ten different assessments, while the three who rank him more or less level will do so for different reasons."

ciation of beauty was, in their opinion, always subjective, and potters remarked with some embarrassment that even the critics were not agreed about what made good pottery and what did not. They re-called that, in the autumn of 1978, Yanagi's son, Munemichi, had come down to Onta and personally picked out twenty-six pots by Ya-mako which he felt were good enough to show at the Folk Craft Mu-seum's annual exhibition. When the pots were judged by a panel of critics in Tokyo, all but one were rejected.

Potters also argued that if there was a "standard" of beauty that could be shared by anyone using direct perception, everyone would, in theory, buy the same pots. This, in fact, did not happen. They, and their buyers, were therefore convinced that direct perception could only provide a *personal* standard of beauty. The appreciation of beau-ty depended entirely on the individual.[2]

Although Sarayama potters and dealers all talked about the con-cept of *mingei* and *chokkan*, they did not pretend to understand many other aspects of Yanagi's folk craft theory. Yanagi's argument that there was a close inverse connection between financial reward and quality—that the more interested a craftsman was in making money, the more his work deteriorated—was accepted by all potters in Sara-yama regardless of their own particular economic level within the community. Haruzō of Yamani and Yūki of Yamako, who have both made a lot of money out of the folk craft boom, agreed with Yanagi's idea. After all, they said, you have only to look at the quality of work in Koishiwara, where some potters are earning ten times as much as themselves, to realize that too much money leads to poor work. Other potters, such as Shigeki of Yamaichi, or Saihito of Yamasai, also agreed with Yanagi's inverse equation between profit and quality. But, instead of citing Koishiwara potters as examples, they told me to look at the pots produced by people like Haruzō and Yūki to see what Yanagi meant.

Many, but not all, dealers agreed with the idea that a craftsman's work deteriorated the more interested he became in financial profit. There was a general feeling that newfound wealth did adversely af-fect the quality of a potter's work, but that this deterioration was not a *necessary* consequence of financial success.

It is true that most outsiders regard the whole community as hav-

2. One can argue that the potters' and dealers' attitude that every individual has his or her personal taste is defensive, in that it licenses them to make and try to sell *all* kinds of pottery in spite of aesthetic criticism.

ing struck gold, but they fail to distinguish at what point avarice is seen to take over to the detriment of the quality of one's work. Mizuo (1971:62), for example, accepts a certain amount of economic improvement, but not too much. Potters themselves are aware of the problem in distinguishing between necessity and luxury. Kazuo of Iriichi and Yoshitaka of Kaneichi both remarked on the differences between rural and urban life-styles; in the country, they said, people had to spend a considerable amount of "waste money" because of the network of personal relations (*tsukiai*) in which they were involved. Thus, the subsistence level for a rural household had to be much higher than that for an urban one. This point was either not understood or not accepted by leaders of the folk craft movement. "Just because money has come into our pockets, they say that our work has grown worse," moaned Yūki in exasperation. A remarkable comment was made to Shigeki by the former director of the Folk Craft Association, Tanaka Toyotarō: "You Onta potters ought to start listening occasionally to what we tell you. After all, it is thanks to Yanagi's idea of *mingei* that you've got rich at all."

Another of Yanagi's theoretical premises was that beauty derived from cooperation. None of the dealers expressed any clear opinion about this idea, although one of them in Tokyo thought that it may have been true of *mingei* in the past. About half of the potters in Sarayama accepted a connection between beauty and cooperation, but added the reservation that, though it may have been true of Onta pottery, they did not regard the idea as universally valid. Thus, potteries could produce good work even though cooperation may have broken down; conversely, a potter who had always been working on his own could still make beautiful pots. Potters were very much aware that their work was praised because they had in the past cooperated with one another, and they were therefore fairly keen on maintaining a "united front" toward the outside world. But, as Kazuo said, cooperation never worked out as well as one would have liked; in some respects, as I have shown, Sarayama's "solidarity" was just for show.

Yanagi's argument that the environment in which the craftsman lived and worked was vital to the quality of folk crafts, and that their beauty depended largely on the craftsman's "closeness to nature," was also only partly accepted by potters. Many of them felt that the environment in which they lived did affect their work without their realizing it, but they did not always agree that their work was good *because* they relied on natural materials and on natural methods of production. After all, people who fired their wares in gas kilns or prepared their clay with pug mills could still make good pots.

Potters were aware that the word "nature" was not easy to interpret, and they were not agreed that they could distinguish between the "natural" and "unnatural" elements of a finished pot. For example, when asked if they knew when a pot had been thrown on a kick-wheel ("natural") and when one had been made on an electric wheel ("unnatural"), they said they could not tell the difference. Similarly, very few potters thought that they could invariably distinguish between wood-fired and gas- or oil-fired pots. There was little agreement that they could distinguish between pots that had been glazed with natural materials and those that had been chemically glazed. It may be, therefore, that potters support the equation between nature and beauty in folk crafts precisely because Sarayama is virtually the only pottery kiln in Japan still relying almost totally on "nature" in its production.

Dealers were more adamant in their opinion of the aesthetic connection between nature and beauty. All but one were convinced that the craftsman made better work if he used natural materials. Some even said that Onta pottery would really go to the dogs if potters started using mechanical methods of preparing clay and gas- or oil-fired kilns. There was a close association in almost every dealer's mind between a man's spiritual attitude, the nature of the environment in which he lived, and the quality of the work he produced. In particular, they envisaged the craftsman as living in secluded, beautiful surroundings undisturbed by the bustle and noise of urban life—a point to which I shall return.

Every potter believed that handicrafts expressed the craftsman's character and that they were therefore imbued with what was called "heart" (*kokoro*). In this respect, potters agreed with dealers in believing that the craftsman's environment and his tools and materials and methods all affected the quality of his wares. Potters did not, however, think that beauty was born *solely* from the craftsman's "heart." They added—and this point echoes their criticism of direct perception—that what they saw in one of their pots and what a critic or buyer saw in the same pot were very different.

Although some of them are becoming well known as individuals because of their success in exhibitions, all potters in Sarayama stressed that they were craftsmen and not artists. They professed not to know anything about the relation between beauty and individualism, but disliked any word that smacked of "art" being used of their work. They made "pottery" (*yakimono*), not "ceramics" (*tōki*), and they objected to people in the folk craft movement referring to their work as a kind of "ceramic art" (*tōgei*). Art was for city, not for country, people.

They were also unhappy about Yanagi's idea that craftsmen should remain uncultivated and unlearned. They argued that, in view of the amount of time critics had spent telling them how they should be making pottery, it was impossible for them to throw pots "unconsciously" any more. Potters said that they had learned to see their pots differently (i.e., they had been "educated") and were now more conscious of their work; it was not surprising that people said it had got worse.

AESTHETIC APPRAISAL AND PRACTICAL PROBLEMS OF POTTERY PRODUCTION

Although Yanagi built his theory around the concept of *mingei*, which included a number of things, from *doro-e* ("mud" or pastel paintings) through joinery to farmers' stray raincapes (*mino*), he was particularly interested in pottery. All the early leaders of the folk craft movement were potters and it would be fair to say that it is potters who have benefited most from the folk craft boom.

Yanagi has written one extended essay about what makes folk craft pottery beautiful. His approach, however, was spiritual rather than strictly aesthetic. Admitting that he knew little about either the historical or the technical aspects of Japanese pottery, Yanagi wrote of his love for the craft: "I live with my heart steeped in its beauty, day and night. By looking at pots I am able to forget my self, to go beyond my self. . . . For me, the realization of belief is also to be found in pottery" (Yanagi 1955b:372).

Yanagi argued that beauty could not exist without love. Beauty was born of the heart, therefore, and if a pot was "unlovable," either it must have been made by a "cold hand," or its appreciator had a "cold eye." Great works were produced when a craft potter's heart was filled with love. Yanagi visualized the potter alone at the wheel, intent upon his work, with no thought in his mind; he lived in the pot and the pot lived in him. They were at one; love flowed between them, and beauty was born.

From this it may be seen that Yanagi was concerned not with pottery in itself but with how pottery was made. Although in evaluating individual pots he isolated such qualities as form, clay, color, line, and taste, it was not the properties of these qualities so much as the way in which they affected the potter that Yanagi thought was important. For instance, clay was seen to be the "flesh and bones" of a pot. But the quality of the clay was linked to the potter's spiritual attitude: the Japanese potters' choice of a softer clay than that found in Chinese porcelain revealed the "soft" and "pliant" nature of the Japanese people (1955b:342).

Yanagi regarded form (*katachi*) as the fundamental element determining beauty. Yet he thought that form was created by the "heart" rather than by the hands. It was not technical accomplishment so much as a spiritual purity that gave rise to beauty. The form of man was to be found in the form of pottery (pp. 334–341).

Form would appear to be the primary criterion by which the quality of pottery is judged at the annual autumn exhibition held at the Japan Folk Craft Museum (Tanaka Toyotarō 1966:10). Since folk crafts are supposed to be functional objects for everyday use, it is not surprising to find that form is emphasized by leaders of the movement. Good form results in good, functional pottery, and functional pottery is beautiful. The question is: to what extent do potters consider form when they make their pots? Do they make pots that are functional but not beautiful in form, or beautiful but not functional? Do dealers, and their customers in turn, purchase pottery because of its form? Or are they more concerned with other qualities such as color and design? These questions need answers because ultimately they will reveal whether there is an aesthetic standard in the appreciation of *mingei*.

Function is often closely tied to form in crafts of any kind. This point has been made by art critics and anthropologists alike (e.g., Keesing 1958:350; Read 1936:126). However, while a basic form may be functional, nonfunctional embellishments may be added as the craftsman seeks to make his work attractive to a buyer. In the case of a pot, there may or may not be a foot-rim, and any foot-rim may be higher or lower, wider or narrower, according to the potter's taste. He may choose to pull out the lip of a bowl or a plate to give variety to the curved body, or he may trim the belly of a bowl square rather than leave it rounded.

The exigencies of function do not, however, necessarily produce what a potter sees as a "good" shape, so that folk craft leaders are indirectly criticized for relying on function as a basis for beauty. For example, when a potter makes a lidded jar, he says that if he is to take the pot's functional purpose into account, he should keep the mouth of the pot wide; the person using the pot can then easily put a hand in to get at its contents. But a broad mouth upsets the balance of the form below, so that in fact the mouth is kept fairly narrow. Similarly, an umbrella stand may look good if it is slender in form, but once it is filled with umbrellas, this shape becomes unstable, and so the pot needs to be swollen at the belly.

In other respects, potters are more faithful to the exigencies of function than their critics might suspect. For example, storage jars have shallow lids which merely cover the mouths of the pots; teapots have deeper lids to allow the pot to be tilted. A bottle-shaped sake pourer (*tokkuri*) should be made as light as possible, so that its user can judge how much wine is left. Such functional aspects of pottery do not appear in the outer form.

While form may be constrained by use, materials and methods of production also affect a pot's form (cf. Graburn 1976:54). Here I shall deal with the nature of the clay, glazing techniques, and methods of kiln loading as they affect Onta pottery.

One fundamental rule underlies the relation between form and function. This concerns the nature of the materials used in a craft, and is often ignored by Japanese folk craft critics. The nature of Onta clay dictates to some extent the final form of its pottery, a form which cannot always be consistent with function. For example, to be functional, pickle jars should be made as cylinders. The pickles will then sink to the bottom of the pot, and they can be easily weighted down. However, Onta clay does not permit this shape for larger pots, for the clay tends to crack at the base. Consequently, most pickle jars must have a narrow base which, while it often gives the pot a streamlined shape, does not guarantee stability in use. Similarly, plates more than fifteen centimeters in diameter cannot be made flat, but have to be curved, so that functionally they become dishes rather than plates.

Another way in which the nature of the clay affects potters' decisions concerning the shapes of their pots can be seen in the addition of foot-rims. According to buyers, *guinomi* sake cups and coffee cups should not have foot-rims at all. Potters prefer to give these pots foot-rims, however, because small pots like these can easily become misshapen during firing.[3]

---

3. According to Yanagi (1955b:371), "the potter's heart is revealed for what it is in the foot-rim, for it is this that determines a pot's final value."

A potter's decision whether to give a pot a foot-rim is often closely connected with his technique of glazing. Sarayama clay does not permit a pot's total immersion in a glaze, and potters do not usually take the trouble to wax-resist those parts of a pot which they do not want glazed. As a result, it is much easier to glaze smaller pots if they have foot-rims. Larger pots are usually not trimmed at all, but some potters leave a ridge at the base of their flower vases. These pots can then be easily held upside down in the fingers of one hand, and glazing is much simpler.

Methods of kiln loading result in various constraints on the form of pottery because potters try to make as economic use of kiln space as possible. The way in which pots are loaded into the kiln also affects the potter's overall decision about what shapes to make and fire. For example, although a potter might like making a rounded, jar-shaped flower vase, this shape can waste a lot of kiln space unless it is counterbalanced by a narrow-necked vase with a fully curved body.

The best way to make maximum use of kiln space is by stacking pots on or in one another. The nature of the clay used in Sarayama permits piling in large quantities, but pots must be given higher foot-rims to ensure that they will not stick to one another if they become slightly misshapen during firing. The custom of stacking in quantity (made possible by the adoption of kiln shelving) has led to potters making their rice bowls and kneading bowls with straight rather than curved sides. They realize that, by doing this, they are making their pots "colder" to look at and less suitable for the functions they serve. Ideally, both rice and kneading bowls should be slightly curved for facility in use.

Larger pots have always been stacked inside one another in a "Chinese box" type of kiln loading. In the old days, when the large pickling jars, water crocks, and pouring vessels were used by shops and farmhouses alike, potters had to adhere strictly to certain measurements. This meant that most of the larger wares had to be of a fairly elongated shape if they were to be stacked inside one another and be functional. More recently, however, with the growth in urban demand for table ware, large pots have come to be made for decorative purposes only. Potters have stopped making their larger wares to measurement, and they strive to create new forms that "look better" (cf. Lathrap 1976:202). These decorative forms are no longer functional and are extremely unstable because of their excessively broad shoulders.

Considerations of kiln space also affect a potter's decision about what glazes to apply to what pots, for certain colors only come out in certain parts of a kiln chamber. The glazes used in Onta pottery are composed of four or five materials: feldspar, wood ash, straw ash, iron oxide, and in some cases copper. Some of these materials are more heat resistant than others. A glaze which contains a higher percentage of materials that are more resistant to heat (e.g., green or white) has, therefore, to be fired at a higher temperature than glazes composed of materials with lower heat resistance (brown or yellow).

The nature of the climbing kiln is such that, at any given time, the temperature inside a chamber during firing will vary along three axes: from side to center, from front to back, and from top to bottom. Consequently, potters must load their kilns so that they can control the melting point of the various glazes during firing.

None of the kilns is quite the same as another, and potters say that each kiln has its "characteristic" so far as glaze coloring is concerned. Some kilns with humidity produce really good colors; others do not. The cooperative kiln is best for brown and transparent glazes; Yamako's produces a good green; Yamani's, green and black; Yamaichi's kiln is remarked for its brown, green, and white glazes, while Kaneichi's is good for all colors except green.

When loading one of the chambers of his kiln, Shigeki of Yamaichi places pots glazed with green and black at the very front of the shelves, copper and transparent over white slip at the back of the front shelves, light green and brown at the front of the back shelves, and brown at the very back of the chamber. On the vertical axis, Yamaichi cannot place green-glazed pots at the bottom of the chamber, because the flames there during firing are extremely "violent," and the temperature fluctuates to such an extent that if the front of a pot did come out green, the back would remain a greyish black where the copper had failed to melt.

The glaze order outlined here differs from chamber to chamber within a kiln. In one chamber of Shigeki's kiln, for example, brown comes out very nicely near the edges, as well as along the back of the back shelves. Shigeki has learned from experience that white and green do not come out at all well in the bottom chamber of his kiln, but will do so best in the second and fourth chambers respectively. Similarly, potters sharing the cooperative kiln know that green does not come out at all well in the bottom four chambers, but it does in the top four, while black works in precisely the opposite way.

All of this may sound too technical for a social anthropological study. But these details of the problems faced by potters in firing their kilns are pertinent because buyers consistently order all sorts of different color combinations. A potter may be asked to fire pots glazed with colors that, given the limitations of the climbing kiln, cannot be combined. Or he may be asked to fire an impossibly large quantity of one or two colors only. Potters point out that technically they cannot meet such requests, but buyers tend to think that this is another lame excuse and that the potters are being high-handed now that there is demand for their work. Relations between the two groups are not improved by such misunderstandings.

AESTHETIC APPRAISAL AND PRACTICAL PROBLEMS OF
POTTERY MARKETING

One major source of conflict between Onta potters and leaders of the folk craft movement stems from their different viewpoints in appraising pottery. While critics are concerned with the appreciation of beauty, potters are trying to make a living from their work. The critics look at the potter's wheel and the *art* of his kiln (*yōgei*) (Yanagi 1955b:365); the potter looks to his kiln for *economic* survival. Even if a potter agrees with the idea that a man's work deteriorates if he is too interested in profit, there comes a time when he himself has to put economic interests before personal aesthetic preferences. However folk craft leaders may evaluate his work, the potter must consider market demand and the interests of his buyers.

When Yanagi first discovered Sarayama, the potters made a selection of wares that were used for the most part in farmhouses round about. These wares consisted mainly of large pickle jars, water crocks, containers for homemade wines and soy sauce. They also made bottles in which sake was sold from shops in Hita, and large, elongated lavatory bowls. Some smaller wares were made—notably the teapot, which first attracted Yanagi's attention in Kurume—but the emphasis was on big pots.

Since the Pacific War, there has been a radical change in market demand. The development of plastics has put an end to the use of really big pots, while rapid urbanization has led to consumer demand for much smaller items that can be used in the modern, often West-ernized, home. Onta potters have found that they must adapt to the new, postwar demand if they are to survive; folk craft leaders, on the other hand, are still primarily interested in the wares that potters pro-duced to meet prewar demand.

Folk craft leaders do not regard many of the pots now being made in Sarayama as truly traditional Onta wares, and they urge potters not to make flower vases, tea bowls, coffee cups, and so on, because they are not traditional. Potters are inclined to agree with their critics on this point, but they add that it is precisely these items that sell well. They thus have little alternative but to continue making such pots. They admit, however, to not knowing what sort of shapes to make. In the past, they relied on dealers to help them, and they also copied photographs of pots from books and magazines (cf. N. Williams 1976:271). Some buyers have on occasion sent potters sketches of shapes that they want made, but potters point out that dealers have often tried to order shapes that cannot possibly be made with Onta clay.

To a certain extent, potters put personal preferences first when they decide on what shapes to throw. For example, although they have been told that a tea bowl should not have a high foot-rim but should "sit low," potters feel that such a shape is entirely unsuitable to the nature of the clay that they use. Hence they continue to give their bowls higher foot-rims than the "experts" demand.

Over the past twenty years or so, potters have been helped both by local government officials and by folk craft leaders in the design of their pots. The Hita Crafts Institute (Hita Shikenjo) drew some flower vase designs for potters soon after Leach had visited the community (Leach himself taught them the medieval English pitcher shape); some of these were later adapted by Miss Y. of the Folk Craft Muse-um. Potters all feel that the shapes they were asked to make were pretty odd and suggest that the schools of flower arrangement must be in a bad way to be advocating such poor vase forms. Instead, they make vases that are fairly straight, tall, and thin in order to facilitate maximum use of kiln space, or rounded with a narrow mouth, so that misshaping is not noticeable.

Almost all the demand for folk craft pottery comes from urban areas. This means that potters not only have to make completely new types of pots, but have to make pots that are specifically for town rather than for country use. For example, there is now an increasing demand for *guinomi* sake cups instead of the much smaller *sakazuki*, although both types have been made in Japan for a long time. People living in urban areas tend to drink sake either on their own or from just one cup when in the company of others; they find a small cup troublesome to fill time and again. In the country, however, nobody drinks sake on his own, but almost invariably participates in an exchange of cups with friends and neighbors. For this purpose, the smaller *sakazuki* is deemed far more suitable, since the larger *guinomi*, favored by townspeople, only hastens alcoholic incoherence and spoils the party.

Potters also find it hard to keep up with the urban demand for coffee cups. They find it too time-consuming to make and attach handles individually to each cup. About ten years ago Miyake Chūichi, leader of the Folk Craft Society, arranged for handle molds to be made for Onta potters, who have used them ever since, fixing them *near* the rims of the coffee cups. Recently, the demand has been for increasingly smaller cups, and potters now attach handles *to* the rims. When the cups are fired, however, they become misshapen.

Obviously, potters could pull their own handles or order new, smaller molds. The fact that they do neither shows that at the moment they are more concerned with economics than with aesthetics. Similarly, a potter whose household does not have a large labor force may refrain from making teapots at all because it takes too much time to make and apply the parts (spout and handle grip). Current demand for Onta pottery allows the potters considerable choice of what to make and what not to make. It is such economic freedom that critics resent.

But if potters must make a lot of new shapes that are patently not traditional, they have also been extremely clever at adapting old shapes to new purposes. The prewar water crocks, for example, have been slimmed down slightly into umbrella stands; the big ash-burning hibachi hand-warmers have been shrunk into ashtrays; and small pickled-plum jars have had spout and handle added to convert into *kyūusu* teapots.[4]

Both dealers and private individuals ask potters to make shapes that may fail to meet their personal or *mingei* aesthetic demands.

---

4. The same sort of thing has occurred in other potteries throughout Japan. In Aizu Hongo, for example, the old herring pickler has been whittled down and adapted into a rectangular ashtray. Gill (in Graburn 1976:109) also reports on Laguna ceramic adaptations of bowls to "ash bowls."

Sometimes potters can refuse to make certain shapes with the excuse that they do not suit the nature of Sarayama's clay (a ploy used by Aborigine carvers in Arnhem Land [cf. N. Williams 1976:283]). At other times, potters are not really interested in the form of a pot, because, as the dealers say, it is not form so much as color combinations, as brought out in pattern and glaze designs, which give a pot its market appeal.

Of twenty-four dealers retailing pottery in northern Kyushu and Tokyo, sixteen said that they placed primary emphasis on glaze coloring and on pattern or design when choosing pottery. Only six said that they chose pottery because of its form. The remaining two men (both with close ties to the Folk Craft Museum) said that they used "direct perception" to select good pots. Of those dealers who placed primary emphasis on form, three were affiliated to one or the other of the two folk craft associations. One of these dealers, who has been buying Onta pottery for more than thirty years, argued that there was no standard by which color could be judged; form, however, did provide such a standard. Another man who expressed a preference for form over color in choosing pots added that this was no more than a personal preference; the general public was, in his opinion, more likely to buy pottery because of its color.

I asked visitors to Sarayama what had made them buy the pots they had bought. If no immediate answer was forthcoming, I asked whether the pot was easy to use, of pleasing design, nicely glazed, or well shaped. Of the 235 people interviewed, 160 answered that they were primarily influenced by color or pattern; only 32 cited form as a criterion of choice. (See table 11).[5] Potters are, naturally, aware of this market demand for good glaze coloring and intriguing patterns, and they decorate almost all their pots with *hakeme* brush strokes, *tobiganna* chattering, or *uchikake* and *nagashi* methods of glaze application, which have all now come to form Onta pottery's hallmark of recognition.

Primarily because they realized that they could apply thicker glazes and hence improve colors, potters started bisque firing in the 1960s. In the past, all pots were "raw" glazed, but now many of the

---

5. Buyers were, incidentally, convinced that their female customers were almost totally influenced by color and pattern in their choice of pots, and that it was only men who "understood" form. My investigations revealed that women are more concerned with form than buyers believe, while men take function into serious account when choosing pottery.

smaller pots, and some of the larger ones as well, are fired to a low temperature before glazing. In theory, the bisque firing is done in order to minimize losses during the main firing, and it is true that customers tend to complain if a pot is misshapen or in some way blemished by firing. In practice, however, potters know that they can apply a greater number of glazes to a bisque-fired surface than to an unfired one. They are thus able to provide a range of color combinations that help satisfy market demand.

Good glaze coloring is a result of the careful preparation of raw materials and the way in which the kiln is fired. Potters admit that they tend to ignore personal aesthetic preferences in deciding what glazes to apply to what forms. Mitsusaburō, for example, dislikes yellow, but argues that it is the only glaze that comes out well at the back of his kiln chambers; Kazuo of Iriichi at one stage glazed a lot of his pots black because of the poor quality of wood ash in his transparent glaze. He said then that he would prefer to glaze his slipped pots with the transparent rather than the black glaze, which he did not see as being in Onta's "tradition."

RETAIL PRICING AND THE CONCEPT OF MINGEI

Earlier I noted that Onta pottery is sold all over Japan, but that the majority of pots are bought by dealers retailing in and around the neighboring town of Hita. Their customers are primarily tourists who buy Onta pots as gifts for friends and relations back home. It will be remembered that Yanagi was convinced that "true" folk crafts should be made in large quantities and sold cheaply. One of the reasons Onta pottery used to be appreciated and bought by local farmers was its extreme cheapness. However, over the years, prices have increased considerably. In 1971 Miyake Chūichi, director of the Folk Craft Society, warned that if prices were to be raised any further, Onta pottery would be in danger of becoming an art craft (*bijutsu kōgeihin*), rather than simply a folk craft (*mingei*). Since then, wholesale prices have gone up three more times. Is Miyake's criticism justified and, if so, on what grounds?

Potters in Sarayama do not make any attempt to cost their work by the weight of clay used, kiln performance, fuel prices, or labor input (cf. Cardew 1971:232–233). Their system of wholesale pricing is therefore "natural" rather than "just," and there is little rationalization in the fixing of prices. Dealers complain that some pots—coffee cups, for instance—are much too expensive, and that it is therefore almost impossible to retail them at anything more than a marginal return (table 12). In private, they also admit that some pots are comparatively cheap wholesale; on these they can make excellent profits.

Even though the price of Onta pottery has gone up considerably over the past two decades, and even though the potters are earning a vastly increased income, it is the dealers' retailing practices—rather than potters' wholesaling—that have led to Onta pottery's ceasing to be cheaply priced folk crafts. The fact that Onta pots are bought by tourists as gifts undoubtedly helps the dealers set high retail prices; people will think nothing of paying ¥5,000 for a really nice tea bowl if it is boxed and wrapped. According to a representative of an Oita department store, the average expenditure on gift pottery is nearer to ¥10,000 per person.

Other factors influence a dealer's decision to retail Onta pottery at very high prices. In the first place, production in Sarayama is limited. Only about 45–50 kiln firings take place every year and these yield pots worth about ¥90 million. In Koishiwara, where apprentices are employed, a potter will fire his climbing kiln six times a year and his gas kiln between four and six times a month. One potter there claims to produce more than the annual output of all Onta potters added together. Dealers are ensured of regular supplies and can therefore afford to retail at reasonably low prices. Onta potters, however, cannot produce enough pottery to meet current demand, because they have not modernized production methods. There are too many dealers trying to buy too little pottery, and the only way the potters can possibly survive is by retailing at very high prices or by branching out into other lines of business.

Second, there is a demand not just for folk crafts but for *handmade* folk crafts. It is because potters in Sarayama do not use up-to-date machinery and because they stick to methods of production that are seen to be old-fashioned and traditional that people want to buy Onta pots. They are also prepared to pay a lot extra because the pots are hand, and not machine, made.

Third, a dealer knows that his customers have individual tastes and that direct perception does not lead to a standard of beauty. He can therefore take advantage of people's different tastes, knowing full well that even if twenty, fifty, or a hundred people think that a pot is too expensive, someone will eventually like it so much that he or she

TABLE 11   Criteria Used by the General Public to Judge the Quality of Onta Pottery

	COLOR	PATTERN	FUNCTION	FORM	OTHER	TOTAL
Female	69 (52.3%)	25 (18.9%)	13 (9.8%)	22 (16.7%)	3 (2.3%)	132 (100%)
Male	52 (50.5%)	14 (13.6%)	23 (22.3%)	10 (9.7%)	4 (3.9%)	103 (100%)
Total Sample	121 (51.5%)	39 (16.6%)	36 (15.3%)	32 (13.6%)	7 (3.0%)	235 (100%)

Note: These figures are the result of interviews conducted in Sarayama during the annual pottery festivals in October 1978 and 1979.

TABLE 12   Wholesale and Retail Prices (in yen) of Onta Pottery, 1979

TYPE OF POT	SARAYAMA WHOLESALE	SARAYAMA RETAIL (MARUTA)	HITA LOW	HITA MEDIUM	HITA HIGH	OITA	NORTHERN KYUSHU	KYOTO	TOKYO	FOLK CRAFT MUSEUM
36 liter jar	18.000	25.000	38.000	45.000	75.000	100.000	60.000	100.000	65.000	60.000
40 cm. plate	4.500	7.500	12.000	15.000	18.500	—	21.000	—	15.000	8.500
30 cm. plate	1.300	2.000	2.600	3.700	5.000	5.000	3.900	—	3.800	3.500
15 cm. plate	310	400	600	850	5.000	1.000	1.350	700	—	600
Teacup	250	450	550	750	1.000	600	750	—	700	—
Coffee cup	550	750	900	1.200	1.300	1.600	1.700	—	—	—
Tea bowl	1.000	4.000	2.000	8.000	25.000	100.000	—	—	—	—
Flower vase (medium)	1.400	2.500	2.800	3.500	8.000	5.900	4.200	—	—	—
Flower vase (large)	4.500	6.500	8.300	16.500	25.000	16.000	20.000	—	—	—
Pitcher	2.000	2.750	4.500	5.000	20.000	5.000	21.000	—	—	—
Incense burner	15.000	22.000	—	35.000	75.000	28.000	—	—	—	—
0.6 liter jar	550	825	1.000	1.200	2.000	1.600	1.650	—	1.500	1.500

will pay the sum demanded. The fact that many of the dealers sell Onta pottery as a sideline allows them to pursue a strategy of selling small amounts of pottery at fairly high prices.

One way in which a dealer will take advantage of individual taste is by not putting any price at all on some pots. Customers are left to name their own prices, and these may often exceed the maximum a dealer would have thought acceptable. One shop owner told me that a customer had once bought a tea bowl for ¥30,000, when he would never have charged more than ¥20,000; another said that he had sold a lidded vase for ¥50,000 when the going price was between ¥30,000 and ¥40,000.[6]

Finally, the retailer can and does take advantage of the *social* value of pottery. Although potters in Sarayama do not rationally calculate ex-kiln prices on the basis of time, labor, and material costs, they tend to price pots according to size and to ignore the pot's purpose. Dealers do not overlook the way in which a pot is used in the home, and they set their retail prices accordingly. For example, an umbrella stand is more expensive ex kiln than a plate forty centimeters in diameter, mainly because it uses more clay and takes up more kiln space. The dealer can, however, sell the plate at a much higher retail price, since it will be "used" as a decorative piece, probably placed on a stand in the *tokonoma*, the sacred place of any Japanese household. The umbrella stand, on the other hand, will be filled with umbrellas, golf clubs, and children's toy rifles and placed "down below" in the hallway of the house. Similarly, flower vases can be retailed at fairly high prices, not only because they will be placed in the *tokonoma* but also because they are an essential part of the aesthetic theory of flower arrangement (*ikebana*), so popular in Japan. Once pots come to be used for artistic rather than everyday purposes, they can be sold at very high prices (¥8 million for a tea bowl by Arakawa Toyozō). Bowls used in the tea ceremony are a good example of the way in which dealers take advantage of a popularly practiced "art" form. Potters sell their bowls for ¥1,000; they think this is too high a price for the amount of work involved and clay used in making a tea bowl; they also know that they have no idea about how a tea bowl ought to be made and copy shapes from photographs in books. When visitors come up to Sarayama, they often refuse to buy tea bowls because they

---

6. Potters in Koishiwara, where retailing directly to the general public accounts for a large percentage of sales, admit to naming prices according to the appearance of their potential customer.

are too *cheap*. Dealers in Hita and other towns in Kyushu retail tea bowls at from five to one hundred times their wholesale price.

The problem here is that potters are primarily concerned about their image as producers of *mingei* pottery. If they sell tea bowls at too high a price, their work will cease to be folk craft, and there is a danger of their being seen not just as craft potters but as artist craftsmen. Dealers are interested, not in Onta pottery as *mingei*, but in the tea ceremony as an "art" form and the fact that a lot of people believe that the more they pay for a pot, the better it must be "artistically." To their credit perhaps, those dealers close to the folk craft movement—Takumi in Tokyo, for example—have never bought pottery that can be used in such popular "arty" pastimes as flower arrangement and the tea ceremony. They have, instead, fallen in line with Yanagi's argument that "men of tea" can ruin folk crafts (cf. Yanagi 1961:4).[7]

CONCLUSION

In this chapter I have discussed some of the practical aspects of folk craft theory, and have outlined what both potters and pottery dealers think about Yanagi's concept of *mingei*. My main aim has been to find out whether there exists an aesthetic standard accepted by, and common to, potters, dealers, the general public, and leaders of the folk craft movement. Two main conclusions have emerged from the material presented: one of them concerns the concept of "direct perception"; the other the problem of whether Onta pottery is an art or a craft form.

First, although Yanagi argued that in theory "direct perception" gave rise to a universal standard of beauty, in practice neither potters

---

7. There is a paradox here that may well have affected the average person's view of the folk craft movement, for Yanagi himself was particularly fond of the tea ceremony. Indeed, it might be argued that this whole philosophy is to some extent a continuation of that put forward by the first great tea master, Sen no Rikyū, at the end of the sixteenth century. Certainly Yanagi's concepts are part of the mainstream of Japanese aesthetic theory. His idea that "selflessness" gives rise to the appreciation of true "beauty" is in many ways a revival of the concept of *yūgen* as put forward by Zeami Motokiyo (1363-1443), "founder" of the classic Nō theatre (cf. Tsunoda et al. 1964:288-291). "The concept of *yūgen* teaches us that in aesthetic experience it is not that '*I* see the work of art,' but that by 'seeing' the '*I*' is transformed. It is not that '*I* enter into the work,' but that by 'entering' the '*I*' is altered in the intensity of a pristine immediacy" (Deutsch 1975:32).

nor dealers were prepared to accept this premise. Although both groups agreed that direct perception was a useful way of appreciating beauty, from their own experience in selling pottery, potters and deal- ers both felt that different people had different tastes. In their opinion direct perception could only provide a personal standard of beauty. On the basis of evidence cited here, I would agree with Forge (1973:xxi) that the existence of a universal human aesthetic is "a mat- ter of faith."

This point is of interest in that it shows how the aesthetic practice of *mingei* parallels the social practice of the potters' ideal of "commu- nity." I have argued, in my discussion of the social organization of Sarayama, that *ideally* the individual is not as important as the prima- ry group to which he belongs—that is, to the household or hamlet in Japanese rural society. I have shown, however, that *in fact* the market- ing of pottery has made the household more important than the com- munity, and the individual more important (to outsiders at least) than the household. The individual does not always put group interests first; he can and does manipulate group ideals to his own personal advantage. Although he is bound to some extent by the social ideals of "harmony" and "all together," the individual engages in bitter fights to satisfy his self-will. The social ideal is not matched by social practice.

I have also pointed out that, according to folk craft *theory*, the de- termination and understanding of beauty is neither arbitrary nor sub- jective. If a man surrenders his self, he can create beauty; if he rids himself of prejudice and uses direct perception, he can appreciate beauty. Beauty is available to all men, regardless of rank or education. But potters argue that *in practice* the appreciation of beauty is always individual, that what is beautiful for one man is not necessarily so for another. Thus the aesthetic ideal is not matched by aesthetic practice.

I have supported this latter argument by a more detailed discussion of the aesthetic appraisal of Onta pottery. I noted that although lead- ers of the folk craft movement were mainly interested in the form of pottery and the way such pottery was used by the consumer, potters in Sarayama were perhaps more concerned with technical consider- ations arising from methods of production. In particular, they had to take into account certain problems involved in glazing and kiln load- ing when they prepared to throw some forms. I showed that although critics may have based their appraisal of Onta pottery on its form, buyers and the general public were primarily interested in glaze colors. This preference for color over form in the selection of Onta's pots is similar to that expressed by buyers of Shipibo pottery in Peru, who purchase wares that rely on large blobs of contrasting colors for visual effects (Lathrap 1976:204).

Potters do not, of course, disregard either form or function entirely when they make their pots. But they do have to contend with a predominantly urban demand and way of life which, as rural craftsmen, they do not fully understand. Form may thereby be affected. This problem is faced by many craftsmen all over the world. Graburn (1969:426), for example, has discussed the way in which Eskimos in Alaska have had to simplify the design and shape of their carvings in response to demands from their North American buyers, who favor objects that are easier to dust! Abramson (1976:256–257) reports on changes in the size and design of Iwam shields in New Guinea when they cease to be used in war and become objects of commerce. Onta potters may not have such problems of hygiene or warfare. They do, however, have to produce for an urban market that increasingly looks upon folk craft pottery as decorative rather than as purely functional.

The increasing interest of the general public in folk craft pottery for its decorative rather than its functional aspects brings me to my second point: that Onta pottery is gradually coming to be seen by the public as a form of decorative art. One indication of this trend may be seen in the extreme concern of customers with the superficial appearance of Onta pottery. In the days when pottery was made to be used, people did not worry if pots were slightly misshapen or bloated from firing, so long as they fulfilled their function. Nowadays, precisely because Onta pottery is used no longer in everyday life but only on special occasions, people complain if pots are not perfect.

The main reason, in my opinion, for Onta pottery coming to be seen as an art form lies in the fact that potters in Sarayama have for the most part chosen to retain traditional methods of production that are "close to nature." On the one hand, the general public wants handmade things because they are novel and comparatively rare; on the other, dealers take advantage of the public's demand for novelty, and of potters' inability to produce in quantity, to retail pottery at comparatively high prices. They are able to do this precisely because of their awareness that every individual has his or her own taste, and that someone will therefore eventually pay the price they demand. Consequently, Onta pottery is no longer bought for daily use by the common people, as Yanagi advocated was necessary for *mingei*. Instead, it has become a luxury item to be used, if at all, on special occasions only. As Beardsley (n.d., p. 31) has noted of Tamba pottery, "It is hard to escape concluding that Tachikui ware and work from certain other similarly known areas have edged into the elite collector's domain." High retail prices, together with the use of individual "tea names" by potters, have led to many people's seeing Onta pottery as an art rather than as folk craft. Other indicators of Onta pottery's increasing aesthetic value include its designation by the Japanese government as an intangible cultural property, the display of select items in museums in Japan and overseas, and its first fakes (cf. Thompson 1979:32).

Potters find themselves in a slight dilemma. Market demand is always changing, and dealers expect potters to introduce new shapes and designs to meet changing tastes and needs. Folk craft leaders, on the other hand, disapprove of novelty and change, and want potters to throw traditional pots. In this respect, potters are treated in much the same way as Eskimo carvers who have to produce "authentic," "identifiably Eskimo" works for their buyers (Graburn 1969:459; 1970:336). Onta potters know that they cannot entirely ignore what the folk craft leaders tell them, even though there is currently enormous demand for their work, because it was their critical appraisal of Onta pottery in the first place which led to such demand. Potters have, therefore, followed one or two pieces of advice given them by the Folk Craft Museum: for the most part they have stopped making incense burners and dragon-embossed vases; they have also almost entirely refrained from using the *yuhada* glaze to which critics for some unknown reason took a violent dislike. Many of the younger potters also copy old Onta pottery forms from the photograph album which the Folk Craft Museum made and distributed to every potter household in Sarayama.

In view of the fact that critics regard the old Onta pots as best and tell potters not to make nontraditional wares, it is perhaps ironical that the folk craft associations have helped redesign the shapes of the old storage jars and *unsuke* pouring vessels, and have given advice about how to create new forms for pitchers, flower vases, and other pots not originally in the potters' repertoire. Paradoxically, by giving help in decorative designs, folk craft leaders have contributed to the degeneration of the folk craft that they are theoretically trying to preserve, in that *mingei* ideals stress that pottery must be used if it is to be really beautiful.

Indeed, the relationship between Sarayama's potters and the leaders of the folk craft movement is in many ways one continuous set of paradoxes. Onta was discovered by Yanagi in 1931; it was made famous by Leach's visit to Sarayama in 1954. Onta pottery was the perfect example of *mingei*. Yet, over the years, everything that had made the potters' work so "beautiful" has been altered by the existence of the folk craft movement: pots are no longer cheap, nor purely functional, nor used by local people in their everyday lives; potters are no longer "unconscious" craftsmen who know nothing of the vice of money. It is sad to relate, but, in a way, the folk craft leaders have been indirectly responsible for almost all the ills that they now bemoan. Their only consolation, perhaps, is that this is not the first time such a thing has occurred, as the following conversation between Edmund Leach and Herbert Read highlights:

Read: Any decay in art, any kind of stylistic
               decadence, to put it more simply, is
               due to the artist becoming self-
               conscious or, if you like, conscious of
               elements and styles which are not
               spontaneous.

Leach: Surely this has the implication that
               the art critic is the destroyer of
               contemporary art because he makes
               the artist conscious of what he is
               doing.

Read: Yes, I would accept that. The art critic
               only appears in decadent periods of
               art. (From Marion Smith 1961:112)

Meanwhile, potters do their best to hold both critics and buyers at a respectable distance. They cling to the concept of tradition both to please the folk craft leaders and to counteract the market demand for novelty and innovation. Dealers always want something different: a coffee cup with combing instead of *hake* slip decoration; a teacup with green overglaze at the lip instead of the customary transparent glaze; red overglaze on a flower vase; a pitcher half brown or black and half green; the requests are endless. In the days when pots did not sell well, potters had to comply with requests like these. But now that the folk craft boom has improved their economic conditions, potters can call on the concept of "tradition" to combat the chaos of market demand and refuse some of the stranger orders, such as those for statuettes of drunken badgers or for double-spouted teapots!

Potters stick to their traditional methods of production and remain acceptably close to nature because their pottery is all the more appreciated by the leaders of the folk craft movement. If they were to mechanize techniques, take in apprentices, and increase production, not only would their social organization disintegrate entirely, but Onta pottery would almost certainly lose its good reputation. Yet the longer they remain close to nature, the more highly their work is appreciated. It seems inevitable that potters will in the end be acclaimed as "artist craftsmen." And yet, ironically, such acclamation would also lead to a disintegration of the community (as I have hinted is already happening). Whatever potters should decide to do in the future, the nostalgia for a "community," which so pervaded their conversation during my stay in Sarayama, will probably never be realized.

Conclusion

This book has concentrated on the relation between ecology and the social organization of a Japanese pottery community, and on the interpretation of that relationship in the context of the Japanese folk craft movement. I have shown that the social organization of Sarayama has to some extent depended on certain environmental limitations. The ways in which agricultural crops were grown and local raw materials were prepared for the production of pottery were seen to bring about cooperation among all households in the community. My description of social organization was partly idealized, since it also depended on an image of the past which those living in Sarayama wished to present to the outside world. At the same time, this social ideal closely corresponded to an aesthetic ideal. Yanagi Muneyoshi, founder of the Japanese folk craft movement, put forward a theory suggesting that the quality of folk crafts derived from "closeness to nature" and a "sense of community." Beauty depended on the natural environment in which the craftsmen lived, and resulted from cooperation among those producing folk crafts.

I have argued that in Sarayama the individual was expected to subordinate his personal interests to those of the household and community to which he or she belonged. The individual was expected to live in harmony with others. I also showed that, according to folk craft theory, not only was beauty divorced from all idea of individualism and the individual artist, but that there was a standard of beauty which could be appreciated by all men, provided that they made use of "direct perception" in their judgment of folk crafts. Beauty was seen, moreover, to result from the mutual cooperation of a folk craft's creator, admirer, user, and critic (Yanagi 1932). Thus, acccording to both social and aesthetic ideals, society was a harmonious entity in which the individual should surrender himself to the ideals of "community solidarity," on the one hand, and of "beauty," on the other.

I described how both social and aesthetic ideals have not been lived up to in Sarayama. First of all, social organization was affected by various changes in the community's relation to its natural environment. For example, potters took advantage of improved communications to stop using some local raw materials and devote themselves to full-time production of pottery. They also made use of such technological developments in the ceramic industry as kiln shelving, the adoption of which led to the breakdown of most forms of household cooperation and to the economic individuation of potting households. The increase in potters' wealth made possible by the purchase of kiln shelving and by an increase in market demand for folk craft pottery brought about a division within Sarayama between potting and nonpotting households.

Second, the community's social organization was upset by potters' contacts with the outside world. I argued that folk craft leaders' interest in Onta pottery not only reenforced the division between potting and nonpotting households in Sarayama, but strengthened the position of younger potters vis-à-vis their elders, thereby upsetting the community's age-grade system of gerontocracy. The situation was further complicated by the fact that the aesthetic appreciation of Onta pottery focused on the individual potter's talent; but I suggested that the community was an egalitarian group of households which, ideally, could not admit to individual talent if it was to operate as a real "community." Consequently, the community as a whole, and the seniority system by which Sarayama had hitherto been run, lessened in importance as ideals, and the individual was freer to take advantage of opportunities to further his own ends.

Changes in Sarayama's social organization affected the critical appraisal of Onta pottery by leaders of the folk craft movement. Thus, the failure by potters to meet a social ideal became simultaneously a failure to meet an aesthetic ideal. In chapter 1 I pointed out that, in Yanagi's opinion, beauty could be adversely affected if (1) the craftsman relied in production on modern technology rather than on local natural materials; (2) he put his own interests before those of the community in which he worked; (3) he became too interested in financial reward and increased production beyond a given point of "equilibrium"; (4) prices were not held at a reasonably low level; and (5) folk crafts became decorative rather than purely functional.

Onta potters did make one or two technological innovations, and they did stop relying altogether on the use of local natural materials. I argued that their newly acquired wealth prompted them to give priority to individual rather than to community interests. Leaders of the folk craft movement interpreted this as meaning that potters were too concerned with financial reward, and argued therefore that Onta pottery had recently deteriorated because of the commercialism surrounding the potters' work.

Because of the demand for folk crafts in general, potters had been able to increase their wholesale, and buyers their retail, prices above what was considered acceptable for *mingei* by folk craft leaders. Although, in theory, *mingei* was to be used in people's everyday lives, Onta pottery had come to be used only for special occasions. Some wares were no longer used at all and served a purely decorative purpose. Strictly speaking, Onta pottery could not be as "beautiful" as it once was, because it was no longer purely functional.

Finally, I discussed the perception of "beauty" itself. Yanagi argued that there was a standard of beauty which could be appreciated by *anyone* in Japanese society, regardless of his or her rank of education, provided that he or she made use of what he termed "direct perception." Fieldwork investigations revealed that this was an ideal which could not be put into practice. Although both potters and dealers thought that direct perception was a useful method of appreciating folk crafts, from their own experience in selling Onta pottery they stressed that different people had different tastes. They consequently argued that the use of direct perception could give rise only to a personal, rather than universal, standard of beauty.

In brief, I have shown that there is a close parallel between the social ideal of how Sarayama should be organized and the aesthetic ideal of how folk crafts should be made. Any social change therefore necessitates a corresponding change in aesthetic appraisal. If potters remain close to nature, their work improves; if they fail to cooperate, their work deteriorates. So-called aesthetic *mingei* ideals are in fact no more and no less than prescriptions for the organization of Japanese society. *Mingei* is in this sense "the autobiography of society" (Mukerjee 1948:57).

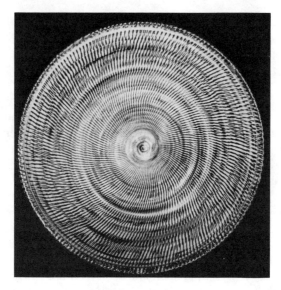

Top view of slipped plate with *tobiganna* chattering. Transparent glaze. Diameter 21 cms.

Old water jar with *nagashi* style overglazing. Height approx. 45 cms.

Unsuke pouring vessel. Height approx. 30 cms.

Old sake bottle. Translucent honey glaze. Height approx. 12 cms.

Teapot and teacups. Copper green glaze.

Large, lidded pickle jar with *tobiganna* chattering and *uchikake* style of overglazing. Height approx. 60 cms.

Close-up of *hakeme* decorated water jar.

Tea jar. Height approx. 45 cms.

FOLK CRAFTS AND SOCIETY

The argument between potters and folk craft leaders concerning the standard of beauty that is provided by use of direct perception leads me to a more general discussion of the relation between folk crafts and society. Essentially, Yanagi and the present leaders of the Japanese folk craft movement have taken the view that beauty is absolute and can be objectively perceived. Potters have countered by arguing that beauty is a subjective state of mind which is relative to the individual. In my opinion, neither the absolute nor the relative view of beauty is tenable. The former is impossible to prove; the latter is overly subjective. Aesthetic standards cannot be purely individual; rather they represent group values instilled in individuals making up the group (Tomars 1940:396). The question is not "what is good *mingei*?" but "what is *mingei* that is good for whom, accepted by what sort of people, and on the basis of what criteria?" In speculating about some of the answers that might be given to this question, I will adopt a position that is neither "absolute" nor "relative" but socially relative.

It has been argued that folk arts and crafts tend to emphasize their communality, which distinguishes them from the arts of other local or national communities (Graburn 1976:4; Tomars 1940:55). I suggested earlier that pottery could be an idiom in which community social relations were discussed. The concept of tradition was important to those living in Sarayama in that it served to give Onta pottery its distinctiveness; if Onta pottery was distinctive, then Sarayama as a whole was a special community which maintained its identity precisely because of its production of pottery.

This point has been made for other societies facing the sort of external pressures that have affected Sarayama's social organization (cf. Brody 1976:76; Gill 1976:113). Graburn (1976:5) has pointed out that what he calls "tourist" or "airport" arts externally define an ethnic boundary with the outside world, while internally they help maintain ethnic identity and social structure. As for Sarayama's potters, of course, Onta pottery is not tied up with problems of ethnic identity. It does, however, become an idiom by which local group identity is fostered and expressed. At the same time, it defines the community, the minimal section in Japanese rural society's system of interlocking groups (cf. Nakane 1970:94).

I would argue that *mingei* does serve an "ethnic" function at the national level. Yanagi often emphasized that his concept of *mingei* was uniquely Japanese and he was concerned that local traditional handicrafts were dying out because of the Japanese people's demand for Western products. I have discussed the relation between Yanagi's ideals and Confucianism in the prewar period in Japan. We should note that *mingei* first became popular in the 1950s, when Japan was going through one of its more fervent periods of Americanization. I suggest that, just as Onta potters make use of the idea of tradition to protect their community from many of the outside influences upsetting their social organization, so the Japanese as a whole have gone back to their traditional arts in order to preserve a national identity in the face of cultural innovations from the West. The fact that the Japanese government now bestows such titles as Intangible Cultural Property, Traditional Craftwork, or Award of Cultural Merit on individual craftsmen or craft communities is an indication of the importance attached by the authorities to the maintenance of a specifically Japanese image, which sets Japan apart from other highly industrialized Western nations.

Although, in this instance, the concept of *mingei* has come to be put to similar social use both by craftsmen living in a rural community and by their public living in predominantly urban areas, a distinction needs to be made between the producer's and the appreciator's overall view of folk crafts. The concept of a "folk" art or craft that emerged in the 19th century was a means of identifying the arts and crafts of a lower class, which was generally rural and nonliterate and followed local traditions. These folk arts were seen to be communal by nature and in direct contrast to the urban, literate, upper-class, fine arts (cf. Tomars 1940:46). We should recognize that folk arts or crafts are at first generally appreciated as art by people living in the "outside" world, and not by their producers. The attitudes adopted by each of these groups towards what they both come to term folk art or its equivalent usually differ to a considerable degree.

One such difference concerns the nature of the art or craft in question. To the potters in Sarayama, *mingei* was not a folk "art" but a folk "craft." In this respect they came close to adopting the purist view of *mingei* espoused by folk craft leaders. I also argued that the term *mingei* had come to be seen by many members of the general public as more closely approximating "art" than mere "craft." I believe that various reasons underlie this difference in opinion and that people's notions of what constitutes beauty or art derive from their social environment. As far as *mingei* is concerned, there appear to be certain dichotomies in the life-styles of those who make and those who appreciate folk crafts. Although none of these dichotomies is entirely independent of the others, I will broadly categorize them as natural/industrialized, rural/urban, handmade/machine-made, and individual/anonymous. It is with the effect of these dichotomies on people's appreciation of *mingei* that I shall now deal.

I have suggested that Onta pottery had come to be seen specifically as an art, rather than a craft form because potters remained close to nature and did not use modern machinery. In considering the concept of closeness to nature which Yanagi argues was a fundamental source of beauty, it will be remembered that both folk craft critics and buyers tended to have an image of Onta potters working alone in undisturbed peace, at one with their natural surroundings. In actual fact, this was hardly the case: potters were constantly interrupted by tourists and other visitors; they spent most of their time "drowning" the silence outside with their radios, and one young man actually threw all his pots at the wheel while watching television. To the rural craftsman nature is not something to be contemplated aesthetically in a detached manner. Rather, it is the environment in which he has to survive; it provides the materials with which he works; it is "the source of his success and of his fears" (Tomars 1940:390).

I think we can say that people idealize nature only when they are not directly involved with it in a struggle for survival. In other words, the aesthetic ideal that associates the quality of folk crafts with closeness to nature derives primarily from urbanization (Tomars 1940:391). Urbanization, usually—though not necessarily—depends on industrialization. The nostalgia for a return to nature arising from urbanism in Japan may be seen not only in modern folk crafts but in the painting and poetry practiced by an urbanized aristocracy during the Nara and Heian periods (A.D. 710-1185). It may also be found in the aesthetic philosophy of Zen Buddhism, by which Yanagi himself was influenced (cf. B. Leach 1978:81), and which came into its own with the construction of the castle towns in the sixteenth century, emphasizing simplicity and quietism during one of the most lavish and turbulent periods of Japanese history. In Europe, landscape painting was to a large extent created by painters of the urbanized Low Countries, while the literary convention of the pastorale developed among writers living in the growing cities of Europe (Tomars 1940:390-391). The painting of Constable and Turner also came just at the time the English countryside was being polluted with the smoke and dirt of the first industrial towns (Mukerjee 1948:210-211). In one sense, the idea of an aesthetic theory centering on the concept of beauty may be said to derive from the destruction of nature which has hitherto accompanied urbanization and—since the eighteenth century—industrialization (cf. Okada 1976:171).

I would argue further that people who buy Japanese folk crafts use the concept of "nature"—perhaps unconsciously—as a means of measuring just how far Japanese culture has progressed (cf. Graburn 1976:13-14). Certainly, when I interviewed one hundred visitors to Sarayama about the relation between nature and beauty in *mingei*, a large majority (70 percent) believed not only that the potters in Sarayama made good pots *because* they used natural materials and means of production, but that potters *ought* to continue to rely on nature and not yield to economic considerations. The moral tone found in Yanagi's concept of nature, and adopted by present folk craft leaders, would appear to extend to a large section of the Japanese public. Potters in Sarayama work in a way in which almost the whole of Japanese society once worked; now that Japanese industry has made such advances, people like to look back and see how far they have progressed. They want potters in Sarayama to stay the way they are, so that they can measure their own and the nation's prosperity. In exchange, they are prepared to accord potters the honor of acclaiming their work as "art."

Coincidental to the main argument presented here, but connected with urban attitudes toward nature, is the relation between art consumption and the female sex. Two Japanese "arts" currently popular and closely associated with the Zen Buddhist appreciation of nature are the tea ceremony and flower arrangement—both of them now largely practiced by women. I have noted that women are the main purchasers of folk crafts in general and, in particular, of the tea bowls and flower vases made by Onta potters. This is of interest because of a theory put forward by Tomars (1940:388-389) suggesting that in a competitive business society, women form the leisure class, which performs the social prestige function of art consumption. Tomars's theory would appear to hold true for Japanese *mingei*; not only are women the major purchasers, they also are a large majority of the membership of the two folk craft associations. It should be pointed out that the part played by women is to some extent to be expected. Ideally, folk crafts are domestic utensils to be used in people's everyday lives; women are thereby more likely to appreciate something like Onta pottery. But although strictly "non-*mingei*" items such as tea bowls and flower vases are bought by women, the really large decorative wares appear to be purchased primarily by men. This shift from female to male control as an object climbs from 'rubbish' to durable art has also been noted by Thompson (1979:33). Evidence from this study, therefore, can give no more than partial support to Tomars's theory that women are the main art consumers in a competitive business society, when applied to Japan.

In an examination of the relationship between art, beauty, and mechanization, my first point concerns the way in which handmade goods are usually extolled by those living in highly industrialized societies. Machine-made goods generally serve their purpose extremely well; they are functional, efficient, and cheap. But their low price makes them available to everyone in society. Hence, their consumption is not—to use Veblen's terms—"honorific" so much as "common." Handmade goods, on the other hand, are not produced with such efficiency; they cannot compete in either quality or quantity with machine-made goods. Yet, precisely because of this, they are seen by some to be "more serviceable for the purpose of pecuniary reputability; hence the marks of hand labour come to be honorific, and the goods which exhibit these marks take rank as of higher grade than the corresponding machine product" (Veblen 1925:159).

The notion of "honorific consumption" affects aesthetic taste in two ways. On the one hand, people place value on the quantitative aspect of handwork. Because handmade things are not generally produced in large numbers, they are comparatively expensive. Veblen argued (1925:128) that people tended to judge a thing's beauty by the amount of money they had to spend on its acquisition. I have noted that Onta pottery was retailed at comparatively high prices—mainly as a result of its coming to be seen as decorative rather than strictly functional ware. I would argue, therefore, that people sometimes regard Onta pottery as beautiful *because* it is expensive; conversely, at other times, they do not think it beautiful *unless* it is expensive (as in the story of the women who thought Shigeki's tea bowls were beautiful until they learned how cheap they were). On the other hand, people are attracted by what they see as the qualitative aspect of handwork. They decry as "unaesthetic" any form of mechanization, any new technological device that might interfere with the "beauty" of hand labor (cf. Tomars 1940:200-201). We have seen this kind of attitude adopted by leaders of the Japanese folk craft movement toward

Onta pottery. Yet, I think it might be argued that because most forms of art are in fact handmade, anything that is handmade—or made by some other form of obsolete technology (cf. McLuhan 1964:ix)—may well come to be seen as "art."

Veblen argued that the qualititive aspects of handwork most appreciated were "commonly, if not invariably . . . certain imperfections and irregularities in the lines of the hand wrought article, showing where the workman has fallen short in the execution of the design" (1925:159). He further suggested that the thought and ideas of people like Ruskin and Morris, who exalted the defective and propagated a return to handicraft and household industry, would have been impossible in an age when the more nearly perfect goods were also more expensive (p. 162). Although Japanese folk crafts usually do contain some slight imprefection of form, it should be realized that the aesthetic attitude which praises the irregular in Japanese art is many centuries old (Keene 1971:18ff). Thus, the notion in Japan that beauty derives from imperfection and irregularity (cf. Yanagi 1955a:53) was not conceived in—although it may be strengthened by—modern industrial society's reaction to the perfection and regularity of machine-made things.

Although Yanagi himself did not object to slight imperfections in *mingei*, he was at pains to stress that individuality was irrelevant to the appreciation of folk crafts which were to be made by and for ordinary people. Paradoxically, nowadays many Japanese see an expression of the craftsman's individuality in the imperfection of his work. In my survey of visitors to Sarayama, I asked one hundred people if they thought that handmade, not machine-made, objects expressed their maker's character. Every person interviewed agreed with this idea. There is a strong association in most Japanese people's minds between handicrafts, imperfection, and individuality, on the one hand, and mechanization, perfection, and impersonality, on the other.

But the idea of individuality connotes again the concept of art. It appears that the individual craftsman is praised because industrialization has given rise to what the majority see as an impersonal and anonymous social environment (Nisbet 1976:134). When people are forced to live in large-scale urbanized societies, they begin to realize, perhaps for the first time, the meaning of anonymity. Then there is a tendency for the individual craftsman to be publicly proclaimed as "artist." Graburn (1976:21-22) has noted that the signing of art works in general was encouraged to offset an increasing impersonality. Although I agree with this argument, I think that the notion of "honorific consumption" should also be taken into account in any discussion of the signing of art work.

Finally, as a gesture to Silbermann's demand (1968:587) that the sociology of art develop laws of prediction on the basis of analysis, I should like to make one hypothesis concerning the relation between folk art and social organization. I suggest that in any highly urbanized and rapidly industrializing society, such as those of northern Europe in the nineteenth and Japan in the twentieth century, an aesthetic philosophy of the kind put forward by William Morris or Yanagi Muneyoshi will be adopted within that society at some stage fairly soon after industrialization begins, and that it will "boom" once a large consumer middle class emerges. In the past it has been possible for such aesthetic ideals to be generated from within a particular society. However, the advance in communications during the past fifty years makes such internal generation practically impossible from now on. Thus, any society's rediscovery of its own folk crafts in the future will doubtless come as a result of external influences—as Graburn's book on ethnic and tourist arts so aptly illustrates.

There is a concluding parenthetical note to be made to Graburn's comment (1976:21-22) that "the world has now become so homogenized and self-conscious that the most folksy arts and crafts are soon identified, glorified, preserved and stultified." Much of the individualism and the glorification of artisan work as art has been fostered by anthropologists, museum curators, art historians, or collectors (cf. Brody 1976:75), who would seem intent upon acquiring the prestigious status normally associated in the West with the words "art" and "artist." This may be seen most clearly when anthropologists call their field of investigation the "sociology of art." How infinitely superior to a mere "sociology of craft" or "anthropology of material culture"! It is because of the potential self-gratification inherent in any anthropologist's ethnocentric notion of art that we should perhaps in future opt for an "aesthetic anthropology" (Maquet 1971:17).

Let me make it clear that I do not intend the "sociology of aesthetics" (as I prefer to call this branch of social scientific research) to concentrate on the study of "art" objects alone. It will address itself to the arts of "exotic" peoples—to woodcarving, weaving, metalwork, and so on—and to those of our own industrialized societies. But it should also cover all other fields in which values of the kind illustrated in this book prevail. The sociology of aesthetics is thus that branch of sociology or anthropology which deals with punk, not just classical, music, with science fiction as well as with Literature (with a capital L), with film, and with dance. More important, its methods can be used to study fashion, certain types of gymnastics, cosmetics, wine, landscape gardening, architecture, jewelry, and cuisine. In short, the sociology of aesthetics should escape the narrow confines of art and reach out to all those other aspects of culture which we have come to link with notions of beauty or taste.

Afterword

One of the advantages of being an anthropologist, and of having an adaptable wife and children, is that I have been able to come back to Kyushu to write this book. Here in a farmhouse a few kilometers below Sarayama, I put the finishing touches to research that I began some four years ago.

Something that I recall being told when I first started fieldwork in Sarayama, but which I did not fully appreciate until my return, was that the period of my study there was but "a drop in the ocean" of the community's long history. Potters had been working in Sarayama for more than 270 years before my arrival; they expected to continue to do so for many decades to come. One or two potters admitted that I had come at a particularly difficult period in Sarayama's history; they also believed that things would get better in the not too distant future.

Their optimism was not unfounded. Upon my return, I discovered that some matters that had struck me as being important three or four years ago had ceased to be problematic. It is true that Mitsusaburō is still doing his utmost not to let the bulldozer have access to the clay pits behind his strip of land; but Saihito has sold Chikara the patch of land in front of his uncle's house, and Shigeki, by an exceedingly complicated arrangement, has received from Kaneyo the land bordering the Gōshiki stream immediately below his clay crushers.

Other changes are more easily perceptible. Haruzō, for example, has persuaded the city authorities, who are always keen to do anything that might increase tourism, to widen stretches of the road from the Ono valley up to Sarayama. Within the community itself, Toshiyasu has arranged with fellow potters to concrete the track up to his house past the cooperative kiln; Mitchan has built a two-story steel-girder-framed clay-crusher shed behind Yamasan; and Yoshi-taka has joined the ranks of those who prefer plastic pipes to wooden gutters to convey the water from their *ize* dams to the clay crushers.

But the most obvious innovation is the construction of an unpaved mountain road along the eastern side of the community, running up into the Gōshiki valley behind Yamako, the dilapidated Yamaka, and Yamaichi. This road is being built with the ostensible purpose of fa-cilitating the felling and transportation of lumber growing on commu-nity-owned land at the top of the valley. It might also be extended for potters to dig their slip clay from Kitanamizu, as they used to do. The road's construction has already made it possible for a bulldozer to dig clay from the old community-owned, rather than private, clay pits, and hence put an end to some of the squabbling among the potters. I am not very optimistic that such changes will in fact take place. Rath-er, I suspect that the presence of this mountain road could lead to oth-er changes that might have more far-reaching effects on Sarayama's social organization. One thing that fieldwork has taught me is to har-bor a deep distrust of roads.

To say that I hope that I am wrong in my suspicion reveals that I am as guilty of nostalgia as those about whom I have written. The two years that I spent in Sarayama have left an indelible image on my mind of the community as it was then. Much of this image is visual, and I regret having visual images destroyed. The recent disappear-ance, for example, of a favorite *taverna* that I frequented nightly when I lived in Athens (long before I had ever heard of the word "anthro-pology"), somehow leaves a hole in my memories that cannot be filled. So with changes in Sarayama. I suspect that people like Yanagi and Leach felt much the same way.

I realize that this nostalgia stems largely from the fact that I have come back to Sarayama after being away from the community for a year and a half. In other words, it arises out of what might be called "discontinuous experience." A lot has happened in my absence that would take me a long time to understand. But for those living in Sara-yama, such changes are part of the continuity of experience.

This continuity is measured in Sarayama with reference to "the past" (*mukashi*). Yet, just as Leach's memory of the "community" is not my memory of Sarayama, so does the content of "the past" differ from one person to the next within Sarayama itself. For Shigeki now, the past means ten years ago; for his sister-in-law, Isae, it is twenty years; for Haruzō, it is the period after the war before Leach came; for his father, Chūzō, now aged ninety-three, it is in the second and third decades of this century. Chūzō and Shigeki are in fact talking about completely different concepts of the "community" when they refer to *mukashi*. The word alone is enough to make them think that they are on common ground. It gives them a shared identity with which to try to come to terms with the present and to plan for the future. Sarayama's inhabitants thus paint a portrait of the past so that the community as a whole may continue to exist (cf. Berger 1979). If this is to be termed "nostalgia," well and good. It is a sense of nostalgia which—unlike that of sociologists and literati—is born out of recognition of continuity, not of change.

Bibliography

Abramson, J. J.
1976   "Style Change in an Upper Sepik Contact Situation." In *Ethnic and Tourist Arts: Cultural Expressions from the Fourth World*, edited by Nelson H. H. Graburn. Berkeley and Los Angeles: University of California Press.

Anderson, J. N.
1973   "Ecological Anthropology and Anthropological Ecology." In *Handbook of Social and Cultural Anthropology*, edited by J. J. Honigmann. Chicago: Rand McNally.

Ariga, K.
1956   "Sonraku kyōdōtai to ie." In *Sonraku Kyōdōtai no Kōzō Bunseki*. Sonraku Shakai Kenkyūkai Nenpo no. 3, pp. 21–49.

Beardsley, R. K.
n.d.   "Stability and Adaptation in Folk Art Production in Japan." Manuscript.

Beardsley, R. K., J. Hall
  and R. Ward   *Village Japan.* Chicago: University of Chicago
1959   Press.

Becker, H.
1978   "Arts and Crafts." *American Journal of Sociology* 83:862–889.

Befu, H.
1963   "Patrilineal Descent and Personal Kindred in Japan." *American Anthropologist* 65:1328–1341.

Berger, J.
1979   *Pig Earth.* London: Writers and Readers Publishing Cooperative.

Bohannan, P.
1961   "Artist and Critic in an African Society." In *The Artist in Tribal Society*, edited by Marion Smith. London: Routledge & Kegan Paul.

Bourdieu, P.
1968   "Outline of a Sociological Theory of Art Perception." *International Social Science Journal* 20:589–612.

Brody, J. J.
1976   "The Creative Consumer: Survival, Revival, and Invention in Southwest Indian Arts." In *Ethnic and Tourist Arts: Cultural Expressions from the Fourth World*, edited by Nelson H. H. Graburn. Berkeley and Los Angeles: University of California Press.

Bunzel, R.
1972   *The Pueblo Potter: A Study of Creative Imagination in Primitive Art.* New York: Dover. (Originally published in 1929.)

Cardew, M.
1971   *Pioneer Pottery.* London: Longmans.

Charlton, T. H.
1976   "Modern Ceramics in the Teotihuacan Valley." In *Ethnic and Tourist Arts: Cultural Expressions from the Fourth World*, edited by Nelson H. H. Graburn. Berkeley and Los Angeles: University of California Press.

Coomaraswamy, A.
1943   *Why Exhibit Works of Art?* London: Luzac & Co.

Cornell, J. B.
1956   "Matsunagi: A Japanese Mountain Community." In *Two Japanese Villages*. Occasional Papers, Center for Japanese Studies, no. 5, pp. 113–232. Ann Arbor: University of Michigan Press.

1963   "Local Group Stability in the Japanese Community." *Human Organization.* 22:113–125.

Cort, L.
1977   "Shigarakigayoi." *Aruku Miru Kiku* 124:3–35.

D'Azevedo, W. L., editor.
1973   *The Traditional Artist in African Societies.* Bloomington: Indiana University Press.

Deutsch, E.
1975   *Studies in Comparative Aesthetics.* Monograph No. 2, Society for Asian and Comparative Philosophy. Honolulu: University Press of Hawaii.

Dewey, J.
1934   *Art as Experience.* New York: Minton, Balch & Co.

Dockstader, F. J.
1973   "The Role of the Individual Indian Artist." In *Primitive Art and Society,* edited by A. Forge. London: Oxford University Press.

Dore, R. P.
1959   *Land Reform in Japan.* London: Oxford University Press.

1978   *Shinohata: A Portrait of a Japanese Village.* London: Allen Lane.

Dore, R. P., editor.
1967   *Aspects of Social Change in Modern Japan.* Princeton, N.J.: Princeton University Press.

Duvignaud, J.
1972   *The Sociology of Art.* Paladin.

Ellen, R. F.
1978   "Problems and Progress in the Ethnographic Analysis of Small-Scale Human Ecosystems." *Man* (NS) 13:290–300.

1979   "Introduction: Anthropology, the Environment and Ecological Systems." In *Social and Ecological Systems,* edited by P. Burnham and R. F. Ellen. London: Academic Press.

Embree, J. P.
1939   *Suye Mura—A Japanese Village.* Chicago: University of Chicago Press.

Forge, A., editor.
1973   *Primitive Art and Society.* London: Oxford University Press.

Frake, C. O.
1962   "Cultural Ecology and Ethnography." In *Ecology and Anthropology: A Symposium. American Anthropologist* 64:53–59.

Freilich, M.
1963   "The Natural Experiment, Ecology and Cul-
                   ture." *Southwest Journal of Anthropology* 19:
                   21–39.

Friedman, J.
1974   "Marxism, Structuralism, and Vulgar Material-
                   ism." *Man* (NS) 9:44–69.

Fukutake, T.
1949   *Nihon Nōson no Shakaiteki Seikaku.* Tokyo: Tokyo
                   University Press.

1956   "Gendai Nihon ni okeru sonraku kyōdōtai son-
                   zai keitai." In *Sonraku Kyōdōtai no Kōzō Bunseki.*
                   Sonraku Kenkyūkai Nenpo 3:1–20.

1967   *Asian Rural Society: China, India, Japan.* Tokyo:
                   Tokyo University Press.

Gamō, M.
1962   "Shinzoku." In *Nihon Minzokugaku Taikei* 3:233–
                   258. Tokyo: Heibonsha.

Gerbrands, A. A.
1957   *Art as an Element of Culture, Especially in Negro
                   Africa.* Medellelingen van het Rijksmuseum voor
                   Volkenkunde, Leiden No. 12. Leiden: E. J. Brill.

Gill, R. R.
1976   "Ceramic Arts and Acculturation at Laguna." In
                   *Ethnic and Tourist Arts: Cultural Expressions from
                   the Fourth World,* edited by Nelson H. H. Gra-
                   burn. Berkeley and Los Angeles: University of
                   California Press.

Graburn, N. H. H.
1969   "Art and Acculturative Processes." *International
                   Social Science Journal* 21:457–468.

1970   "The Eskimos and Commercial Art." In *The So-
                   ciology of Art and Literature,* edited by M. Al-
                   brecht et al. New York: G. Duckworth.

Graburn, N. H. H., editor.
1976   *Ethnic and Tourist Arts: Cultural Expressions from
                   the Fourth World.* Berkeley and Los Angeles: Uni-
                   versity of California Press.

Hamada, S.
1965   "Onta no karausu hoka." *Mingei* 147:8–9.

Harmon, M.
1974   "Folk Visual Arts." *Encyclopaedia Britannica, Macropaedia,* vol. 7, pp. 470–481. Chicago: W. Benton.

Harris, M.
1968   *The Rise of Anthropological Theory.* London: Routledge & Kegan Paul.

Haselberger, H.
1961   "Methods of Studying Ethnological Art." *Current Anthropology* 2:351–384.

Hatae, K.
1970   "Mukei bunkazai to wa donna mono ka?" *Nihon no Mingei* 180:4–9.

Isoda, S.
1951   "Sonraku kōzō no futatsu no katachi." *Hōshakaigaku* 1:50–64.

Johnson, E. H.
1967   "Status Changes in Hamlet Structure Accompanying Modernization." In *Aspects of Social Change in Modern Japan,* edited by R. P. Dore. Princeton, N.J.: Princeton University Press.

Jugaku, B.
1935   "Iriamu Morisu to Yanagi Muneyoshi." *Kōgei* 50:1–30.

Keene, D.
1971   *Landscapes and Portraits.* London: Secker & Warburg.

Keesing, F. M.
1958   "The Aesthetic Aspect of Culture." In *Cultural Anthropology: The Science of Custom.* New York: Holt, Rinehart & Winston.

Kitano, S.
1963   "*Dōzoku* and *ie* in Japan: The Meaning of Family Genealogical Relationships." In *Japanese Culture,* edited by R. Smith and R. K. Beardsley. Chicago: Aldine.

Koyama, F.
1967   *Nihon no Kōgei,* vol. 9: *Tōji.* Tokyo: Tankō Shinsha.

Kumakura, I.
1979   "A Tocsin for Our Times: The *mingei undō.*" *Japan Interpreter* 12:445–448.

Lathrap, D. W.
1976   "Shipibo Tourist Art." In *Ethnic and Tourist Arts: Cultural Expressions from the Fourth World,* edited by Nelson H. H. Graburn. Berkeley and Los Angeles: University of California Press.

Leach, B.
1960   *A Potter in Japan.* London: Faber & Faber.
1972   "Introduction." *The Unknown Craftsman,* by S. Yanagi. Tokyo: Kodansha International.
1976   *Hamada, Potter.* Tokyo: Kodansha International.
1978   *Beyond East and West: Memoirs, Portraits, and Essays.* London: Faber & Faber.

McLuhan, H. M.
1964   *Understanding Media: The Extensions of Man.* New York: McGraw-Hill.

Maquet, J.
1971   *Introduction to Aesthetic Anthropology.* Reading, Mass.: Addison-Wesley.

Mason, J. W. T.
1935   *The Meaning of Shinto.* New York: E. P. Dutton.

Matsukata, S.
1955   "Hita kikō." *Mingei* 27:15–17.

Matsumoto, T.
1961   *Nihon Chihō Chishitsu-shi: Kyūshū Chihō.* Fukuoka: Asakura Shoten.

Mead, S.
1976   "The Production of Native Art and Craft Objects in Contemporary New Zealand Society." In *Ethnic and Tourist Arts: Cultural Expressions from the Fourth World,* edited by Nelson H. H. Graburn. Berkeley and Los Angeles: University of California Press.

Mendieta y Nunez, L.
1957   "Sociologia del Arte." *Revista Mexicana de Sociologia* 19:67–84.

Mizuo, H.
1966 "Gendai to mingei." *Geijutsu Shincho*, vol. 17 (5).

1968 *Gendai Mingei-ron.* Tokyo: Shinchōsha.

1971 "Yakimono no bi—17:Onta." *Nihon Bijutsu Kōgei,* vol. 392

1972 *Minyō no Tabi.* Tokyo: Geisōsha.

1974 "Teshigoto ni tsuite." *Mingei* 252:6–10.

1978 *Yanagi Muneyoshi. Nihon Minzoku Bunka Taikei,* vol. 6. Tokyo: Kodansha.

Morris, W.
1902 *Hopes and Fears for Art.* Five lectures delivered in Birmingham, London, and Nottingham. London: Longmans, Green & Company.

1947 *On Art and Socialism: Essays and Lectures.* J. Lehmann.

Mukerjee, R.
1948 *The Social Function of Art.* Bombay: Hind Kitabs.

Nakamura, K.
1956 "Sonraku kyōdōtai." In *Sonraku Kyōdōtai to Kōzō Bunseki.* Sonraku Shakai Kenkyūkai Nenpo no. 3.

1977 *Nihon no Sonraku Kyōdōtai.* Tokyo: Japan Publishers.

Nakane, C.
1967 *Kinship and Economic Organization in Rural Japan.* London: Athlone Press.

1970 *Japanese Society.* London: Weidenfeld & Nicolson.

Nakano, T., and K. Brown.
1970 "Changing Rural Japan." In *The Study of Japan in the Behavioral Sciences,* edited by E. Norbeck and S. Parman. Rice University Studies, vol. 56, no. 4, pp. 195–206.

Netting, R. McC.
1965 "A Trial Model of Cultural Ecology." *Anthropology Quarterly* 38:81–96.

Nisbet, R.
1970 *The Sociological Tradition.* London: Heinemann.

1976   *Sociology as an Art Form.* New York: Oxford University Press.

Noma, Y.
1955   "Onta no Sarayama." *Mingei* 27:6–9.
1965   "Ontagama shinken." *Mingei* 147:13–16.

Norbeck, E.
1954   *Takashima: A Japanese Fishing Community.* Salt Lake City: University of Utah Press.

1961   "Postwar Cultural Change and Continuity in Northeastern Japan." *American Anthropologist* 63:297–321.

1977   "Changing Associations in a Recently Industrialized Japanese Community." *Urban Anthropology* 6:45–64.

Okada, J.
1976   "Applied Arts and Handicrafts in Japan." In *Dialogue in Art: Japan and the West,* edited by C. Yamada. London: A. Zwemmer.

Osborne, H.
1955   *Aesthetics and Criticism.* London: Routledge & Kegan Paul.

Plath, D.
1967   "*Japanese Rural Society* and *Asian Rural Society.*" Book review. *Japan Quarterly* 14:518–520.

Rappaport, R.
1971   "Nature, Culture, and Ecological Anthropology." In *Man, Culture, and Society,* edited by H. L. Schapiro. London: Oxford University Press.

Read, Sir H.
1936   *Art and Society.* London: Faber & Faber.
1961   "Comments" and "A Personal Point of View: Summary of Proceedings." In *The Artist in Tribal Society,* edited by M. Smith. London: Routledge & Kegan Paul.

Ruskin, J.
1963   *The Genius of John Ruskin: Selections from His Writings,* edited by J. G. Rosenberg. London: Allen & Unwin.

Sakamoto, K.
1953   "Suiden shakai no seikaku." *Jimbun Gakuho*
3:143–164.

Seki, K.
1962   "Nenrei shūdan." In *Nihon Minzokugaku Taikei*,
vol. 3, pp. 127–174. Tokyo: Heibonsha.

Shimpo, M.
1976   *Three Decades in Shiwa: Economic Development
and Social Change in a Japanese Farming Commu-
nity.* Vancouver: University of British Columbia
Press.

Silbermann, A.
1968   "A Definition of the Sociology of Art." In *Arts in
Society: International Social Science Journal*
20:567–588.

Smith, M., editor
1961   *The Artist in Tribal Society.* London: Routledge &
Kegan Paul.

Smith, R. J.
1956   "Kurusu." In *Two Japanese Villages.* Occasional
Papers, Center for Japanese Studies, no. 5, pp.
1–112. Ann Arbor: University of Michigan Press.

1961   "The Japanese Rural Community: Norms, Sanc-
tion, and Ostracism." *American Anthropologist*
63:522–533.

1978   *Kurusu: The Price of Progress in a Japanese Village,
1951–1975.* Stanford: Stanford University Press.

Smith, T. C.
1959   *The Agrarian Origins of Modern Japan.* Stanford:
Stanford University Press.

Smith, W. W.
1973   *Confucianism in Modern Japan.* Tokyo: Hoku-
seido.

Steiner, K.
1956   "The Japanese Village and Its Government." *Far
Eastern Quarterly* 15:185–199.

Steward, J.
1955   *Theory of Culture Change: The Methodology of
Multilinear Evolution.* Urbana: University of Illi-
nois Press.

Suenari, M.
1972

"First Child Inheritance in Japan." *Ethnology* 11:122–126.

Sumiya, K.
1953

"Sonraku kyōdōtai to yōsui kyōsei." *Shakaigaku Hyōron* 3:39–60.

Takahashi, T.
1958

"Nihon ni okeru nenrei shūdan soshiki no shoruikei." *Tōyō Daigaku Kiyō*, vol. 12.

Tanaka, Takashi
1969

"Onta e no osasoi." *Mingei* 195:44–48.

1971

"Arita to Onta ni miru dentō." *Mingei* 225:16–25.

Tanaka, Toyotarō
1961

"Kyūshū no minyō." *Mingei* 101:6–10.

1966

"Nihon mingeiten nyūsen sakuhin kōhyō: tōki." *Mingei* 160:10–13.

Tanaka, Yōko
1965

"Onta no tōgyō." *Mingei* 147:17–25.

Terakawa, Y.
1975

"Ontagama no rekishi" and "Ontagama nenpyō." In *Onta no Dentō to Tōgi*. Oita-ken Bunkazai Chōsa Hōkoku-sho.

Thompson, M.
1979

Rubbish Theory: The Creation and Destruction of Value. Oxford: Oxford University Press.

Tomars, A. S.
1940

Introduction to the Sociology of Art. Mexico City.

Tonomura, K.
1965

"Kawaranai Onta-gama." *Mingei* 147:10–12.

1973

"Yanagi Muneyoshi to Uiriamu Morisu." *Mingei* 247 and 248.

Tsuchiya, Y.
1965

"Sonraku shakai no hendō—seisan to shōhi o chūshin to shite." In *Shiga Daigaku Gakugei Gakubun Kiyō*, vol. 15.

Tsunoda, R., W. de Bary, and D. Keene
1964

Sources of Japanese Tradition, vol. 1. New York: Columbia University Press.

Tsurumi, S.
    1976   *Yanagi Muneyoshi*. Tokyo: Heibonsha.

Umeki, H.
    1973   *Ontayaki—Yakimono no Mura*. Oita: San'ichi Shobō.

Veblen, T.
    1925   *The Theory of the Leisure Class*. London: G. Allen and Unwin.

Williams, N.
    1976   "Australian Aboriginal Art at Yirkala: Introduction and Development of Marketing." In *Ethnic and Tourist Arts: Cultural Expressions from the Fourth World*, edited by Nelson H. H. Graburn. Berkeley and Los Angeles: University of California Press.

Williams, R.
    1958   *Culture and Society 1780–1950*. London: Chatto and Windus.

Wittfogel, K.
    1955   "Developmental Aspects of Hydraulic Societies." In *Irrigation Civilizations: A Comparative Study*, edited by J. H. Steward. Washington: Pan-American Union.

Yanagi, M.
    1931   "Hita no Sarayama." *Kōgei* 9:1–11.
    1932   "Sakubutsu no kōhansei." *Kōgei* 15:52–71.
    1946   "Mingei undō wa nani o kikō shita ka?" *Kōgei* 115:1–22.
    1947   *Teshigoto no Nihon*. Tokyo: Seibunsha.
    1949   *Folk Crafts in Japan*. Tokyo: Kokusai Bunka Shinkōkai.
    1954   *Kōgei Bunka. Selected Works*, vol. 3. Tokyo: Nihon Mingeikan.
    1955a   *Kōgei no Michi. Selected Works*, vol. 1. Tokyo: Nihon Mingeikan.
    1955b   *Cha to Bi. Selected Works*, vol. 6. Tokyo: Nihon Mingeikan.
    1961   "Ontagama e no kenen." *Mingei* 101:4–5.

Yoneyama, T.
1965   "Kazoku to ie no shakai jinruigakuteki kenkyū
                yosetsu." *Jimbun Gakuho* 21:129–152.

1967a   "Kaminosho: A Farm Village Suburban to Osaka
                in South Central Japan." In J. Seward, ed., *Con-
                temporary Change in Traditional Societies*, vol. 2.
                Urbana: University of Illinois Press.

1967b   "Kurikoma: A Farm Village in the Mountains of
                the Tohoku District of North Central Japan." In
                Contemporary Change in Traditional Societies, vol.
                2. Urbana: University of Illinois Press.

Yoshino, M.
1971   *The Japanese Marketing System: Adaptations and
                Innovations.* Cambridge, Mass.: MIT Press.

Index

Adoption, 45, 52–53, 60, 62

Aesthetic: appraisal, 3, 43, 150, 177, 193*n*, 196–205 passim, 228; criticism and social change 180–181; ideals, 6, 49, 215–217. *See also* Aesthetics; Folk craft, theory and practice of

Aesthetics: moral aspects of, 18, 20–22, 26, 182; and society, 3, 6, 24, 27, 164, 210, 215–230 passim; sociology of, 229–230. *See also* Aesthetic; Art; Beauty

Age: associations 65–69; grade seniority, 48, 70–71, 150, 162–165, 176–177, 216

Agrarianism (*nōhonshugi*), 12

Agricultural: community, 2, 44, 46–49, 71, 73, 92; cooperative, 69, 143

Agriculture, 92, 111, 121, 124, 125–126, 131–132, 141, 143, 151, 164, 176, 215; and folk craft ideals, 137; and irrigation, 2, 73–74, 83. *See also* Environment

Airport art, 223

Ancestors, 44, 51, 62; return of, 51, 67, 68, 109

Anonymity, 178, 225, 228–229

Aquinas, Thomas, 25

Arishima, Takeo, 13

Arita, 28, 32, 94, 127*n*, 137

Art: absolute and relative concepts in, 25, 223, 224; and anthropology, 3–4, 229; and capitalist society, 10–11, 148*n*; folk crafts as, 3–4, 16, 21*n*, 22–23, 224, 229; handmade, 227–228; and industrialization, 225–226; Onta pottery as, 196, 205, 208, 209, 211–212, 226; women's appreciation of, 17, 226–227. *See also* Beauty; Folk craft; Nature

Artist, 3, 6, 14, 22, 149, 179–180, 195; vis-à-vis craftsman, 161, 214

Arts and crafts movement, 9–11, 23

atarishiki mura, 13; new village movement, 12

Beauty, 1, 10, 16, 149, 183, 192, 195, 196, 201, 210, 224, 230; absolute and relative concepts of, 223, 224; and consumerism, 147–149; and cooperation, 2, 4, 20–21, 49, 120, 121, 181, 182, 194, 215; functional aspects of, 6, 10, 16, 22, 197, 212, 217; and individual, 20–22, 192–193, 195, 207–208, 210, 217, 228; and intellectualism, 22, 192, 196; and nature, 2, 6, 11, 20, 137, 181, 194–195, 215, 225–226; standard of, 15, 26, 192–194, 209–210, 215, 217, 223; and tradition, 2, 6, 121; and truth, 10, 192, 209*n*; Yanagi's concept of, 13–14, 18–23, 181, 215, 216–217. *See also* Art; Environment; Folk craft; Yanagi, Muneyoshi

Bisque firing, 50, 95, 185, 204–205

bon. See Ancestors

buraku. See Hamlet

butsudan, 51

Buyer. *See* Pottery, dealer

Carlyle, Thomas, 9–10

Cash, social concomitants of, 131–132, 136, 138

chokkan. See Perception, direct

Compositor: Miller Freeman Composition
Printer: Braun-Brumfield, Inc.
Binder: Braun-Brumfield, Inc.
Text: 10/12 Palatino
Display: Palatino